Beaches,
Blood,
and
Ballots

Beaches, Blood, and Ballots

A Black Doctor's Civil Rights Struggle

Gilbert R. Mason, M.D.,

with James Patterson Smith

University Press of Mississippi / Jackson

Margaret Walker Alexander Series in African American Studies

www.upress.state.ms.us

Library of Congress Cataloging-in-Publication Data

Mason, Gilbert R.
    Beaches, blood, and ballots: a black doctor's civil rights struggle /
Gilbert R. Mason, with James Patterson Smith.
        p. cm. (Margaret Walker Alexander series in African American
studies)
    Includes bibliographical references and index.
    ISBN 1-93411-028-0 (cloth : alk. paper)
    ISBN 978-1-934110-28-7

    1. Mason, Gilbert R.   2. Afro-Americans—Civil rights—Mississippi—
Biloxi—History—20th century.   3. Afro-American physicians—
Mississippi—Biloxi—Biography.   4. Afro-American civil rights workers—
    Mississippi—Biloxi—Biography.   5. Biloxi (Miss.)—Biography.
    6. Biloxi (Miss.)—Race relations.   7. Civil rights movements—
    Mississippi—Biloxi—History—20th century.   8. Mason family.
    I. Smith, James Patterson.   II. Title.
    F349.B5 M37   2000
    976.2'00496073'0092—dc21
    [B]   00-024664

British Library Cataloging-in-Publication Data available

For Natalie

Social Worker

Plugs at day, plugs at night,
Helps the wrong, helps the right,
Sometimes works without desire
Works so well must retire.

See my baby working hard,
Got to make it says the Bard,
Getting up early hitting the clock,
Go six miles like going a block.

Going to places smelling like rum,
Visit the elite or visit the slum,
There she goes never a shirker,
That's my baby, Social Worker.

Gilbert R. Mason
May 30, 1950

Cogito, ergo sum.

René Descartes

Gil's Prayer

Thou hast sown in the fertile
Bayous of the Father of Waters,
Thou hast tendered the bloom
In the garden of martyrs.
Thou hast shepherded the foundling
When none other bothered,
Now Lord, spare the promise
From premature barter.

Thou hast embellished the spur
And given it splendor,
Thou hast given it strength,
But made it tender.
Thou hast placed in its hands
An unfulfilled agenda,
Now Lord, give it stay
To praise the sender.

Gilbert R. Mason
April 14, 1954

Contents

Foreword

On Thursday, May 14, 1959, eight months before four students from North Carolina Agricultural and Technical College launched the Greensboro lunch counter sit-ins, nine black citizens of Biloxi, Mississippi, ventured onto a forbidden spot on a twenty-six-mile-long segregated beach in open and conscious defiance of Mississippi's Jim Crow practices. Police removed these swimmers from the Mississippi Gulf Coast beach and warned them against returning. At a time when, out of approximately ten thousand black residents of Biloxi, three were members of the NAACP, there followed months of mass meetings, public petitioning, and community-wide planning to challenge the banning of blacks from the beach through civil disobedience and federal court cases. Additional wade-ins at Biloxi the following April triggered the bloodiest race riot in Mississippi history and produced the first significant U.S. Justice Department intervention in Mississippi to challenge the state's segregation laws in federal court.

On April 30, 1960, New York-based reporter James L. Hicks of the *Amsterdam News*, in a front page feature series of articles on the Biloxi wade-ins, wrote a piece entitled "This Man Mason." Hicks, who had covered civil rights activities throughout the South, led his story with this statement: "Little Rock has its Daisy Bates; . . . Martin Luther King rose up out of the racial turmoil of Montgomery, Alabama, and now Biloxi, Miss., has its Dr. Gilbert Mason." With this salute, Hicks recognized the Biloxi wade-ins as marking the beginning of the civil rights movement in Mississippi. In retrospect, it is now clear that these wade-ins heralded the opening salvo in a sustained series of Mississippi Gulf Coast wade-ins and lawsuits that for the first time successfully challenged the state's segregation laws.

Almost simultaneously, the local organizers of the Biloxi wade-ins began working on one of the earliest Mississippi school desegregation suits, a suit which, in 1964, for the first time anywhere in Mississippi, opened the doors of public schools to black children and white children on a nonracial basis. The local moving force behind all of these Mississippi civil rights milestones was Dr. Gilbert Mason of Biloxi. Dr. Mason, a black medical doctor and native Mississippian, was the founder and president of the Biloxi branch of the NAACP and for thirty-three years was a vice president of the Mississippi Conference of the NAACP while Aaron Henry was its president.

This book is Dr. Mason's, presenting his story from his point of view. In the larger sweep of civil rights historiography, Dr. Mason's firsthand account illuminates a neglected but profoundly important level of the civil rights movement and civil rights leadership. Without the inspiration, determination, courage, and harrowing sacrifices of countless individuals working at the local level to dismantle Jim Crow limb by limb and branch by branch in small cities and towns across the South, the success of the civil rights movement would have been truncated and of limited significance. Beginning with the 1954 *Brown* case, the U.S. Supreme Court destroyed the legal doctrine underpinning racially segregated schools and brought into question the legality of a wide array of other segregationist laws and practices long thought to be deeply ingrained in a distinctive southern way of life. The national heroes and spokesmen of the civil rights era are well known. Dr. Martin Luther King, Jr., Roy Wilkins, and James Farmer, and the national organizations which they represented, have long been associated in the public mind with the moral, legislative, and legal crusade to banish racial discrimination and segregation from American life.

Change in the law at the national level created opportunity for a revolution in political and social practices in the South. However, the realization of this opportunity required committed individuals in hundreds of cities and towns across the South who were willing to face up to the fearsome task of challenging entrenched segregationist power structures at the local level to claim the rights and benefits guaranteed under the constitution and laws of the United States. Challenging long-lived social customs or power arrangements is never easy. That Jim Crow's peculiar and demeaning system of back-of-the-bus mandates and practices including racially separate and unequal schools, waiting rooms, parks, drinking fountains, rest rooms, and public accommodations was swept away in less than a generation is largely due to the idealism, intelligence, and long-suffering perseverance of countless local leaders who rose to the occasion, took new ground, and made change a reality in cities and towns across the South.

As a primary source document, Dr. Mason's memoir contributes to an evolving historical understanding of several important questions. First, why did individuals at the local level decide to risk jobs or careers, personal safety, and even their lives for the movement? What types of men and women became local civil rights leaders? What models or ideals guided them? How were their ideals shaped? What did they expect to gain through the risks and sacrifices they undertook? Second, this memoir offers insight into the origins of local strategy and tactics. How did local leaders build the clusters of local followers and supporters necessary to sustain their efforts over a period of years? How did the organization of the local civil rights struggle evolve? To what extent were local civil rights activities spontaneous and indigenous to the communities in which they arose, and to what extent were they prompted by leaders and issues beyond the local community? Who determined the points of attack? Was local or national leadership in control? Finally, from the point of view of a front-line veteran in the civil rights struggle, were the achievements of the movement worth the price paid? How did those who risked themselves in the campaign for desegregation view the emerging voices of black separatism? In addressing these and other questions, Dr. Mason's story offers a local activist's eyewitness assessment of the incredible local changes through which Mississippi, the South, and the nation passed in the 1960s and 1970s.

Dr. Mason's account has further value as an important document illustrating African American life in Mississippi and the Deep South during the period from the 1930s through the 1990s. In tracing Dr. Mason's childhood in Jackson, Mississippi, it sheds light on the life of first-generation urban, black, working-class families who remained connected to their roots on farms near the emerging cities of the South. The impact of the great migration on African American families is also seen here from the point of view of family members who remained in the South, but maintained close personal relationships with relatives in Chicago and other northern cities. Dr. Mason speaks of the higher education experiences of black physicians and of their adjustments to the restrictive circumstances under which they practiced medicine in the waning days of the Jim Crow era in the South.

This book had its origins in a long series of tape-recorded interviews which Dr. Mason undertook in the spring and summer of 1998 for the Center for Oral History and Cultural Heritage at the University of Southern Mississippi. Before becoming committed professionally to the lengthy interview project, I had known Dr. Mason politically, as we had both served on the state executive committee of the Mississippi Democratic Party and the Harrison County Democratic Executive Committee at vari-

ous times between 1984 and 1998. As a historian, I knew that Dr. Mason
had made important stands in Biloxi and that he had endured the fire-
bombing of his office and the burning of an automobile in the struggle
for the desegregation of the beach. However, I knew little of the detail of
these stories. In recent years in Democratic Party life, we have most often
seen Dr. Mason as our local and state party parliamentarian, in which role
he was insistent, correct, strong, and unwilling to accept slipshod methods. Party executive committee members saw his strength and respected
his obvious expertise in parliamentary procedure. Where we did not follow his advice, we often came to regret it. Like many of the younger
members of our committee, I saw the bold strength and determined perseverance of Dr. Gilbert Mason in political settings and knew little else about
him as a man. Not until the 1988 Democratic National Convention in
Atlanta did I catch a glimpse of the inner man, the idealist combating in
the arena of politics for convictions deeply held. One evening after a long
convention session, Dr. Mason and I, along with Mayor Gerald Blessey of
Biloxi, wound up in a hotel barroom sitting together at a table discuss-
ing—of all things—the Sermon on the Mount. In this setting, I discovered
that the black doctor from Biloxi was also an armchair philosopher who
was much concerned with Christian ethics and who was at home in theo-
logical discussions.

Over the next few years, as a professor of history at the University of
Southern Mississippi, I occasionally sent students working on papers related to the civil rights movement to see if Dr. Mason might give them a
few moments out of his busy day for a first-person interview. He routinely
declined these and most other requests for interviews. I was therefore
somewhat surprised when Judge Robin Alfred Midcalf telephoned me to
ask if I would be willing to assist Dr. Mason with a book about his life. I
suggested to Judge Midcalf that a good starting place for such a project
would be a series of oral history interviews that could be transcribed for
posterity. If the working relationship proved satisfactory to Dr. Mason
and to me, we could then decide whether to take the project forward to
produce a book for publication. From March through July of 1998, we
undertook weekly interview sessions, which were usually conducted in Dr.
Mason's home. From sixty hours of taped interviews, five hundred typed,
single-spaced pages of transcripts were produced. Over the months I
gained genuine admiration and deep respect for Dr. Mason as a man of
great courage, genuine faith, noble dreams, and tremendous endurance.
In an atmosphere of mutual respect, we developed a good working relationship and agreed that we would continue working together to trans-

form the interview material, enriched by Dr. Mason's personal papers and contemporary newspaper stories, into his first-person account of the civil rights era.

In preparation for each interview session, I constructed an agenda of questions to guide our discussion. Sometimes the information related in one session would suggest areas for fuller discussion in the next. In several instances, I decided to ask for a second account of an important episode in order to clarify events. Often, the second account produced new and richer details on tape. As we worked to organize and construct the book, fresh memories continued to be evoked and noted as enrichments to the raw interview accounts. Dr. Mason's review of his papers, old newspapers, the Mississippi State Sovereignty Commission files, and drafts of proposed chapters often produced even greater detail, new recollections, and fresh insights from him that were then incorporated into the revisions of chapters. My work as a historian has been to pull Dr. Mason's recollections together into a narrative form that presents his point of view, his interpretations, and his understanding of the situations through which he has lived. This process has resulted in a document that brings us face to face with what it meant to be black in Mississippi in the days of Jim Crow, what it cost local leaders to challenge that system, and how the success of that challenge nurtured a genuine hope for the future of America in the heart of this embattled veteran of the civil rights struggle in the South.

James Patterson Smith

Acknowledgments

First of all, I wish to acknowledge and thank God Almighty for my life and for the strength that made this book and all things possible. Second, I want to thank the Mississippi legislature for funding the oral history projects proposed in the budget of the Mississippi Department of Archives and History under the leadership of Mr. Elbert Hilliard, executive director, the trustees, and the Honorable William F. Winter, president of the board. With their support and leadership the capable professional staff at the Mississippi Department of Archives and History has been able to continue and expand Mississippi's fine Oral History and Cultural Heritage Project working through the Center for Oral History and Cultural Heritage at the University of Southern Mississippi.

This book grew out of an oral history project involving more than sixty hours of interviews with me conducted by Dr. James Patterson Smith of the University of Southern Mississippi's Department of History. Sincere thanks therefore go to the University of Southern Mississippi, Dr. Horace Fleming, president, and to Dr. Charles Bolton, director of the university's Center for Oral History and Cultural Heritage, whose staff members, Ms. Marie Sykes and Ms. Shana Walton, graciously typed and proofread almost five hundred single-spaced pages of interview transcriptions in an efficient and timely manner. Further, I want to thank the university for permitting Dr. Smith to use his sabbatical leave to assemble, extract, and refine the contents of the basic interview materials in an academic and coherent literary and historical manner. I am grateful for the many hours that he has spent researching, organizing, and editing the story of my life. I wish to acknowledge Dr. James "Pat" Smith and to thank him for being coauthor of my life story.

I also thank Natalie Mason, my wife of almost half a century, who not only made my life far richer than it ever would have been without her, but who also patiently sat in on and participated in most of the original interview tapings. I thank Dr. Smith's wife, Mrs. Jeanette Smith, who courteously tolerated my many telephone calls to her residence and proof-read the book manuscript for us.

I certainly thank my family for the generous information they provided about family matters and genealogy, much more of which is recorded and available for posterity in the transcribed interview at the McCain Archive at the University of Southern Mississippi than could be included in this book.

I want to acknowledge my older brother, Willie Louis Mason, a retired longshoreman, who has been my tutor and mentor from childhood, and his wife, Elnora, who advised and encouraged me when I was in junior high and high school during World War II while my brother was away serving the nation in the U.S. Army on the battlefields of Europe. Later, as I worked my way through college, they opened their home and allowed me to stay with them while I worked on the Mississippi River for half the summer of 1948.

I am eternally grateful to the whole NAACP family for their long history of dependable support for human rights endeavors. I want to especially thank the Biloxi branch of the NAACP for its many courageous and visionary stands over the years, and I thank my successor as its president, Mr. James Crowell, for his grace, his constancy as a friend, and his dauntless personality. I want to thank Samuel Yette, author of *The Choice: The Issue of Black Survival,* for his brotherly advice over the years.

Moreover, I owe a debt of gratitude to my office staff, who served not only in a medical capacity but also as civil rights activists. For their work in both of these areas over the years, I want to thank Mrs. Cornelia Saucier and Mrs. Melvina Davis Smith, who served during the terrible days of the sixties. I also thank Mrs. Blanche V. Elzy, Mrs. Virginia Lewis Holmes, Mrs. Linda Carrier, Mrs. Cheryl Collins Brimage, Mrs. Beverly J. Owen, and Mrs. Pearl N. Bradford Hopkins. Most of these nurses and receptionists also served as typists and archivists for NAACP activities in Biloxi at one time or another. I want to thank the employees of the Modern Drug Store who worked for me and with me under hazardous conditions in the early sixties, namely Mrs. Alicia Coleman, our pharmacist, Mrs. Annette Seldon Sizor and Mrs. Betty Pat Vereen, our clerks, and William "Little Bill" Bradford, Jr., who rode his bicycle through perilous byways in order to make deliveries. I want to acknowledge the role that Mrs. Rose Juzang played in the documentation and typing of documents and correspondence for me when she served as secretary for the Harrison County Community Action Agency in the early years of that organization and later as chairperson of the Harrison County Democratic Executive Committee.

I certainly want to thank the physicians who covered for me so that I could attend various conferences, conventions, committee meetings, NAACP events, and Boy Scouts of America camps, camporees, and jamborees over the past forty-five years. Especially do I thank Dr. Frank Gruich, Dr. Charles Gruich, Dr. Billy Wansley, Dr. Jerry Adkins, Dr. Frank Martin, Dr. James Martin, Dr. Jefferson McKenney, Dr. Lance Barnes, Dr. Alfred McNair, Dr. Jesse Ezzell, Dr. John McKee, Dr. Richard Furr, Dr. Lee Morris, and Dr. M. A. Anwar. I owe a debt of thanks also to many hospital support staff members, including Mrs. Linda Raines at Gulf Coast Medical Center and Mrs. Mona Duncan, Mrs. Nelissa Sturgis, Mrs. Leslie Johnson, Mrs. Sherry Berry Allen, Mrs. Freda Newman, and Mrs. Mary Dell Rosetti, director of medical records, at Biloxi Regional Medical Center.

For their rich advice I thank Judge Fred Banks and attorneys Melvin Cooper, Joseph Hudson, Robin Alfred Midcalf, and Gerald Blessey. I thank broadcaster and businessman "Rip" Daniels for his vision of a new day. I want to express my gratitude to Mr. Leo Russell for the gift of copies of the photographs of the 1963 wade-in which were used in evidence in court and which he saved from destruction.

Finally, I must acknowledge and thank Adam Atwood Mason Owen, Mrs. Mary Thigpen, Mrs. Katherine Egland, Gilbert Mason, Jr., and the members of the NAACP family whose urging and many encouragements caused this book to be written.

Beaches,
Blood,
and
Ballots

ONE

Beginnings

Train up a child in the way he should go: and when he is old,
he will not depart from it. —Proverbs 22:6

"DR. MASON, WHEN DID YOU BECOME A CIVIL RIGHTS AC-
tivist?" This is the question a white nurse posed last spring when, after
practicing medicine in Biloxi, Mississippi, for forty-three years, I found
myself a hospital patient. Many people in Mississippi know that Gilbert
R. Mason, the black doctor from Biloxi, was for thirty-three years a vice
president of the Mississippi Conference of the NAACP and a close associate of Medgar Evers and Aaron Henry. Medgar Evers's last Sunday night
on this earth was spent at my house, and I served as a pallbearer at his
funeral. In Biloxi they know that I was one of the founders, and for thirty-
three years the president, of the Biloxi branch of the NAACP. Local folks
know that I organized Mississippi's first nonviolent civil disobedience
campaign, the wade-ins on Biloxi beach beginning in 1959, to gain equal
access to God's Gulf Coast beaches for all of his children. We endured and
persevered to victory through a tidal wave of threats, violence, and reprisals from mad-dog segregationists. Local people will recall the success of
our targeted economic boycotts against the encouragers and perpetrators
of assaults on and intimidation of black citizens engaged in peaceful protest on the beach. Many in Biloxi remember that in 1960, well before the
freedom summers and the federal Voting Rights Act of 1965, we undertook
successful voter registration drives in Biloxi that gave black folks the
power to replace their worst enemies in the local political establishment.
Many also recall that in August of 1964, Biloxi's schools became the first
in Mississippi to admit black children to formerly all-white classrooms.
School desegregation came first to Biloxi because I joined early with
Medgar Evers and Mrs. Winston Hudson in the first lawsuit challenging

Mississippi's system of enforced racial segregation and inequality in public schools. For over forty years, local people have seen this black doctor from Biloxi uphold the cause of human rights before local, state, and national boards and commissions. These are some of the facts of my life. My nurse knew most of the bare facts. She wanted to understand more.

"So, Dr. Mason, when did you become a civil rights activist?" Many people ask me such questions because they really want to know why I and other local leaders across the South became involved in the civil rights struggle, why and how we took the risks we took, and why and how we achieved success against a white power structure steeped in a vile and sinister racist ideology. Born in the 1920s and 1930s we were the "freedom boomers," not baby boomers, arriving on the scene with a yearning for freedom and equality burning in our breasts. From where did our commitment come? Thankfully, the new generation has no memory of the most vicious and humiliating aspects of legally enforced segregation and its corollary of legalized second-class citizenship against which my generation struggled. Still, the ugly and hurtful residues of racism remain. This book represents my personal effort to reach out to a new generation of black and white youth to help build understanding and to affirm that, having weathered many dangers, storms, and fears, I still have hope for Mississippi and hope for America.

"So, Dr. Mason, when *did* you become a civil rights activist?" It seems such a simple question, but the answer is complicated. I didn't just become a civil rights activist one day. We are individuals, you know, and there is so much that goes into making the individual: the way you live; your parents and family; the nurturing and examples you receive from neighborhood, community, church, teachers, preachers, Scout leaders; the faith and the ideals you develop; the people you adopt as heroes. All of these play a part in making us who we are.

I am a native Mississippian, born at home at 113 Riggins Alley between Monument Street and Farish Street in Jackson, Mississippi, on October 7, 1928. I was delivered by a black midwife and born into a thoroughly segregated and racist society. From early childhood I realized that discrimination and segregation were not right. As a schoolboy I could not reconcile the practices of Mississippi with the promises of the U.S. Constitution and the Declaration of Independence. By the time I was in high school, I had begun to believe that we should defy segregationist laws and customs wherever possible.

The world I saw as a child left no doubt in my mind that segregation and humiliation went hand in hand. In 1932, when I was four years old, my daddy and a local grocer with some other friends decided that they would go to Chicago to see Joe Louis fight the Uruguayan boxer Uz Gudan. Though my grandparents had moved to Chicago, I had never been to see them. My daddy got his friends to agree that I could go along. I got into the backseat of that new Chevrolet sedan and went to sleep. When I woke up, I could sense something wrong. As we got closer to Illinois near the Ohio River, the men began to whisper. Cairo, Illinois, had a reputation for beating up on black folks and for race riots and lynchings. I remember they told me to get down on the floor. I got down on the floor. We went on to Chicago safely, but getting down on that car floor had made an impression.

Back home in Jackson, at some point in early childhood I discovered that legal segregation, or the Jim Crow system, meant that I could not use the public parks or swimming pools. Battlefield Park was the public park nearest to me, but we as black folks couldn't play there. Because black kids in Jackson had no public pools available to us, I learned to swim in an old swim hole called the "bowlegged weed" where a storm-ravaged tree bent out over a dangerously steep bank descending to a stream running south from the Goudy brickyard pond. I remember being distinctly disturbed as a Boy Scout because my friend Joseph Debro and I had to wait six months to get the merit badge in lifesaving and camping because the black Boy Scout camp, Camp Lubaloo near Clinton, did not have any certified lifesavers to train us. Our scoutmasters had to appeal to the area Scout executive to allow certified lifesavers from the white Scout camp, Camp Kickapoo, two miles down the road, to certify us. Successful completion of those badges after a long and frustrating wait meant that Joseph Debro and I became Eagle Scouts; it was the first time blacks had done so in Jackson and the second time in Mississippi.

Everywhere we went, Jim Crow laws told us what we could and could not do. Of course, all of the restaurants in Jackson were "white only." I don't recall being able to even walk up to a window to get served. Many department stores would not let us try on clothes before buying—not even ladies' hats. Some stores on Capitol Street wouldn't serve black people at all. As late as 1958, when I was already a practicing physician, I went down on Capitol Street to buy a tie to wear for my daddy's funeral, and the store wouldn't even sell me a tie. Hotels and motels routinely refused us accommodations if we traveled. Gas stations had "colored" rest rooms and "colored" water fountains, and there were "colored" waiting rooms in bus and train stations and in white doctors' offices. Streetcar and bus drivers sent us to the back and placed moveable signs on the seats marked "colored" on one side and "white" on the other. The signs were moved backward and forward depending on how many white folks were aboard. If seats were in short supply, whites sat while blacks stood up for the ride. At Baptist Hospital sick black patients got treatment only in the basement until R. H. Green, a white businessman with a lot of black employees, donated the money to build the R. H. Green Annex so there would be a decent place where colored people could be sick and die. I remember my folks took me there once when I fell out of a tree and they thought I had broken a collarbone.

I finished high school in Jackson's segregated and unequal public school system. Oh, I had many wonderful and dedicated teachers at Sally Reynolds Elementary School, Jim Hill Junior High School, and Lanier High School. Still, we knew that our teachers were not paid fairly and that our equipment was second-rate compared to what the white schools had. In high school particularly, I became aware that we were getting the hand-me-down chemistry instruments—used flasks, retorts, and Bunsen burners—and we even got used desks. We did not go to the white public library. We used the little library at our school or went to the one at Jackson State College. In football we received the thrown-off togs, jerseys, helmets, and shoes from Central High School, which was a so-called white high school in Jackson. The shoes, I remember, were badly used. Many times they had missing cleats or no cleats at all, so we would repair them, then dye and polish them up.

The all-black Lanier football team practiced on a cinder-ridden field in back of the school. The cinders had been covered with a layer of dirt, but every now and then a cinder would come through and cut you when you hit the ground. I carry scars now from that practice field. We did not have a school stadium, so we played all of our games at Jackson State's stadium or at what was called the Mississippi Colored State Fairgrounds. That's right, there was a "colored" fair and a white fair. The Mississippi Colored State Fairgrounds was out on Highway 49 near what is now Medgar Evers Boulevard. We played before a black audience mainly, but our games were well supported and open to all people. Since there were no bleachers, people usually just stood on the sidelines, so there wasn't a question of white versus black seating. We did not have a gym at Lanier either. We played our basketball games at Holy Ghost High School gym on Ash Street, or we played at Jackson State's gym. Holy Ghost was the all-black Catholic school about a block and a half from our campus. I don't recall ever going to see Central High or any other white school play in Jackson.

We had problems sometimes because our Lanier school colors were maroon and white like Mississippi State's, and like them, we called our team the Bulldogs. If you lettered at Lanier, you became a member of the "L" Club and wore a maroon-and-white jacket with a bulldog and a big "L" stitched on it. My older brother was a four-year letterman, but I was usually a second string end and only lettered one year. Downtown on Capitol Street, there were occasions when white guys calling themselves Mississippi State alumni would try to pull the maroon-and-white Lanier jacket off one of our boys, even though there was plainly an "L" and not an "M" on it.

In this environment, when did I become a civil rights activist? I know that as a boy I got into a lot of fights in my own neighborhood. As a little fellow I had wrestled with my big brother, who was six years older. Bullies in our section of town knew that I'd fight them in a minute. They didn't pick on me. Many times though, I fought to defend a little timid friend of mine, Charlie Magee, on Cox Street (I lived on Booker), or because people were picking on my cousin, Christia B. Ratliff, who lived behind me. Bullies have a tendency to pick on people of gentle character or who look weak. After I was grown and in medical practice, a childhood friend dropped by the office one day and told me that a Jackson minister's wife, the widow of Reverend Steen, who had lived across the street from me back then, was asked what I was like as a boy. This preacher's wife said, "He won't lie, he won't cheat, he won't steal, and he don't take no shit." That was my reputation as a boy. The bullies didn't pick on me, because I didn't "take no shit."

Segregation was a legalized bully system. Even before I went to high school I saw how, in the minds of some white people, legalized Jim Crow qualified black people for capricious humiliation and degradation. When did I become an activist? Was it that day when I was twelve years old and bent over to pump air into my bicycle tires at a Gulf station on Terry Road, and a big white guy slipped up from behind and kicked me over? When I turned to ask, "Why?" his smug answer, " 'Cause I wanted to," made a lasting impression. His interpretation of Jim Crow gave him a special privilege to bully. I soon started doing small things to defy the system.

Under Jim Crow the law dictated some aspects of race relations— seating on buses, separate schools, and the like. Still, you just never quite knew when some white person's unique idea of racial etiquette/degradation would jump up to entangle, humiliate or threaten you. As a thirteen-year-old, I got a job delivering groceries on my bicycle for Ritter's Grocery in a white neighborhood on Terry Road near its intersection with Silas Brown Street. One evening near dark I made a delivery to a white lady. As I stood on her porch trying to make change in the dark, she got mad because I was too slow to suit her. "Give me that money," she snapped, "I'll count it myself." I said, "Lady, I can count," and handed her the correct coins. Offended, she snarled, "That's what's wrong with you smart-aleck young niggers," and she called the store to complain. The next day at the store, my white boss's wife issued a reprimand punctuated with a veiled threat. "Gilbert, be careful," she warned. Then, pointing down the road toward the Pearl River, she added these ominous words: "They took one colored boy down there, and they never heard from him again." What hard words for any mother's young son to hear come from the mouth of an adult. Even at age thirteen, I knew that the Pearl River had become the premature grave of many blacks. I knew the boss's wife intended to intimidate me with that threat. White folks, she made clear, would not put up with uppitiness from me. With my boyish reply to a white customer's impatience, I had inadvertently broken the rules of racial subordination to the extent that my life was threatened.

Some days later the peculiarities of segregationist racial etiquette ran me afoul of the white store manager himself. My daddy, a strong-willed man that white folks didn't mess with, had taught me to be polite and respectful to all people but subservient to none. He insisted that I address grown-ups, black or white, as "Mr.," "Mrs.," or "Miss So-and-So." When called or questioned, I was to reply, "Yes, Mrs. Smith" or "No, Mr. Smith." This ran square into the peculiar ideas of my white boss at Ritter's Grocery. It took awhile, but one day he noticed that the words "sir" and "ma'am" were never in my vocabulary when answering his customers. Once he caught on, he confronted me and insisted that I address his wife as "ma'am." I defied him. I called her "Mrs." He turned and hit me upside the head so hard that it burst my eardrum. Hurting, enraged, I instinctively reached for the pocketknife I sometimes carried for protection against mugging. In pain, I fumbled with the pocket but couldn't get the knife out before the white man walked off. But for the grace of God, what might have become of me if in that moment my hand had found that knife? I left that store and never went back. My dad wanted to sue, but the only witness was afraid to testify.

I tried working for a while as a carhop at a burger joint near the intersection that used to be called Five Points (where Medgar Evers Boulevard joins Woodrow Wilson Avenue). The attitude of the customers got to me. I did not like people calling me "nigger" or "boy." They would yell,

"Hurry up, boy," or "Boy, turn your hat around so you'll look like you're coming all the time." I soon quit the carhop business. I wouldn't "take no shit," but was I a civil rights activist yet?

In high school I took a notion to go to the *white* state fair in Jackson. As I have said, in those days Mississippi state fairs were segregated. The two fairgrounds were miles apart. The black state fair had animal displays and traditional rides, cotton candy, and hamburgers with onions. But I decided to see the *white* state fair. I got in okay, and I was walking down the fairway when some big white guy came up—he was bigger than I was, and he just willy-nilly hit me in the jaw and muttered, "You're not supposed to be here. You got your own fair." That was my first and last time going to the so-called white fair.

However, I had other scrapes with Jim Crow insanity. In high school I rode the city bus to school. The bus route was called Whitfield-Mill-Lynch and ran from an industrial area on Mill Street, where it picked up some white riders, to Ash Street, turning onto Lynch into a black neighborhood where the all-black Jim Hill School used to be located and where the black Masonic Temple is now. On that route in the 1940s, many times I and others my age defied the driver and the laws of Mississippi to sit in front of the "colored" sign. The driver would get angry and yell, "You're violating the law. You can't sit in front of that sign." I remember distinctly one day when there was a white man sitting in front of the sign; some of my schoolmates and I got up and went forward to his section. He said, "You can't ignore me, I'm a white man." We said, "So what." He got up. The driver stopped. The white man got off.

We got away with it, but this kind of bucking of the system on buses could be quite dangerous. Twenty years later the burned-out buses and mass arrests of freedom riders showed the risk. However, long before that era, young Medgar Evers defied the color line, riding a bus from Meridian to Jackson in front of the sign. The driver stopped the bus and beat Medgar with his fists. When Medgar still wouldn't move, the driver called the police and had him arrested. One of my fraternity brothers tells about riding a bus to Camp Shelby at Hattiesburg, Mississippi, for induction into the army. Once the bus passed through the gate to the base, one of the black men stood up and said, "Well, we're on a federal reservation now. I'm not gonna sit in the back of the bus anymore," and he moved to the front. The driver stopped and called a white MP; they beat this young fellow unconscious. Or, as my friend put it, "They beat him so bad that he lost his manners."

In Jim Crow days in Mississippi, you just never knew what might come down on you. You could be brutalized unexpectedly. If you struck back, it was almost guaranteed that you would be arrested, manhandled, and further brutalized by the authorities themselves without any real opportunity to prove your case. A good deal of exhaustion comes from anticipation or expectation of unpredictable brutality. You didn't have to imagine racial brutality in Mississippi. Insults, humiliations, beatings, rapes, and lynchings were very real. They are well documented. And as older children we knew about them. Having been personally subjected to a part of that as a child, I can assure you those things existed.

Jim Crow segregation was a heavy burden for the soul, even if it did not always bend your body down. The title of a Bettye Parker Smith short story included in *Fathers' Songs: Testimonies by African-American Sons and Daughters* is "God Didn't Live in Mississippi Then," but, in spite of it all, I think he did live here even back then. God was here then, or we wouldn't be here now. God showed up in loving families and in concerned neighbors and community leaders. He gave us true churches, strong heroes, and a faith so powerful that our dreams never died. You couldn't explain why I and others became civil rights activists without understanding the importance of these gifts in shaping us.

I am happy and thank God for having grown up in a Christian family. My mother, Alean Jackson Mason, was a gentle and wise person. As a girl she had attended a little one-room public school in Hinds County called Orange Hill School. As far back as I can remember, she worked at home as housewife and full-time mother. My mother sang spirituals and religious songs from her heart, and she could sing them one right after the other. Her gentleness and sensitivity were in the songs she sang. The first I ever heard of the *Titanic* and all those sad deaths was when she sang the song "The Day the Titanic Went Down." Then she sang about the great flood of 1927 and the great storm in 1928 in Tupelo, and all the people who had nowhere to go. From Mother, I heard about a lynching that she had seen or was told of as a child. She said that to keep the poor victim from crying out, the lynchers had stuffed his mouth with mud. What a thing for a mother to have to share with a son.

My father, Willie Atwood Mason, lived the Golden Rule: "Do unto others as you would have them do unto you" (Matthew 7:12; Luke 6:31). The sayings of Jesus—"Seek ye first the kingdom of God, and his righteousness; and all these things shall be added unto you" (Matthew 6:33) or the greatest commandment, "Love the Lord thy God with all thy heart, and with all thy soul, and with all thy mind, and with all thy strength," and the second like unto it, "Love thy neighbor as thyself" (Mark 12:30–

31)—were my daddy's credos. He was an upright man who wouldn't let me as a teenager work in any downtown hotel because "things go on there that a boy's eyes should not see." My parents saw to it that I grew up going to Sunday school and church at the St. James Missionary Baptist Church on the corner of Jones and Cleveland in Jackson.

But, now, my daddy was a fighter. He talked freedom as far back as I can remember. In fact, there have been fighters in my family all of my life. My daddy, my brother, and, long before me, my grandfather and great-great-grandfather had the reputation of fighting for freedom and liberty. My father, Willie Atwood Mason, started out as a farmer, as had his father, Walter Harrison Mason. Both eventually became barbers and moved from rural Hinds County to Jackson. My dad and his family moved to Chicago in 1922 as part of the great black migration north looking for jobs. After working at the American Can Company for a while, my daddy decided to return to Jackson in 1926 or '27 and resume barbering. He worked for two barbershops before he got his own place, called Mason's Barbershop, which was and still is located in back of the Alamo Theater in the historic Farish Street district. He eventually moved out on Hamilton Street, where he worked until he died in 1958. When the spies of the Mississippi State Sovereignty Commission started investigating me in the late fifties and early sixties, they reported that I was "the son of Willie Atwood Mason, the prominent barber on Hamilton Street."

My father stood for excellence and was beyond reproach. He believed in excellence in all things. Regardless of who you were, black or white, if you were not doing right, if you did not do well or if you did not do the best you could, you would incur the wrath of a gentleman who, in no uncertain words, would let you know that you could do better. He would preach excellence to you. On the other hand, if you did well at something, he would compliment you, white or black. So he gave praise without racial bias, and he gave criticism without bias. He had a clean shop, and his customers came first. Willie Atwood Mason would not stand for mediocrity, and he would not stand for any vulgarity, loudmouthing, or rowdy conduct in his shop. He had a way, a demeanor of command, of uprightness and straightforwardness. I gathered some of that, I think, from him. My daddy was very well respected, so white folks didn't fool with him.

My grandfather, Walter Harrison Mason, had farmed and barbered before moving to Chicago, but he was also a Baptist preacher. A horse trade reveals my grandfather's scrappy nature. It seems that, as a youth, my daddy once bought and paid for two horses from two white crooks. Claiming that my dad hadn't paid, the white men came to my grandfather's place to try to take the horses away from him. The confrontation got heated, and my grandfather produced a shotgun. "Get on the porch, Atwood," my grandfather ordered. Then, to the white men he said, "If you come in the yard, I'll let you have it," meaning he would shoot to defend his son's property. The white men left. My daddy kept his horses.

In due course, I learned about my great-great-grandfather, Harrison Mason, born a slave in Virginia in 1792, but transported before the Civil War to Mississippi, where he became the slave of D. M. Birdsong. I never knew Harrison Mason personally, of course, but I knew that it was said that when the Civil War fighting came to Mississippi, Harrison Mason, though up in years, went to the Union lines. He enlisted as a private in Company H, Eleventh Louisiana Colored Infantry, and fought for freedom. After the war, we know he signed a sharecropper's contract with D. M. Birdsong. In spite of the harsh terms of his sharecropper's contract, by selling his labor and that of his children off the Birdsong plantation, Harrison Mason saved enough to buy 360 acres of his own near Bolton, Mississippi. He died at ninety-eight years of age in 1890. Our family patriarch was a distinctive figure around Bolton. Even though two of his sons had reportedly shot a sheriff of Hinds County and escaped to the hills, Harrison Mason himself commanded respect and admiration from a variety of people. Harrison Mason kept to his agreements. He paid his debts conscientiously. My aunt Lois, my dad's oldest sister, now in her nineties, says that the Indians around Bolton at the turn of the century still remembered the old man as "tall like a pine tree, black like tar, and talk like a radio." That was Harrison Mason, my great-great-grandfather.

As I grew up in the 1930s, the sufferings of slavery were still living memories much talked about by the old folks in our family. I actually met my great-grandfather on my father's side, Jeremiah Trotter, who was born a slave in 1850, and I met my great-grandmother, Jenny Brown Trotter, who was born a slave in 1857. On his deathbed in a sparsely furnished room warmed by a potbellied stove, old Jerry Trotter urged us, his great-grandchildren, to gather close so he could see us. I was only eight or nine years old, but my memory of the scene still moves me to tears. I knew more about Jenny Brown Trotter, who lived to be ninety. Jenny's father and her owner was a white man named Hastings Sandridge. Her mother was a slave woman named Eliza. We called Jenny, our great-grandmother, "Maw." She was a great church worker and community worker in her prime. She was also very aggressive. It is said that, as a child six years old, Jenny had the audacity to order federal troops off *our* plantation. I could just see her doing it, too. Maw died in Chicago in 1946. I learned that my great-grandfather on my mother's side, Calvin Augustus Jackson, Sr., a slave, also had a white father, a man named Addams, who seems to have kept a white family in Natchez and a black family around Yazoo City. We think Addams was a Republican National Committeeman after the Civil War. In freedom, Calvin Augustus Jackson, Sr., had the character to choose to act as father to a little girl not his own, my blond, blue-eyed, light-skinned, great-aunt Delia, who came into this world when a white overseer raped her mother (my great-grandmother) in a cornfield. When freedom came, Calvin Augustus Jackson, Sr., would not take his father's white family name, Addams. He chose instead to call himself Jackson. In freedom, Harrison Mason also refused to take the Birdsong name of his last master. I am proud to be descended from strong black men and women. As a child, how could I know them or know about them and not breathe in some of their spirit?

I grew up in poverty, but I didn't know I was poor. We lived in an urban neighborhood, but we did not have electricity until 1938 or '39 when I was ten or eleven. We used outhouses almost all of my childhood. We did not have indoor toilets or indoor running water at our house until 1943. We had one spigot on the back porch and one in the front yard but no indoor sink or commode. We were too poor for luxuries like birthday parties or birthday gifts. My wife, Natalie, made me my first birthday cake after I was grown. I was the baby in our family. I had a brother, Willie Louis Mason, six years older than I, and an older sister named Rozelia. Still, my parents managed to afford some kindergarten for me at a sort of daycare/kindergarten called Robinson's Kindergarten in a private home on Booker Street. My father made it a point every year to buy each of his children his or her own separate set of school textbooks. When we brought home our teachers' book lists, if we all had a dictionary on our list, then each of us got a new Thorndike dictionary, the red-backed ones. There were no hand-me-down textbooks either. Daddy made sure we each had new books every year until the state started providing them free in the 1940s. There was no doubt that our parents placed a premium on school and expected us to do our best.

We had close ties to a large extended family of aunts, uncles, and cousins. This definitely gave us a real sense of security. It also gave us many warm, good times. I had the advantage of knowing both of my grandmothers well. My mother's mother, Mary Williams Jackson Evans, or Sis, as we called her, lived on a farm in the Orange Hill community near Bolton-Edwards about thirty-two miles from Jackson. She is buried in the little Orange Hill Baptist Church cemetery along with both of my parents.

My brother, sister, and I spent some of our Christmas vacations with Sis. I'll always remember that she had a dogtrot house. That is a house made up of two cabins side by side under a common roof but with an open air hallway, or "dogtrot," down the middle between the front and back porches. My grandmother had a kitchen and rooms on one side of the dogtrot and bedrooms on the other side. The walls were plastered with newspaper held up with glue made from flour, but the floors were immaculate. They had been scrubbed such that the grains in the wood stood out as if they had been hand polished. Knowing her, they probably had been. Sis had a big fireplace where we would roast potatoes. We wrapped potatoes in mud, then buried them in the hot coals in the fireplace and sat around, and Sis would tell us stories of things near and far. From Sis we heard about the Civil War battle at nearby Champion Hill, when Grant marched on Vicksburg. Or we heard about the *Titanic*, or the great Mississippi flood of 1927.

I saw my share of cotton growing on Sis's farm, and I would go in late summer to help pick it for her. Those dry bolls, when you reach to take the cotton out, go up under your fingernails and stick you and give you sore fingers. I stayed one whole summer in the country with Eugene "Uncle Buddy" Wallace and his family. The Wallaces were relatives on my mother's side. They gave me many good times, taught me to love molasses and gravy, and took me to a Full Gospel Baptist church. (The Full Gospel movement among black Baptists emphasized worship in which tambourines, drums, cymbals, trumpets, and other musical instruments were used, as sanctioned in Old Testament accounts of the dedication of Solomon's temple in 2 Chronicles 5:13 and in the exhortations to praise found in Psalms 150:3–6.)

When I was sixteen years old, I started spending summers working in Chicago, where I lived with my dad's mother, Effie Trotter Mason, or "Little Mama," and with Dad's sister, Lois. I am so grateful for the gift of my extended family. With so much love and acceptance and support from these and so many others around me, how could I not develop a strong sense of dignity and self-respect? Isn't that the starting point for respecting others and for respecting all human rights?

There were also important saving graces in the larger black community that surrounded me as I grew up. Housing, of course, was generally segregated all over Jackson. We lived in the black section in southwest Jackson called the Washington Addition, which had its own post office that we called Goudy. We took pride in Goudy as a distinct community where we had the only swimming hole in Jackson. Black kids from all over Jackson came to swim at our hole, and, of course, many friendly fights broke out. The best swimmers in Jackson, though, came from the Washington Addition. Without any formal training, I was able to make the Tennessee State swimming team when I went to college. We were proud of Goudy, and I was proud that folks there called my assistant scoutmaster, Albert Powell, "the unofficial mayor" of Goudy.

Mr. Powell is an example of what was wholesome and good in that community. There were men and women who were dedicated to the development of our youths. There were black ladies in Jackson who stood for something in civic life and civil rights, and there were men who were doing things with boys, and who were preparing boys to do things. Because my own high school teachers and even the professors at Jackson State College would go the extra mile beyond the call of duty, they gave me a full life as a high school student in spite of a Jim Crow budget. We had several English teachers who wanted us to be as adept in literature as we were in grammar. They had us memorize poems like "Invictus" and "Crossing the Bar" or lines from Shakespeare. When I was in seventh grade, I could recite Lincoln's Gettysburg Address. My son, Gilbert, Jr., learned it at age five. These and other literary and Bible passages committed to memory have served me well over the years. One of my English teachers, Ms. Mabel Wesley, a graduate of Rust College, especially caught my attention during World War II as she taught us *Macbeth* and its relevance to understanding the struggle for power in the world. She also pointed us to thoughts from Frederick Douglass, who maintained that power does not respect anything but power—never has, never will. From Frederick Douglass I came to understand that you might not get all that you pay for in this life, but you will pay for all you get. You cannot reap the crops without plowing up the ground. So Frederick Douglass concluded that struggle it must be, whether physical or mental. I was a good student who generally made all A's, and I certainly understood the implications of Shakespeare and Frederick Douglass.

When several of us decided to form a club called Boys' Forum at Lanier, we found Coach Ben Allen Blackburn II willing to give up his time to sponsor it and to bring us together with people from various walks of life; we talked and learned etiquette, protocol, and hygiene. Later, when a number of us in Boys' Forum organized another club called the SPECs, or Social, Political, and Economic Club, Professor T. B. Ellis of the Jackson State athletic department took time to meet with us and mentor us. For the first few meetings of the SPECs, Professor Ellis presided until we elected Walter Washington, later to be president of Alcorn University, as our club president. Now, I had a bad habit of sometimes undiplomatically interrupting people in meetings if I wanted to know something. One night I undiplomatically interrupted Professor Ellis. He shot back, "Mr. Mason, do you rise to a point of personal privilege?" I said, "No, sir." "Do you rise to make a motion to adjourn, or take a recess, or fix the time at which to adjourn or any other privileged motion?" I said, "No." He said, "Well, what you are saying is out of order." "Why is it out of order?" I asked. He said, "Because *Robert's Rules of Order* says it's out of order." I said, "Who's Robert?" The next day I bought myself a copy of *Robert's Rules of Order*, and I studied it. From that point in high school on, you would not find *Robert's Rules of Order* too far from me, nor would you find my Bible too far from me, and that still holds. I was glad when they named a building for Professor Ellis at Jackson State.

Others in the community took time with me when they didn't have to. College Hill Baptist Church sponsored Boy Scout Troop 58, my troop. Mr. James White, my scoutmaster, got me a job throwing the *Jackson Daily News*, which gave me a chance to know virtually all of south Jackson in the Washington Addition, including some subscribers in bars and honky-tonks. Mr. White was in the forefront of teaching us to be self-sustaining and aware of economics. He played the violin and taught me to love classical music. Many men and women volunteered as merit badge counselors. Mr. T. C. Elmo, a letter carrier, worked with us on aviation badges, and Mr. John Bates, my high school coach and shop teacher, helped with the wood carving badge. Mr. M. M. Hubert, the cooperative extension agent, helped us with the agriculture badge. Professor Price took me to his lab at Jackson State many evenings to go through various experiments for the chemistry badge. Mrs. Shirley, a biologist, and her husband, Professor Hardy, would take time for Saturday field trips. I thought I knew something when I could call every plant on the Jackson State campus by its Latin name. One summer I got a job landscaping and pouring sidewalks on that campus. The nurse at Jackson State worked with us Scouts on the personal fitness merit badge. It was she who first diagnosed my nearsightedness, which in turn led to my first pair of glasses at age thirteen. Professor J. Y. Woodard worked with us before school, after school, or any time you could get to him. Before I finished high school they even had me mentoring younger boys as a merit badge counselor for some badges and working as a summer camp senior counselor.

Scouting was so good to me, but so was my church. Our church, the St. James Missionary Baptist Church, had Sunday school each Sunday morning and BTU (Baptist Training Union) each Sunday evening. I seldom missed any service. The first pastor I really knew was a lady, Reverend Crawford, who wore a long black dress, and she could really preach. Deacons like Brother Earl Martin, Sr., taught us in Sunday school and BTU. After going over a lesson in small groups, we reassembled, and I was often called on to summarize the lesson for the younger kids. This helped me gain a lot of confidence in public speaking.

The two great events of my childhood happened almost simultaneously when I was twelve years old. I joined the Boy Scouts, and I "got religion" and joined the church. We had a revival meeting in our church, and I made a profession of faith. I made a vow to change—not that I was all that sinful, but I felt that I could change to adopt the ways of the Lord and embrace his teachings. Reverend T. C. Simmons baptized me outdoors in the Goudy brickyard pond. As the congregation sang "On Jordan's stormy banks I stand. . . ," the candidates for baptism assembled in white robes made from sheets and waded out into the water. I was a good swimmer and had no fear, even though Reverend Simmons believed in immersing you three times in the name of the Father, the Son, and the Holy Ghost. Joining the church and joining the Scouts were two great events that just dovetailed for me. I took the Boy Scout oath seriously: "On my honor, I will do my best to do my duty to God and my country and to . . . help other people at all times." And from church I knew that if I was going to be godlike, it also meant helping other people at all times.

Beyond building my self-confidence, the teachers, preachers, and Scout leaders I encountered gave me strong positive role models with powerful ideals to guide my life; they gave me heroes. When we sat around the fire at Scout camps and sang, "Softly falls the night of day, / While our camp fire fades away; / Silently each scout should ask / Have I done my daily task? / Have I kept my honor bright? / Can I guiltless rest tonight? / Have I done and have I dared / Everything to be prepared?," I believed in those words, and I felt them. I still do as an adult. When we sang, "My country 'tis of thee, sweet land of liberty," I believed it, and I believed in freedom even when it was being denied to me as a young black boy. Yes, I believed. And I believed in the ideals of Patrick Henry and Nathan Hale and the Declaration of Independence and the U.S. Constitution. I believed the words of the Bible that God is just and loves all of his children equally. And when my scoutmaster, James A. White, and my Scout troop committeeman, Reverend R. L. T. Smith, Sr., talked freedom and civil rights to the boys, I listened. I also learned from their deeds. I knew that Reverend Smith stood for lofty principles and was a founder of the Mississippi Conference of the NAACP and of the Jackson branch. I knew that he and

James A. White ran an unofficial voter registration office, printing pamphlets and flyers and talking freedom in Mr. White's garage in the 1940s. I knew they had kept on even when their jobs as letter carriers were threatened. I knew that my coach, John Bates, and his wife, Gladys Noel Bates, had lost their jobs when they filed suit to equalize teacher pay for blacks and whites in Mississippi. I knew that Mrs. Rose McCoy, a teacher whose dentist husband help found the Mississippi NAACP, cared enough to bring the great black opera star Marian Anderson to sing at Lanier High School, because black kids couldn't go to events at the city auditorium. Along the way, some caring soul also brought the great singer and actor Paul Robeson to sing on the steps of Sally Reynolds Elementary School in Jackson in 1943, while we assembled on the lawn, our spirits soaring with the crescendos of freedom's melodies. Because someone cared enough to bring him to the ears of a poor boy in Jackson, Mississippi, Paul Robeson inspired me in his songs and in his life. In Paul Robeson I found my greatest black hero.

Paul Robeson was a genius. The son of a black preacher from Philadelphia, Robeson finished first academically in his class at Rutgers, lettered four years in college sports, and in both his junior and senior years was named a college All-American in football. Robeson went on to Columbia Law School and finished tops in his class there, but decided on a career as a singer and actor. What a vibrant, warm bass voice. He sang spirituals, he sang opera, he sang in several languages, and he sang freedom. No one can sing about Joe Hill "going on to make men free" like Paul Robeson. To this day, when I hear Paul Robeson sing the lines of the old spiritual— "One of these mornings bright and fair, / I'll spread my wings and cleave the air, / And I know my robe will fit me well, / Because I tried it on at the gates of hell"—I hear an authentic voice of the African American experience. His statements against injustice and his singing for liberty and for justice to labor got him in trouble with the House Un-American Activities Committee in the 1950s, but he stayed true to his conscience. Paul Robeson became my great living black hero.

How could you be around, be with, sit at the feet of people who love liberty and not absorb some of it yourself? So many people in my childhood were inspirations to me. They reminded me, as one of the poets said, that I, too, could leave behind me "footprints in the sands of time." They helped me believe that I, too, should try to make a difference. They helped me to find myself and to find my calling.

I had wanted to be a doctor from at least the time I was in elementary school or as far back as I can remember. I think the impetus toward medicine really grew out of my own inner makeup, although I had the good fortune to have seen and known some black physicians and dentists as a child. I visited in the home of my friend O. F. Smith, a fellow Boy Scout, whose father was a dentist. I knew about men like Dr. Miller, who ran the Afro-American Hospital at Yazoo City, and Dr. C. B. Christian and the young Dr. A. M. Hall in Jackson. On Farish Street a black physician had founded the Sally Harris Clinic, which most black families in central Jackson used for outpatient treatment rather than going to Baptist. Dr. Miller came from Yazoo City to take my tonsils out at the Sally Harris Clinic. I admired physicians and dentists, but I liked medicine because medicine was disciplined and orderly. As a child, I liked animals, and I liked the body. The mystery of life and of living functions always fascinated me. I wanted to become a doctor because doctors were scientists, and scientists explored things, and I wanted to explore things. At church I learned that Jesus wanted us to serve others, and when I became a Boy Scout and we pledged "to . . . help other people at all times," that just sealed it. I truly wanted to help other people at all times. The first high school term paper I wrote was "What Is This Thing Called First Aid?" I wanted to become a doctor for the science involved and for the Good Samaritan acts that I could do to help other people, to relieve suffering, to save lives, and to prevent disability. I knew that to serve humanity in this way meant going to college, something no one in my immediate family had ever done.

I had heard that Howard University was the best black university in the country, and that it had a good premed curriculum and a medical school. Being a straight-A student, I was qualified, but I knew that Howard was too expensive for our budget. Tennessee State was my second choice, because I had heard that they, too, had a good premed program. However, out-of-state tuition made Tennessee State too expensive. My daddy urged me to go to Tougaloo, where he could pay the cost. I didn't want to go to Tougaloo; not that I had anything against Tougaloo, but I wanted medicine. Seeing my resolve, Daddy found a way. "Well," he said, "you can go to Chicago and work and live with my mother, and she won't charge you any board. If you stay with her summers, you can save enough to go wherever you want to."

So it was that I prepared to go to Chicago to work that summer after high school graduation, and to go on to Tennessee State in Nashville that fall. I was going into the wider world to prepare for the service to humanity that all of my ideals, my curiosities, and my faith in God called me to do. However, these same ideals and the powerful examples in the lives of the people I knew in southwest Jackson also pointed me toward leadership and toward a life committed to community activism. As I stood on the platform ready to board the train to Chicago, my daddy reached for the arm of his sixteen-year-old son, grasped it strongly, and said with emphasis, "Gilbert, be strong, steadfast, unmoved, and trust in God." My dad's hands grasped me again nine years later in a train station in Washington, D.C., to remind me emphatically of these same words. More inspiration was to come from the world outside Mississippi.

TWO

Preparation for Service

[T]herefore get wisdom: and with all thy getting get understanding. Exalt her, and she shall promote thee: She shall bring thee to honour, when thou dost embrace her. —Proverbs 4:7–8

I WAS ONE SORE DUDE THE NIGHT I GOT ON THE TRAIN to make the trip from Jackson to Chicago to stay with Little Mama, my dad's mother, and work in the summer of 1945. I was sixteen years old and had just graduated from high school. That day I had gone out to Sis's farm to say good-bye. I had made the mistake of riding old Dan one last time. Old Dan was the horse my daddy owned and kept at my grandmother's place. Old Dan was in one of those moods where every time I got a little distance from the house, he would take off at a gallop back to the house as fast as he could go, despite my fervent efforts to reign him in. When I thought I had him stopped, he would take off again. So, before I could finally dismount, old Dan had made me physically sore. In a sense, riding old Dan was like riding the unpredictable vicissitudes of segregation in Mississippi. Old Dan's effect had been physical. Racism's effect was more subtle. My physical soreness I felt when I got on the train in Jackson. I did not understand the restrictive soreness imposed by segregation until I got off that train and breathed the freer air of Chicago.

My older sister, Rozelia, who had been to Chicago many times, accompanied me on the trip. When we rolled into the Twelfth Street station, Rozelia announced that we were going to catch the El, Chicago's elevated public transit system, out to my grandmother's apartment. When I got on the El, the only two vacant seats together were beside white folks. Now, here I am from the heart of Mississippi in 1945, and "you don't be sitting by no white folks in Mississippi." I was not familiar with integration at all. Anxiety hit me. I said, "Sudda, Sudda, where do I sit?" (We called my sister Sudda.) She said, "Sit anywhere, fool," and she sat right down beside those white folks. Thoroughly intimidated and not quite knowing what to expect, I sat down beside her, and we rode uneventfully to our destination. That was an experience. My anxiety and fear had come from a soreness created by riding Jim Crow all those years in Mississippi.

My grandmother, Effie Trotter Mason, or Little Mama, as we called her, welcomed me into her home, a basement apartment at 2722 Indiana Avenue on the South Side. The apartment was noisy with streetcars going by at eye level outside and with all sorts of things going on in apartments above us, but Little Mama allowed me to work and save whatever I could for college. During my first two summers in Chicago I stayed with her. My grandmother stood less than five feet tall, but she had a powerful religious faith. Her husband and my grandfather, Walter Harrison Mason, had been a Baptist minister, and one of my uncles, Reverend Abraham Mason, was pastor of a Full Gospel Baptist Church in a converted store-front on South State Street near Comiskey Park. Little Mama and I had many long talks about religion. She was a great singer of spirituals and hymns, and she actually wrote and published several gospel songs. Her song "O Who's Goin' to Lead Me?" affirmed the faith that "Jesus goin' to lead me, / O Jesus goin' to lead me through this unfriendly world." Little Mama's "Hide Me, Jesus, in the Solid Rock!" was her sung prayer that "When trouble comes, as sure it will, / . . . Let thy light be guiding still, / Hide me, Jesus, in the solid rock." Thomas A. Dorsey, the famous composer of the hymn "Precious Lord, Take My Hand," did the musical arrangements for Little Mama's songs and published them. Little Mama and I went to Sunday services at Pilgrim Baptist Church on Indiana Avenue and Thirty-third Street, where she was a member of the one-hundred-voice Pilgrim Gospel Chorus.

The day after I arrived in Chicago, I went out looking for a job. I remembered that in 1922 my daddy had gone to work for the American Can Company in Chicago. As fate would have it, the first plant that I went into was a can company, the Crown Can Company. I told the manager that I was only sixteen but that I wanted to go to college in the fall and needed a job. He said, "Have you ever worked a slitter machine?" I said, "No." I didn't want to ask what a slitter was, but he showed me the machines and how they worked in the can-making process to cut large sheets of tin-coated steel into pieces the width of a can. I got the job as a slitter operator and learned to feed the machine, pushing the sheets through the cutters at just the right time every few seconds. We worked from can to can't—that is, from the time you can see until the time you can't. I caught the streetcar to work and back each day.

At the Crown Can Company in Chicago, I also developed my first real friendships with fellow workers outside my own race. Each day three of us sat down to lunch together, a young Mexican-American fellow, an Italian-American girl, and me. From my Mexican friend I learned about bean sandwiches with chile peppers. From my Italian friend, who smoked on every break, I learned that some people smoke just because they like it. In Chicago, I got to know these two friends from other races without trepidation. This is something that would not have happened in Mississippi at that time.

I gained a sense of public freedom in Chicago that I had not known in Mississippi. I got to know about my uncle Thurston, an army officer, who was one of the first blacks to break the color barrier at Inglewood High School in an exclusive all-white Chicago neighborhood. Chicago was not a perfect city. Its neighborhoods were rigidly segregated, but not its public accommodations. I took great pleasure in being able to walk down State Street in Chicago and just literally go into every store. Unlike in Jackson, Mississippi, in Chicago every store had its door open to black people and all people. Madison Avenue and State Street in the Loop had everything you might want—Brooks Brothers, jewelry stores, the Merchandise Mart. If you love having fun in a big shopping center, as I do, go to the Merchandise Mart in Chicago. Now, I was not about to buy a Brooks Brothers suit or any expensive jewelry, but I could and did go in and look whenever I wanted. I especially delighted in Chicago's public parks, where I could walk freely and enjoy the beauty of God's creation unrestrained by man-made segregationist prohibitions. There is something basic in human nature that makes you yearn for that kind of freedom. Beyond this, I saw my first black policemen in Chicago in 1945. That was somehow reassuring. And even Chicago's white policemen seemed friendlier, or at least they were more polite and courteous to black citizens than what I had seen in Jackson. I came to believe that if I should get into a dispute with a white person in Chicago, I would have an equal opportunity to prove my case with the police or in court. That belief was liberating. In the segregation era in Mississippi, so much of the black man's fear, or at least caution, in the presence of white people came from the fact that Mississippi law enforcement and Mississippi courts gave whites a free hand to intimidate, threaten, beat up, and brutalize blacks. Simple conditioning in such a hostile environment was enough to create anxiety and fear. In Chicago, I lost that fear. I felt free to just wander around the city, something that I wouldn't do now. But back then, it was a great place for the sore spirit of a black teenager to stretch and heal.

Here, as in Jackson, I also gained security from being surrounded by a large extended family of aunts, uncles, and cousins. They gave me an education outside the classroom. My aunt Lois, who had no children of her own, became my guardian angel in Chicago. She worked at Lakeside Press for many years. I actually stayed with Aunt Lois my last three summers in Chicago. My aunt Ruby was an artist and sculptress. For several years, Aunt Ruby had pursued a modeling career in New York, but she had returned to Chicago. Ruby took me to my first formal piano concert in a big hall on State or Wentworth. I dressed in black tie and black suit. She had a big collection of records and taught me to love Billie Holiday and Rachmaninoff. I collect Billie Holiday and Rachmaninoff albums to this day. Ruby was well read and also introduced me to the Rosicrucian idea of reincarnation. My aunt Geneva took me to my first pro football game, the Chicago Bears versus the College Allstars. One of her friends took me to my first White Sox baseball game, where the pregame festivities featured my hero, Paul Robeson, singing several numbers.

Then there was my uncle Stance. Only six years older than I, Stance was my dad's baby brother. In his teen years, Stance had given his folks a rough time, and, to try to help him straighten out, my grandmother had sent him to Mississippi to live with us for a while. Stance was athletic, having been a boxer, but he had settled down to become a professional waiter on trains running from Chicago to Omaha. I admired Stance as a man of the world, and in Chicago, he took me under his wing. One day he decided to show me the city. We started at about Forty-seventh and South Parkway, going east to Cottage Grove where one of his friends lived. He took me into every bar on Forty-seventh, and we crisscrossed from side to side, working our way down the street. Stance showed me off at every stop as his nephew who was studying to be a doctor. Now, I was too young for anything but Shirley Temples, but Stance drank beer. When we got to his friend's place on Cottage Grove, Stance drank a beer or two and suddenly noticed the time. "You know, I'm going to miss my train to Omaha," he said, and we ran to wave the streetcar down, but the motorman wouldn't stop. Stance ran along and tried to "Bogart," running up to the door. The driver slammed the door on Stance's fingers. It hurt Stance for me to have seen this car close its door on him. So, he reformed. Stance did not take another drink of beer or liquor that whole summer.

Stance, who had never finished high school, could converse on every-thing from jazz and bebop to philosophers like Plato, Aristotle, and Karl Marx. I was an avid reader, a member of the Book-of-the-Month Club and the Classical Club, but Stance really introduced me to Karl Marx, Plato, Aristotle, the Epicureans, and Marcus Aurelius before ever I studied them in college. In Chicago I read Carter G. Woodson's pioneering works on black history and discussed them with Stance. Stance told me the first I ever heard about LSD and marijuana and their effects. From Stance I also learned about Charlie "Bird" Parker. Stance took me to the magnifi-cent Regal Theater to hear and see such greats as Duke Ellington, Cootie Williams, Rochester Anderson, Clarence Muse, Louis Armstrong, Moms Mabley, Ella Fitzgerald, and Sarah Vaughan. Then we would sometimes look in at the Savoy Ballroom and catch Billy Eckstine or Count Basie. Stance had worked all over the country, so he told me about many things I would never have thought about. Stance was a beautiful person, a genu-ine good and protective human being. For a while he was my hero, and he was always more like an older brother than an uncle.

Each summer Chicago was an education in itself, but I did not forget my great goal of medicine. My walking and wandering about the city often took me down by Michael Reese Hospital at Thirty-first and Lakefront. And there I would sometimes just stand and dream and hope and pray that, Lord, one day I would be in this hospital or one like it. To me no building had ever looked so pretty as the Michael Reese Hospital. Occa-sionally seeing that hospital helped keep my dream alive through long days of tedious summer labor.

Then each fall, I headed down to Tennessee State in Nashville and back into Jim Crow country to study chemistry, biology, and math. Now, racial discrimination in downtown Nashville in the late forties was just as bad as in Jackson, but I stayed on campus most of the time. In those days, the Tennessee State campus was almost totally self-sufficient, with its own farm, laundry, and cafeteria. You really had little reason to leave the cam-pus, and if you did, you had to walk to town. There were plenty of social outlets to go along with an excellent academic program in chemistry, biol-ogy, and math. Most important, during my freshman year at Tennessee State I met and fell in love with the best thing in my life, Miss Natalie Lorraine Hamlar of Roanoke, Virginia, to whom I was married for forty-eight years. I remember that we went to some segregated movie theaters in Nashville, but I was so much in love that it didn't make any difference as long as I could just be somewhere sitting next to her.

When Natalie and I started courting, and it got serious, I wanted to give her some token that would symbolize our being engaged to become engaged. The usual was a fraternity pin, but I didn't belong to a fraternity. My Eagle Scout pin was the most precious thing I owned, and Natalie knew that. I gave her my Eagle Scout pin. Natalie knew that I was serious about her. However, Natalie's dream was social work, a major not then available at Tennessee State. My heart broke when she transferred to Howard in Washington, D.C., during our sophomore year so that she could get a social work major. Still, we kept in touch and I managed to get up to D.C. in the fall of 1947 to see her. By this time, I had joined the prestigious Alpha Phi Alpha fraternity, and I had a new fraternity pin. Most Alpha men in those days would not give a girl their fraternity pin. I made a switch, though. I took my Eagle Scout pin back and gave Natalie the Alpha pin.

With Natalie gone to Howard, I threw myself into a full and active extracurricular student life at Tennessee State. To make ends meet financially, I worked in the cafeteria, took up meal tickets, and picked up trash. For a time, I washed and ironed other students' shirts for money, but I eventually connected with a laundry in town that gave me forty cents on the dollar for picking up and delivering for their laundry service on campus. These jobs, along with a Tennessee Valley Authority research assistantship in the chemistry department, supplemented my summer savings to sustain me. I made the swimming team and was elected vice president of the freshman class. After two weeks, the president got sick, and I took over as president for the remainder of the year. Then, I was elected president of my sophomore, junior, and senior classes. In Alpha Phi Alpha, I was chapter secretary. I was inducted into Beta Kappa Chi, a scientific fraternity, and became its president and the vice president of Alpha Kappa Mu, an academic honor society sometimes known as the Phi Beta Kappa of black colleges. I was editor in chief for our college yearbook, the *Tennessean*, in 1948 and 1949. On Sundays I stayed busy, too. We had chapel and Sunday school on campus, and I served as class president and assistant superintendent of the Sunday school. All of these offices gave me valuable leadership experiences, more confidence in public speaking, and additional motivation to really study the parliamentary procedure that Professor T. B. Ellis had induced me to learn about in high school.

Of all of these activities, Alpha Phi Alpha meant the most to me. Its fraternal ideals struck a deep chord within me. Alphas pledged to "Ask not what the fraternity can do for you, but what you can do for the fraternity" long before John Kennedy turned his version of the phrase. And the Alpha fraternal ideal stressed that lasting benefits accrue to oneself and one's family in direct proportion to the service one performed for community and fraternity. I had been infused with the service ideals of the Boy Scouts of America, so this just resonated with me. I jumped from the Scouts into Alpha Phi Alpha. Outside of the church and the home these two organizations were, and still are, my molding guides.

The academic program at Tennessee State in chemistry and biology was challenging. We had a good faculty. Dr. Carl Hill and Professor Townes had written textbooks in chemistry. Townes had also worked on the Manhattan Project, as had Professor Dillard, my physical chemistry teacher. In biology we saw a lot of visiting lecturers from Meharry Medical College. Chemistry and biology students at Tennessee State also took joint seminars with students at Fisk and Vanderbilt. Fisk had one of the greatest black chemists of this century in Professor St. Elmo Brady. Tennessee State students were lucky to be able to take classes with St. Elmo Brady. Even white students from Vanderbilt and other Nashville colleges came up to Fisk to take St. Elmo Brady's classes. And in the late 1940s, I attended integrated seminars at Vanderbilt as part of my Tennessee State science curriculum. Segregation in higher education in the upper south was eroding.

I took eighteen hours of pure science my first semester at Tennessee State and made the swimming team. I did well with the load. The second semester I made all A's. They said I was the first male student in twenty-five years to have done so. During my sophomore year things got rougher with quantitative analysis. The swimming coach, Professor Hughes, promised that if I would go out for the team, I would letter my second year. I said, "Coach, if I work to make the swimming team again, I'm going to flunk quan." I made up my mind that since I was going to school to become a doctor, not a Johnny Weismuller, I would quit the swim team. I have had a little regret from time to time for not having earned an athletic letter from Tennessee State, but I made the right choice. I had an excellent science program in front of me, and I couldn't waste that opportunity.

Of course, study in the humanities was required of everyone. I particularly remember sophomore literature classes which reintroduced me to Emerson, Thoreau, and Whitman. Emerson's essay "Self-Reliance" and the poem "Forbearance" made a deep impression on me. I carry a copy of "Forbearance" in my wallet. Thoreau's "Civil Disobedience" had already captured my imagination and had become my credo. On two occasions twenty and more years after leaving Tennessee State, I have gone out of my way to visit Thoreau's grave in Massachussetts, which is for me a shrine. Whitman's love of democracy and his tribute to Lincoln in "O Captain! My Captain!" remains meaningful to me. I especially remember a lit class at Tennessee State in which the professor tried to push us to define this thing called democracy, which Whitman so celebrated. After some students ventured the standard textbook definitions, I shocked the lady with an answer that boiled up from my own painful awareness of the great gulf between this nation's ideals and its practices. "Democracy," I exclaimed, "is a farce!" Alarmed, the professor grasped her lips with both hands. "It is a farce," I said, "when its benefits are entrusted to some and denied to others." These sentiments were shocking to some faculty members in an all-black college in the South in 1946, but they are a good example of my evolving social and political thinking as a student.

I finished Tennessee State with "high distinction" in 1949. I earned a double major in chemistry and biology with a strong minor in math. Natalie and I had become engaged at the beginning of my junior year, so I hoped that I would be able to go to medical school at Howard University in Washington, D.C., where she was starting her master's in social work. My MCAT scores and grades made me confident that I would be admitted to medical or dental school somewhere. I applied at Howard, Meharry, Harvard, Washington University, and St. Louis University, but Howard was my first choice. The waiting lists were long, and it took a year for me to gain admission to medical school after college graduation. In the late summer of 1949, I decided to move from Chicago on down to Washington to be nearer to Natalie and to enroll in some graduate chemistry and anatomy courses at Howard to keep my scientific aptitude sharp. Natalie was staying with her sister and brother-in-law and working, but I had no money, so marriage was out of the question for the time being. I had to find a place to live and a job in D.C.

Once again my extended family came to my rescue. Little Mama, my grandmother in Chicago, had brothers living in the Washington, D.C., area. Decatur Trotter, my great-uncle, gave me a place to sleep and fed me until I could find a job and housing on my own. Decatur Trotter worked at the U.S. Naval Yard near Washington and received many citations for innovations and improvements on tools that the navy used. Decatur was a deacon in his church, active as a Boy Scout leader, and all around a grand man. Decatur and his wife, Bernice, introduced me to Bernice's father, Reverend Caesar Alexander, a retired Methodist minister and widower with a big house and a little room to rent. Reverend Caesar Alexander, or Papoo as we called him, became one of my heroes and a molding influence in my life.

For seven dollars a week, I rented the little room from Papoo. It was just big enough to walk into and back out of. You couldn't turn around. I was grateful for the room, and I soon realized how fortunate I was to be in the presence of Caesar Alexander and to sit at his feet and learn from his life. I mean I was fortunate. Reverend Caesar Alexander had read and seen and heard and associated with the great black leaders of his generation. To sit at his feet and hear him describe Booker Washington and the speech Washington made at the D.C. Farmer's Market or to hear Papoo's vivid descriptions of Marcus Garvey and what he said at Lafayette Square in front of the White House was fascinating. The life and message of Marcus Garvey about pride in who you are and about the absolute necessity for black entrepreneurship and black economic empowerment came alive for me. The lives of great men have always inspired me—Paul Robeson, Marcus Garvey, and W. E. B. Du Bois. I was so fortunate to be in the presence of living history because of Caesar R. Alexander. You never know the impact of your example on another person. Reverend Alexander and so many others have given me so much. The old Nelson Eddy recording of "Pilgrim Song" says it all: "And bless the staff that hither bore me, / The alms that helped me on my way, / . . . Lovers, strangers or foes, would that I / Might clasp them in fervent rapture to my heart." In the still and quiet of my little room at Papoo's house I had time to read and think and reflect and even write some poetry. In Washington, D.C., I became a physician and a better man.

In 1949, the city of Washington, D.C., was filled with contradictions. As our nation's capital it was rich in the symbols of freedom and our highest ideals. However, Washington was also a southern city shackled with segregation and white supremacy. I could just wander around and gain inspiration amongst the monuments and museums. I'd go out looking for a job and wind up in the Library of Congress. I'd go out again the next day and end up at the Smithsonian, or the Armed Forces Medical Museum, or the National Archives, or the botanical garden, or the natural science museum, or the Capitol, or Frederick Douglass's home. It was big time business to me. I would go into the Capitol rotunda with its great monuments and just look around. Every child should visit the nation's capital and its historic sites. That's one Washington, inspiring you with the ideals and greatness of the country at its best.

Then, there was the Washington that was as full of segregation and racial discrimination as any other city in the South. In 1949, segregated theaters, hospitals, hotels, and schools were the rule in Washington, D.C., just as much as in Jackson, Mississippi. There were department stores in

Washington that would not serve blacks. When I arrived in D.C., Mary Church Terrell, founder of the National Association of Colored Women and charter member of the NAACP, and a group of ladies were picketing Woodard and Lothrop because they wouldn't serve blacks. This was long before the Montgomery bus boycott or the North Carolina lunch counter demonstrations. Before I left D.C. in 1954, Mary Church Terrell had succeeded in a lawsuit to end discrimination in Washington hotels, restaurants, buses, and other public facilities. What a role model! A graduate of Oberlin College, daughter of an ex-slave from Memphis who had become a millionaire, Mary Church Terrell was a well-educated, wealthy, beautiful, elegant, stately lady pounding the pavement for human rights and dignity.

I began making it a point to try different businesses in Washington to see which ones would serve me. Natalie told me about this fabulous store off G Street called Julius Garfinkel. She said, "They won't serve black folks." I said, "We're going to find out." It was around Christmastime, and Natalie's birthday was coming up. I wanted to give her a nice gift, so off to Julius Garfinkel's I went in a defiant mood, thinking, "They're going to serve me." I broke in there with my southern self and looked around the store, waiting for somebody to tell me to get out. I found a stylish dark-blue umbrella with simulated reptile skin on the handle, just perfect for Natalie. So, I took it to the white sales clerk and said, "I want to buy this." She looked at me, looked at the umbrella, and hesitated; then, as if to say, "It's Christmas," she sold it to me, and wrapped it up. I gave this surprise to my love, saying, "Julius Garfinkel *will* serve you."

My main concern was finding a way to support myself until I could be admitted to medical school. In 1949, I got a temporary summer job with the Census Bureau. When that played out, I found work sweeping the floors and putting together toys for twenty-six dollars per week at a national chain store noted for its bicycles, auto parts, tires, and appliances. Near Christmastime as business increased, I worked assiduously. However, the white store manager, who was about my age, insisted that I call him "sir." I had refused to use this form of address as a teenager in Jackson, and as a college graduate in Washington, D.C., I was not about to use it on someone my own age. Segregationist etiquette took its course once again. On a cold Christmas Eve in Washington, D.C., this bigoted young white store manager fired me for refusing to call him "sir." Segregation and degradation went together in D.C. just as they had in Jackson.

I soon landed another job washing dishes for twenty-six dollars a week at the Roger Smith Hotel, which used to stand at 1700 Pennsylvania Avenue, just down from the White House. I walked past the White House every day going to work. The president was staying in Blair House while they renovated the White House. I happened along just minutes after the Puerto Rican nationalists attempted to assassinate President Truman at Blair House, and I saw the security activities in the aftermath as I walked on, spellbound, to my job at the Roger Smith. After about three months, I switched to the very elegant old Shoreham Hotel, where I continued to wash dishes for twenty-six dollars per week.

I got more human rights education at the Shoreham, which at that time still catered to a "white only" clientele. There were certain parts of the hotel that were off limits to black employees, even in emergencies. Hurrying one day, I snagged my finger on a stainless steel runner on the dish slide and opened a deep gash in my finger. The hotel had a resident doctor, but I was made to go a very roundabout way to the doctor's office to keep me out of the "white only" areas of the establishment. However, I got a different kind of human rights education at the Shoreham and the Roger Smith. In this post–World War II era, there were several displaced persons from Hitler's concentration camps working at these hotels alongside me. One in particular impressed me. He had been a philosophy professor at the University of Heidelberg before the Nazis took over. He used to pick through the garbage for food. He knew that I wanted to be a doctor and that I was waiting to get into med school. He used to say, "Mason, you know, sometimes you have to step down before you can step up." I learned firsthand some of the things that had gone on in the concentration camps and what had happened to Germany. Stark fear still haunted the minds and memories of these Holocaust survivors whose gaunt bodies bore witness to the awful fruits of unchecked bigotry everywhere.

At least I was working and taking graduate courses in chemistry at Howard, but medical school was still my dream. Both Meharry Medical College back in Nashville and Howard's dental school in D.C. let me know fairly early that I would be admitted to their fall 1950 classes. Howard's medical school was what I really wanted, but it was slow in acting on applications. With time running out for me to commit to Meharry or the dental school, I reved up my courage and went to Dr. K. Albert Hardin, chairman of the Howard medical school's admissions committee, and told him my dilemma. God was with me. They called a special meeting of the admissions committee, and I was literally the first applicant admitted to the entering class at Howard University College of Medicine for 1950.

Natalie and I married on July 29, 1950. My finances eased some that summer, as I got a job with the Census Bureau. I had again applied for summer work there but was at first rejected. Then, I ran across a friend from Tennessee State who had completed his sophomore year and landed a Census Bureau job. It appeared to me unreasonable that I, an honor graduate of Tennessee State, should be rejected in favor of a college sophomore. I decided to go to see Senator John Stennis of Mississippi. The senator graciously gave me an audience, and I told him my needs and my frustration with the Census Bureau. "I am a Mississippian," I said. "I want a job." The senator said, "Go back tomorrow." I did just that, and found immediate employment as a GS-3. I soon found that my friend who had not finished college was a GS-4. I went back to Senator Stennis and told him. "How did you vote last time?" he asked. Now, 1948 was the year the Dixiecrats bolted the Democratic Party and Mississippi had gone Dixiecrat, but I truthfully replied, "I didn't vote. I was too young." "Go back tomorrow," he said. The next day, I was promoted to GS-5. Years later as a physician, I was in Washington lobbying for Head Start. I recounted this story to Senator Stennis, and he claimed to remember it. He said, "Well, I was right. I believed in you, and you amounted to something." I learned something about the importance of patronage and personal friendships. How many talented people get passed over who have no connections, or who lack the courage to go to power with their qualifications and needs?

In the fall came medical school. For once, Mississippi's Jim Crow system favored me. Because there was no opportunity for its black citizens to attend graduate school or medical school inside the state, Mississippi offered to pay black medical students a five-thousand-dollar stipend in monthly installments over four years on the condition that recipients return to Mississippi to practice for at least five years after med school. Natalie had a similar but smaller stipend from the state of Virginia to support her master's of social work studies at Howard. Our finances were spread thin, but somehow we managed. On Christmas breaks, I worked for the U.S. Postal Service delivering in the snow or sorting the Christmas mail surge.

Medical school was rigorous, and Natalie's graduate work was demanding. So, we had to study all the time. We had no car. We had to walk to school. Still, in all those years we never missed a class, and we were never late for a class, not even a 7:30 A.M. roll call. The Howard faculty was superb. Natalie's great professor was Ina Bell Lindsey, one of the nation's pioneers in the field of social work. One of the greatest teachers I ever encountered was my anatomy professor, Dr. W. Montague Cobb, a graduate of Amherst with an M.D. from Howard and a Ph.D. from Case Western Reserve. Dr. Cobb was a real scholar. He published research in anatomy, and he must have quoted the Bible as much as any theologian. He was editor in chief of the *Journal of the National Medical Association* for many years. As a professor and as a man, Dr. W. Montague Cobb had a powerful influence on me. The overall program was well organized, thorough, and focused on excellence. The entering first-year medical students were assigned to five-person support groups arranged alphabetically. My group consisted of Marius from New York, Mason from Mississippi, Mulvaney (a woman) from New York, Magee from Washington, D.C., and Newton from New Jersey. It was tough.

Howard's program gave med students in their last two years many excellent clinical experiences or externships to back up that power in the classroom. Freedmen's was a black hospital that took Howard externs, interns, and residents. However, segregationist traditions imposed certain limitations. For example, some traditionally white hospitals would allow Negro medical students to go on rounds and hear cases presented, but would not allow them to "put on hands" to examine white patients. Public hospitals in the Washington, D.C., area began desegregating while I was at Howard. We did pediatrics at Gallinger, now D.C. General, which had previously been "white only." When my class went to Gallinger to do our pediatric training, the hospital had accepted its first black resident, Dr. LaSalle LeFall, only one year earlier. LeFall broke the color barrier for black doctors, and our class broke the color barrier at Gallinger for black medical students. Between my junior and senior years I was lucky enough to be one of five Howard medical students hired as externs at the Maryland state mental hospital called Crownsville. We were the first black students to work there. There were two German-trained Jewish staff physicians at Crownsville who were displaced persons from Nazi Germany. We learned a lot of medicine from them, especially from Dr. Mendal, who passed on a lot about Jewish sufferings under the Hitler regime. Dr. Mendal taught me how to do spinal taps. I stayed on campus at Crownsville one night a week to answer emergencies. Here we quickly learned to suture, because the patients fought or got cut frequently. We also learned to evaluate a patient's reality orientation and to administer appropriate sedatives when necessary.

During my last semester at Howard in January of 1954, my son, Gilbert, Jr., was born at the historic Freedmen's Hospital established in 1867. At about the same time, I got a job as an extern at St. Elizabeth's, a psychiatric hospital in Washington, D.C. I was the first black anything there—extern, intern, or physician. I got off the bus every day right in front of Frederick Douglass's house and walked to work surrounded by history. My job was to give annual physical examinations to patients, many of whom had not had physicals in years. In doing this, I discovered that even the minds of the mentally ill can be permeated with racism. As I examined one elderly white man, he looked up at me and asked, "Are you a doctor?" I said, "Yeah, I'm a doctor." He said, "Well, I'll be damned. A nigger is a doctor." I asked him how long he had been in the hospital, and he told me that he had been there since 1898. I said, "Well, nowadays we have Negroes driving buses, teaching school, and flying airplanes." He did not want to believe me. "I'm going to have to check that with Dr. Willis," he snorted. Dr. Willis was white. This patient's racial stereotypes were still intact despite his psychosis. Even in the confused mindscape of mental illness, he wasn't going to believe a black man.

In the spring of 1954, I graduated from Howard Medical School with honors, and I received the top award in neurology for a paper dealing with nomenclature in psychiatry. I was ready for an internship, but there were still only a handful of hospitals in the United States that would take black interns. I applied at Michael Reese, the hospital of my dreams in Chicago, but I wound up at Homer G. Phillips Hospital in St. Louis. This turned out to be good for me, because my internship at Homer G. Phillips gave me a much broader base of practical experience than I might have gotten elsewhere. As an intern, I worked hard, seventy-two hours on, twelve hours off. It was rough. They paid me $155 per month. Natalie and Gilbert, Jr., stayed in Mississippi for the first part of my internship. I lived at the interns' dormitory, which was connected to the hospital through a tunnel. I saw almost everything there was to see in medicine: infectious diseases, pediatrics, adult male and female medicine, male and female surgery, ob-gyn. I delivered babies and learned to do cesarean sections and tubal ligations. We wired jaws, set legs, and treated gunshot wounds and all types of traumas from automobile and industrial accidents. I got little sleep, but these were great experiences for someone like me who wanted to be a family practitioner back home in Mississippi.

Eventually, I got an apartment in a home near King's Highway on Labadie Street, and Natalie and the baby joined me for my final few months of internship. I had little time to really see or get to know St. Louis, but in 1954 the city was desegregating its streetcars and buses, and black and white hospitals had begun to exchange personnel. By Christmas of 1954, we had some white medical students at Phillips from St. Louis University and Washington University, but there was not yet reciprocity for black students and interns at the white hospitals except for occasional lectures or seminars. Still, as I finished my internship in 1955, old patterns of segregated race relations were changing, if slowly, in both St. Louis and Washington, D.C.

With a rich and tough internship under my belt at Homer Phillips, I felt well prepared to set up a medical practice. I had seen Chicago, Washington, Nashville, and St. Louis—four big cities in the world outside Mississippi. In 1954, my dad made the trip to Washington for my graduation from medical school. When I took Daddy to the train station for his return trip home, an older black man heard that Daddy was headed back to Mississippi. "Man, if they let you out of Mississippi once," he questioned, "why in the world would you go back?" Daddy's reply was simple. "It's my home," he said, "and I want to go back." A year later in 1955 as I completed my internship, my idealism also drew me back home to Mississippi. In the atmosphere that was Howard University in the 1950s, I had gotten a solid medical education, but I also got an education in humanity. Washington had surrounded me with the history and idealism of freedom. Howard just drove it home. Mordecai Johnson, the first black president of Howard University, was still there. He brought champions of freedom from around the world to lecture and speak at graduations. Mordecai Johnson always gave spellbinding introductions that made you know the importance of the philosophy behind any speaker he presented. The historian John Hope Franklin and the writer E. Franklin Frazier were teaching at Howard in those days, and while I could not sit in their classes, I heard them give talks. I heard James Nabritt III, the dean of the Howard University Law School and one of the lead attorneys for the 1954 *Brown v. the Board of Education of Topeka* desegregation case. So, I had sat at the feet of giants inside and outside the classroom. Freedom and public service were just in the air at Howard. My beloved anatomy professor, W. Montague Cobb, was more than just a physician and scholar. As national president of the NAACP for many years, Dr. Cobb lived his commitment to freedom and community service for all to see. He used to tell us, "Go south, young man." Black physicians' services and black physicians' influence for social uplift were most needed in the South. Dr. Mordecai Johnson, the president of Howard, echoed this in his talks with students. The South was my home, and I wanted, above all, to serve. The Howard ideal was that physicians were not just healers but teachers who should become a part of their community. Howard inspired us with the notion that medicine had to do with healing the soul, the heart, and the spirit as well as the body. Thus, by the time I finished my training, medicine and the struggle for human freedom and dignity seemed synonymous. I concluded that dedication to one required dedication to the other. The Boy Scout oath has always meant a lot to me. I had a clear sense of duty both to my patients and to the world in which we all must live. As a boy in Mississippi, I had also learned about an oath that Athenian youths took to "transmit this city far more beautiful than it was transmitted to me." Howard reinforced these ideals. I believed deeply in the words of these two oaths when I decided to come home to Mississippi to practice medicine, to teach, and to become a part of the community.

THREE

Going Home to Serve

*[B]ut whosoever will be great among you, shall be your minister: And whosoever
of you will be the chiefest, shall be servant of all. —Mark 10:43–44*

IN THE SUMMER OF 1955, I CAME HOME TO MISSISSIPPI
to practice medicine. I wanted to come back. Mississippi's infant mortality
rates were high. At the time of my decision to return, I expressly pointed
out three guiding goals for my medical practice: I wanted to see healthy
babies, healthy mothers, and good housing for my mothers and babies.
This meant good prenatal care, safe deliveries, and good neonatal care. I
needed to be able to get staff privileges in a hospital to deliver babies. For
black doctors at this time, hospital staff privileges were rare, whether you
were in the South or the North. In Mississippi the black-owned Taborian
Hospital in Mound Bayou and the African-American Hospital in Yazoo
City granted black doctors staff privileges. In 1955, no white-run hospital
in the state's capital city, Jackson, had ever granted a black physician staff
privileges of any kind. Nonetheless, I believed, perhaps naively, that my
training at Howard Medical School and Homer Phillips Hospital made
me especially well suited to treat the conditions I would encounter in
Mississippi's impoverished communities. An all-white local Mississippi
hospital board might not see it that way. Still, I knew that I was needed,
and, after all, I had signed a five-year obligation to practice in Mississippi
when I had taken the state's five-thousand-dollar grant for medical school.
I hoped and prayed to find a place in Mississippi where I would be allowed
to serve to my fullest potential.

I believe that providence, acting through a cafeteria worker at Homer
Phillips in St. Louis, opened the doors that allowed me to set up a practice
in Biloxi, Mississippi, a coastal town with about ten thousand black citizens out of a total population of some forty-three thousand. In 1955, Biloxi

was losing its only active black physician, a woman named Dr. Velma Wesley. Off up in St. Louis finishing my internship, I had no reason to know this, but I had made friends with a cafeteria worker who happened to be from Pass Christian, another Mississippi coast town near Biloxi. On duty at about 2:00 A.M. one morning, I went to the cafeteria to snack. My friend was working this shift, and we talked. When she found out that I was from Mississippi, this cafeteria worker told me about a Dr. Felix Dunn, a Meharry graduate from Mississippi who had come through Homer Phillips a couple of years earlier and gone back to practice in Gulfport, Mississippi. I had never met or heard of Dr. Dunn, but I took his name and wrote to him to inquire about prospects for my setting up a practice on the Mississippi Gulf Coast. Unknown to me, Dr. Dunn forwarded my letter over to Dr. Velma Wesley, who was about to leave her general practice in nearby Biloxi. So, out of the blue, one day as I was making rounds in St.Louis, I got a long distance phone call. On the line, Dr. Wesley introduced herself and said, "I'll be leaving here in May, and I'd like to sell you my equipment and if necessary my practice." We talked further, and I discovered that I knew Dr. Wesley's husband, who had been a medical student at Howard one year behind me. She had been in Biloxi for eighteen months and was planning to rejoin her husband in Detroit, where he planned to intern and where she wanted to do a residency.

With alacrity, I caught a train to Mississippi. Dr. Wesley showed me around Biloxi, and introduced me to the office landlord and to some of my future patients. I took out a note to buy her equipment, but I declined to buy her practice. I said, "I'll earn a practice, if I merit one." Before heading back to St. Louis, I called Dr. Dunn to thank him for passing my letter along.

I finished my internship and returned to Biloxi in July of 1955 to open my practice at 439½ East Division Street. Located in a predominantly black neighborhood, my first office was a wood frame building with a sand-stone-colored, simulated-brick tar paper finish. I had one examining room, a consultation room, a lab, a rest room, and a waiting room. The building was small but efficient, and, as a State Sovereignty Commission agent later reported, it was air-conditioned. I rented this little building for sixty-five dollars per month from Mr. James Pollard, Sr., a local black businessman. I hired Mrs. Gilmore, an LPN, to work as my receptionist and nurse, and Natalie helped with insurance forms. Little did I know that within eight years this little building would withstand two attempted firebombings.

I found that Mississippi was as segregated when I came back in 1955 as it had been when I left in 1945. There were only forty-seven black physicians in the state when I left in 1945, and there were exactly forty-seven when I got back. When I had made a trip down to take my Mississippi State Medical Licensing Exams at the "white-only" King Edward Hotel in Jackson in 1954, I sat for the exam in the room with the white interns and examinees. However, when break time came I literally had no place to go. I could not go with the white doctors to the coffee shop or to get a soda. Those places were off limits to blacks. I decided to try to relax on a sofa in the second-floor lobby. A white attendant quickly told me that blacks were not allowed in the lobby, and that I would have to remain in the testing room alone during breaks. Whatever may have been going on with the U.S. Supreme Court, or in Washington or St. Louis, Jim Crow had no chinks in his armor in Mississippi in 1954.

I soon found that Biloxi was just like any other Mississippi town in this regard. Its schools were segregated and unequal. To accommodate servicemen stationed at Keesler Air Force Base, there were separate white and colored USOs. Everywhere there were separate but unequal white and colored waiting rooms, rest rooms, and drinking fountains. Poll taxes and fear of capriciously administered literacy tests kept most blacks from voting. All public accommodations in Biloxi and Harrison County legally discriminated against Negroes. In courtrooms, whites sat on the left side of the aisle and blacks sat on the right. White political candidates would not address integrated audiences. On the transit system, my wife was sent to the back of the bus. The beachfront hotels, restaurants, and tourist entertainments were "white only." And a beautiful twenty-six-mile-long white sand beach was strictly forbidden territory for blacks, except for a few dozen yards in front of the Gulfport Veterans Hospital.

What did Biloxi-style Jim Crow mean to my medical practice? It meant that I almost never saw a white patient for the first twenty-five years that I practiced. It meant that white doctors maintained separate colored waiting rooms and separate colored entrances to their offices. Jim Crow Biloxi-style meant that in 1955, when I responded to a chamber of commerce membership drive by sending in a check for thirty-six dollars, Mr. Anthony Ragusin returned my check to me in person, explaining that the Biloxi chamber just wasn't ready for a black member—not even a black doctor. Jim Crow meant that a few local pharmacists refused to type "Mr.," "Mrs.," or "Miss" in front of my patients' names on their medication containers. More seriously from a medical standpoint, Jim Crow meant that Negro patients admitted to the Biloxi Hospital were sent to the so-called annex instead of the main part of the hospital. The annex was a two-room wooden building with a brick veneer. Each room contained a four-bed ward. Regardless of their ailments or relative medical conditions, whether infectious or life threatening, men were confined in one room and women in the other. New mothers, if they were black, were confined in this exposed ward with their newborn babies. When pregnant black mothers presented themselves in labor at the hospital emergency room, they were sent to the annex rather than to any specialized labor room. This was risky. When they were ready to deliver, my mothers had to be rushed around a corner to catch an elevator to the third-floor delivery room in the main hospital complex. Many times we didn't make it that long distance to the delivery room. The baby would be born while we waited for the elevator, or on the way up to the third floor. Newborn black babies and their mothers were sent back to the annex and were exposed to whatever illness might be in the next bed over on the ward. White babies, on the other hand, went to the nursery. No black baby went to the nursery unless it was critically ill or near death.

Almost everywhere in the country a black physician would have expected difficulty getting hospital privileges in 1955. Thankfully, I had no trouble getting hospital privileges in Biloxi. Ms. Emma Lou Ford, a white hospital administrator, was very receptive to my affiliation with the Biloxi Hospital. She had looked carefully at my record from Howard and Homer Phillips. Senior white physicians on staff respected the breadth of my training as an intern and told me that I could do any procedure that I was big enough to do and had been trained to do. While I could practice in the hospital, Jim Crowism made my status a little strange. The hospital had three categories for approved staff physicians: active, courtesy, and emeritus. Only active staff members voted in hospital staff meetings. Courtesy and emeritus staffers could attend staff meetings, but were not allowed to vote. From 1955 to 1966, I was a courtesy staff member. Medically, they would let me do anything I was big enough to do, but they would not give me the title of active staff member, not even when I completed advanced certifications. The old racial stereotypes were strong. A black doctor practicing in the hospital was astounding to white folks and even to black folks. I remember a white LPN who met me at the hospital door one day, her arms akimbo. I said, "What's the matter?" She said, "I never saw one before." I said, "What do you mean you never saw one?" She said, "I never saw a black doctor before." Even the other physicians had not seen enough black doctors to feel comfortable giving me the voting rights that went with active, rather than courtesy, staff status. On the other hand, I could practice in the hospital, something no black doctor in Jackson could do at the time.

I also found fellow physicians in Biloxi—white physicians—who were willing to assist my professional development. Hospital regulations required any doctor who had not served a residency in a specialty area to do a preceptorship under a senior staff physician to gain certification to perform senior procedures in that specialty. I sought and gained certification for senior procedures in ob-gyn and surgery. In this setting I actually struck up genuine friendships with some of the white physicians— friendships that endured over the years and proved precious. Dr. Frank G. Gruich, Dr. Clay Easterly, and Dr. W. L. Sekul came to be high on that list of valued white friends. Gruich and Easterly were the specialist preceptors under whose supervision I gained senior certifications. Sekul was a pediatrician. Since I was getting hospital privileges and professional development assistance from these men, it seemed that my prayers for the opportunity to serve to my fullest capabilities were being answered. Frank Gruich and Clay Easterly documented my ob-gyn and surgical competence, covered my patients for me when I was out of town, and stuck by me courageously in the most difficult moments of the 1960s civil rights struggle.

Gruich and Easterly could and did certify my professionalism. They could not get me voting privileges on the hospital staff. Nor could they get me membership or voting privileges in the Mississippi State Medical Association or its local affiliate, the Coast Counties Medical Society. Because I, as a Negro, could not gain the status of voting member in these local or state organizations, I could not become a member of the American Medical Association. Nationally, in 1895, this absurdity in the AMA had led black physicians to organize the National Medical Association, which, though predominately black, held its membership open to all races. In Mississippi our small professional community of black physicians, dentists, and pharmacists formed the Mississippi Medical and Surgical Association. Locally, black medical professionals across the Mississippi, Alabama, and Florida gulf coasts came together in the black Gulf Coast Medical, Dental, and Pharmaceutical Association. Thus, from our own resources, we saw to it that black practitioners did not work in total isolation. Regular meetings in each of these medical groups, white or black, involved a business session, a social gathering or a dinner, and a scientific session. Our black association typically met in members' homes, since restaurants and hotels were closed to us.

As a professional, I thought my patients deserved the benefit of my keeping up with the science available in all of these groups. I decided to apply for membership in the white Mississippi State Medical Association and its Coast Counties Medical Society affiliate. Dr. Milas Love in Gulf-port also applied. Under pressure, these white organizations created the category of "scientific member" to accommodate interested black doctors, but they denied us any voting rights. They informed us that we could attend scientific sessions whenever the white state or local associations met, but we could not attend their dinners, dances, or business sessions. Dr. Love and other black physicians refused to be embarrassed or humili-ated with this second-rate status and would not participate. Not me, though. My attitude was get your foot in the door. Go, see, be seen, and find out what's going on. So every time the Mississippi State Medical Association or the Coast Counties Medical Society met, I showed up if I possibly could. As the only black physician in attendance, I was in many a lonely place.

On the coast, though, I took some comfort in my evolving friendships with white physicians. I will never forget the day in 1959 when four white doctors stood up for me as a fellow professional and a fellow human being against their own executive committee at a Coast Counties Medical Society meeting at the Biloxi Yacht Club. Because I, as a black, was banned from meals and business sessions, I arrived and waited outside in the hallway that day, while the white voting members finished eating. The scientific session, which I was permitted to attend, was to follow the meal. Lo and behold, out comes a member of the executive committee inform-ing me that the speaker was to be Rubel Phillips, the Republican candidate for governor, and that "Mr. Phillips said that he will not speak to an integrated audience. So, you're going to have to leave."

As a scientific member, I protested my eviction from this session. At about that time Dr. Frank Gruich, Dr. Charles Floyd, Dr. A. K. Martino-lich, and, I believe, Dr. D. L. Clippinger came to the hallway in my sup-port. With an unpleasant scene developing in the hallway, the executive committee called me into a room. I continued to insist on my rights as a scientific member. The full wrath of the executive committee now erupted. They threatened to go after my medical license if I didn't get out of that place. At this point, my four white colleagues arose almost as one body in righteous indignation and said, "If you put Dr. Mason out, we go, too." The committee threatened me so viciously that eventually I said, "Fellows, let's go." So we left—all five of us, one black and four coura-geous whites—in Mississippi, in 1959. Those gentlemen, those champions of human rights and justice, those four white physicians recognized me, a

black man, as a fellow physician. In the face of humiliation and ridicule
from their own colleagues, they came out with me, and I wasn't even a
voting member. I left frustrated and angry but also gratified at my friends'
support.

I kept on showing up at the local white medical society's scientific
sessions. To gain information and succeed with my patients, I could endure humiliation. I was even ready to pay double dues to learn from both
the white and the black professional groups. Jim Crowism put the white
medical association's moral and professional integrity on trial, not mine.
Seven years later, in March of 1966, I received an unusual and somewhat
puzzling personal letter from this group summoning me to a meeting at
the Pass Christian Yacht Club. I went as I was directed, and, to my surprise, I found that Dr. Milas Love was also there in response to a similar
mysterious letter. A business session opened, and we were duly inducted
into the formerly all-white Coast Counties Medical Society as full voting
members. After eleven years of persistence, the walls came tumbling
down. I was finally free to benefit from full association with other professionals on an equal basis. With this barrier removed, I followed through
and joined the AMA and the formerly all-white Mississippi State Medical
Association. At the same time in the Jackson area Dr. Al Britton and Dr.
Robert Smith, both black physicians, were admitted into the formerly all-
white local and state medical societies. In 1972, I became the first black
delegate ever elected to officially represent his local affiliate society at a
meeting of the Mississippi State Medical Association.

Things were by no means perfect, but I could and did practice good
medicine in Biloxi. Patients began knocking on my door in July of 1955,
and they have never stopped knocking. In a small city like Biloxi, people
observe a doctor. They see how many of his patients walk into the hospital
and how many get carried out. By the grace of God, I didn't lose that
many. I did prenatal care and delivery, took care of neonates, did infants'
and children's immunizations and the like. I treated infections, wired
broken jaws, set fractures, and, after completing my preceptorships, did
C-sections, appendectomies, and minor surgeries. I did only what I was
prepared to do, but that included an array of treatments and procedures
that would be unheard of for a family practitioner today. I got a reputation
for being concerned and for being a pretty good baby doctor. When one
of my mothers went into labor, even if I had twelve people waiting on me
at the office, I would stay with that laboring mother every minute until
the baby was delivered. One of my personal goals, of course, was to make
an impact on Mississippi's terrible infant mortality rate. In my first twenty-

five years of practice, the period when I was delivering babies, I delivered nearly three thousand. I had some sick babies, but only one child that I delivered died in its first year of life. I attended some very sick mothers, but they all pulled through. Part of that is attributable to my educating the mothers. Part of it is due to the fact that I insisted on hospital deliveries. I strictly would not deliver babies at home. Once I did deliver a set of twins in my office, but only because we could not make it to the hospital. Another part of my success is due to good consultative support from white specialists practicing in Biloxi and Gulfport. To their professional credit, no local specialist ever denied advice, consultation, or services to my patients based on race.

Of course, I kept up a steady pressure to improve conditions for my patients at the hospital. A few months after I began practicing I was working with a patient in the colored annex debriding a wound. Sometimes when I am reflecting I will look up. I looked up and noticed that pieces of the ceiling were falling. I looked down at the floor and there was nothing but bare wood. I turned to the nurses working there and said, "By God, I hadn't noticed this before." I went straight to the new administrator, Mr. S. E. Grimes, and requested that the hospital at least set aside two private rooms in the main building for black mothers to use after their deliveries so that the babies wouldn't be placed on that exposed and crumbling ward in the annex. Mr. S. E. Grimes later proved to be a hard man to deal with on race issues. That's why I started calling him SEG, a nickname that used the phonetic sounds his initials made to symbolize the pernicious principles for which he openly stood. However, this time, in 1956, Mr. S. E. Grimes conceded me the two private rooms for postdelivery black mothers and their new babies. All other black patients still went to the open wards in the annex. Separate and unequal conditions continued to exist in the hospital until we moved into a new building and changed the name to Howard Memorial in 1964. Even then, we had to fight a rearguard action against a few white staffers who still wanted to confine black patients behind the doors on the south side of the new hospital. However, we spoke up and got some principled white support. So, Biloxi-style hospital Jim Crow died in 1964. From this point on, both black and white newborns went to the hospital nursery where they could be watched closely. I know that this, too, saved lives. The first black baby that I placed in that new nursery is now a Biloxi city councilman.

With Jim Crow medicine or Jim Crow anything, you made your way daily through a maze of indignities, small and large. My dad had taken out a little insurance policy for me through a company called United.

When I took over paying on the policy, I found that their correspondence to me was always addressed simply to "Gilbert Mason," without any preceding form of address such as "Mr." or "Dr." I wrote the company headquarters to inform them that I wished to be addressed as Dr. Gilbert Mason. To my chagrin, I received curt replies first from their state president and then from their national one, both bluntly informing me that as a Negro I would never be called "Dr." or "Mr." in the state of Mississippi. I immediately canceled the policy.

Sometime after Mr. S. E. Grimes took over as hospital administrator, I became aware of a directive he had sent to all departments ordering them *not* to put "Mr." or "Mrs." in front of black patients' names on medicine labels and other paperwork. That same directive went on to order that "Mr." and "Mrs." be put in front of white patients' names and that even white children should have a "little master" or "little miss" placed in front of their names. SEG had earned his nickname. Of course, I was not sent the directive, but I found out about it, and confirmed it with a white friend, Mrs. Westmoreland, who worked in the lab. Again, I went to Mr. S. E. Grimes. "Man, this is improper," I protested. S. E. Grimes replied, "It's something I've always done, something I'm doing now, and something I'm going to always do." Old SEG could have written lines for George Wallace.

I did not stop, though. I took the "Mr." and "Mrs." issue to a white attorney who was on the hospital board. He seemed sympathetic, but he would give me no support. "Well," he said, "you may be able to do that in Chicago, but you can't do that in Mississippi. This is a Mississippi tradition. We don't call black folks Mr. or Mrs." I kept coming back, though. When I discovered a few local pharmacies dropping the "Mr." or "Mrs." from my prescriptions, I called them to protest any change made by a pharmacist to a doctor's prescription. I brought the issue to the hospital staff. After all, I argued, if I wrote "Mr." or "Mrs." on a prescription and some pharmacist removed it, this was the equivalent of illegally altering the prescription. I kept on making those protest statements for some time. Then the hospital staff, my white fellow physicians, finally started working on old SEG. Eventually, SEG sent down a new edict that there would be no title whatsoever put in front of anybody's name. This was a sort of a victory, but I wasn't looking for a victory. I was looking for equity and respect. I sought respect for the sanctity of a black physician's prescriptions and respect for the dignity of black patients and white patients alike.

In February of 1960, at about the time that we resolved the "Mr." or

"Mrs." issue at the hospital, Natalie and I organized the Modern Drug Store, Inc. We rented a unit on Main Street in the building that now houses the offices of lawyer Curtis Hays. I had always taken seriously Marcus Garvey's exhortations for black entrepreneurship. Natalie and I already owned a laundromat, and the time was right to start the drugstore. We hired a young black Xavier University pharmacy graduate, Mrs. Alicia Coleman. Biloxi had not seen the likes of a black pharmacist. On my part, this was a business decision and a principled experiment with black entrepreneurship. As with any business, its start-up involved risk. We had given the hard facts of business risk and opportunity serious consideration before we launched Modern. This being the case, I find the Mississippi Sovereignty Commission spy files very insulting in their false accusation that I organized Modern Drug Store as some kind of maladroit protest at the refusal of others to use "Mr." or "Mrs." on their medication labels. The timing of the opening of our pharmacy had nothing to do with the hospital's "Mr." or "Mrs." controversy. I would point out that Modern's start-up came at the end, not the beginning, of that little struggle for dignity at the hospital. And even this was by coincidence, not by design. Moreover, it was rare that any private pharmacies altered names, titles, or forms of address on my prescriptions. In reality, the drugstore was a big investment for us. We had to sell the laundromat in order to manage the pharmacy. Natalie was the president, and I was the secretary-treasurer. The pharmacy was well received. By this time, we were even allowed to join the Biloxi Chamber of Commerce. We found that some white-owned pharmacies were willing to help us when we ran short on supplies. We reciprocated when asked. So from 1960 to 1963, we successfully operated the Modern Drug Store. Unfortunately, Alicia Coleman, our pharmacist, and her husband, Emile, moved away in 1963. We chose to close Modern Drug Store, Inc., at that time in order to concentrate on other activities. At about the same time, I invested in a new, black-owned savings and loan that organized in Mobile, and Natalie's brother helped start a black-owned bank in Virginia. All of these ventures, including the drugstore, were, in my mind, about Garveyism and black entrepreneurship, about our future—not about segregationist stupidities, as the state's anti–civil rights spies imagined.

Meanwhile, my medical practice grew, and I made a living and a life for myself and for Natalie and Gilbert, Jr. Some were surprised that I did as well as I did, given the fact that I treated more than my fair share of indigent patients. Now, I did not get all of the black patients. There were two white doctors in Biloxi who had as many black patients as I did. When

I had first arrived, Dr. W. P. Kyle, a seventy-seven-year-old retired black physician living in Biloxi, told me that the white doctors would have a tendency to direct the poorest black folks to the black doctor and retain for themselves those black patients most able to pay. Therefore, I knew that I would have to work hard to earn a paying practice that could sustain me financially as I undertook the disproportionate load of charity cases that would come my way. Locally, some doctors were charging four dollars for a house call and three for an office visit. I set my normal fees a little higher at seven dollars for a house call and five dollars for an office visit. Few of my patients had employers who provided health insurance. If they had any insurance, it was likely to be what they called "street insurance" with premiums of a few cents collected weekly at your door. Companies like United, Independence, Security, and Universal operated that way. When a policy holder was sick, I filled out a form and wrote a note to the insurance company stating the amount of time the patient would need off from work to recover. The company then paid the patient fifteen or twenty dollars a week for as long as they were laid up. The patient was then supposed to pay me. Some paid, and some didn't.

Members of black lodges and black benevolent associations sometimes got similar benefits through their lodge or association. On the coast in Biloxi we had the United Benevolent Association, the Order of the Odd Fellows, the Courts of Calanthe, the Household of Ruth, the Elks and Masons, and Masonic auxiliaries such as the Daughters of Isis. Catholics had the Order of the Blessed Martyr Peter Claver and the St. Vincent de Paul Society. I well remember old Mrs. Amelia Bertrand, who lived on Bohn Street and headed up the local St. Vincent de Paul Society. One day Mrs. Bertrand came in and asked me if I would become St. Vincent de Paul's designated physician for three dollars an office visit and four dollars a house call. It was much like negotiating with a modern HMO. I accepted her offer. Notwithstanding these creative grassroots approaches to health care finance, most of my patients needed credit and paid their doctor bill in installments. Despite their poverty, despite their lack of insurance or low insurance benefits, my patients were good to me. Many people have been surprised to learn that my collection rate was actually greater than that of the average family practitioner, white or black, on the Mississippi Gulf Coast. My patients gave me a decent living in return for my services. For this I am grateful. By the grace of God, we served, we survived, and we prospered.

The ideal of service that had inspired us at Howard pointed beyond the examining room and the hospital ward to the needs of the community.

The concept of the physician as a part of the community, a teacher as well as a healer, was always before me. The preamble to the constitution of the National Medical Association exhorts doctors to serve as a "nexus" to the general population. Natalie, as a social worker with a master's degree, saw and actively supported the larger role implied in these concepts. Therefore, from the beginning of our service in Biloxi, we made every effort to become a part of the community. We became active members of the First Missionary Baptist Church in Biloxi. Through friendships with John Pettus, P. I. Green, and Joseph Austin, I immediately became active on the Boy Scout Council, first as an assistant scoutmaster and then as scoutmaster for Troop 416. Though we had no daughters, Natalie became active in Girl Scouts. We joined the P.T.A. long before Gilbert, Jr., even started to school, and I became the team physician for the Nichols High School Tigers. I joined the Masonic Lodge and the Elks Lodge; Natalie joined their ladies' auxiliaries. Sidney Clark, a childhood friend and fellow Boy Scout from Jackson, had become an instructor at Keesler Air Force Base in Biloxi. Sidney was trying to form an alumni chapter of Alpha Phi Alpha on the Mississippi Gulf Coast. I became his seventh man and a charter member of the coast's Zeta Mu Lambda chapter of Alpha Phi Alpha. I had the honor of being asked to join Sigma Pi Phi, the world's oldest black professional fraternity. Natalie helped found the Mississippi Gulf Coast's alumni chapter of Delta Sigma Theta sorority. Through Mr. Alphonse Jenkins, the Sportsman's Club, a black men's fishing club in Biloxi, reached out to include me in their deep-sea fishing and social outings. We were also quick to join the Gulfport branch of the NAACP, then led by Dr. Felix Dunn. I later became associated with the NAACP's Medical Committee for Civil Rights, and in 1960, I became founding president of the Biloxi branch of the NAACP.

I found gracious friendships and much-needed camaraderie in all of these groups. These lodges, fraternities, and associations were service oriented. The Alpha Phi Alpha motto, which derived from the gospel of Mark—"First of all, servants of all, we shall transcend all"—summed up the spirit of many black fraternities, lodges, and benevolent organizations in those days. My Masonic lodge, for example, sponsored and financially underwrote my Scout troop. During the civil rights struggle our adversaries failed to calculate the true strength that came to the movement through black lodges, civic groups, fraternities, sororities, and professional associations. White racist calculations relied on numbers and locations of NAACP chapters or numbers of people believed to be on official NAACP membership rolls. This was a faulty measure of black sentiment. Black people have always been very creative in dealing with white pressure. In the 1940s and 1950s, Mississippi public school teachers were required to list all organizations of which they were members. An NAACP membership could get them fired. Many of our brothers and sisters faced similar intimidation and threats from white employers if they joined the NAACP. The NAACP or its members were the white racists' target. The white establishment tried to make people fearful of joining, and then followed a silly logic to conclude that black folks did not want the equal rights for which the NAACP stood. If we did not have a chapter in every city and county they thought we were not there or had no local support for the cause of civil rights. However, black people in Mississippi were like water. When we were blocked in one direction, we just moved in another, always with our eyes on the prize. We had stealth fighters that the segregationists and kluxers never saw. The truth is that almost every black organization of which I was a part was also giving financial support to the NAACP. The United Benevolent Association in Biloxi hosted many NAACP meetings. Many who felt that they could not personally join the NAACP supported NAACP group memberships for their lodges, fraternities, sororities, civic clubs, and professional associations. There were seldom any employer threats attached to membership in a black civic club, fraternity, sorority, lodge, or professional association that bought an organizational membership in the NAACP. Antagonistic white employers never caught on to the connection, so they never understood our strength. Each organization was itself a kind of "nexus" in the community giving communications networks and strength to the civil rights struggle.

I did my best to support the many groups I joined. Scouting, P.T.A., and NAACP work wound up getting more of my time than the others. However, each group nurtured me with some of the true friendships and psychological support which I needed in order to survive in the troubled times of the 1960s. Because of black friends, the isolation and loneliness that Jim Crowism might have imposed on a black physician never really enveloped me. Occasional balls and parties lightened our lives. Some of our social events were strictly *custom de rigueur*, black tie and tuxedo affairs. On the other hand, many organizations met in people's homes because restaurants and hotels denied us accommodations. Jim Crow drove us out of sight of the white community, but meeting in people's homes cemented our friendships. This practice, along with the brotherhood and sisterhood we shared in being black and together in hostile times, built a special closeness. In the NAACP and in the Gulf Coast Medical, Dental, and Pharmaceutical Association, Dr. Felix Dunn and Dr. J. O.

Tate became trusted friends. Clare and Tommy Rhodeman, G. Jack and Rosa Martin, James and June Crawford, Alexander Bellamy, Herbert Caliste, Rehofus Esters, Wayne F. Calbert, and many others from all walks of life befriended us and stood with us through thick and thin.

Little by little we became a nexus in back-of-town in Biloxi. As we gained people's trust, they sought our advice on all kinds of personal and community problems. On the evening when I was inducted into the Masonic Lodge, my older brother, Willie Louis, came over from New Orleans for the event. There in that lodge hall people from every walk of life surrounded me, a young twenty-seven-year-old physician still wet behind the ears, asking me questions not only on health and medical conditions, but on all manner of issues and concerns. It was apparent that the folks had not only inducted me into the lodge as a first-degree Mason but had also taken me to their bosoms. My brother pulled me aside and said, "Man, this is the place you ought to be." My brother's words struck a chord within me. In that instant, from the mysterious depths of a grateful heart, I, too, knew that I had found my destiny, my place of service. The boundaries of that service soon expanded.

FOUR

The Beach

Jabez called upon the God of Israel, saying, "Oh that thou wouldest bless me and enlarge my border, and that thy hand might be with me, and that thou wouldest keep me from harm so that it might not hurt me!" —1 Chronicles 4:10

FRIENDS AND FAMILY MEMBERS IN CHICAGO AND WASH-ington had told me that I would not tolerate the limits that Jim Crowism would impose on my life if I returned to Mississippi. In 1955 the world was changing, and I knew it. The courts were ruling in case after case that segregation violated the equal protection clause of the Fourteenth Amendment to the U.S. Constitution. As an idealistic young physician, I had no intention of living my life or seeing my son live his life within the narrow confines laid out by racist segregation laws. Thus, in May of 1959, four years after I started my medical practice, I led nine black people to take their first steps onto the "white-only" public beach in Biloxi, Mississippi. The Biloxi police promptly ordered us off and threatened us with arrest. This 1959 wade-in and the series of sustained protests which followed marked the beginning of Mississippi's first nonviolent civil disobedience campaign. As the instigator of the first wade-in, I became the prime mover and chief organizer of an eight-year struggle to open Harrison County's twenty-six-mile-long public beach to the full enjoyment of all citizens. Almost overnight, I became a recognized local civil rights leader. As a result, I and my family, along with friends who supported this cause, became for years the targets of vile threats, intimidation efforts, and fire-bombings. My name appeared on KKK hit lists alongside those of Medgar Evers and Aaron Henry, and I was the target of at least one bungled assassination attempt.

From the time that I arrived in Biloxi in July of 1955, the thought that the twenty-six-mile-long Mississippi Gulf Coast beach was closed to me and my family because of skin color did not sit well with me at all. According to Harrison County and the city of Biloxi, my little son could not legally swim in the warm waters of the Gulf of Mexico that lapped the shore just a few blocks from our home. Local practice reserved God's sunrises and sunsets over the glistening waters and white sands of Biloxi beach for the exclusive enjoyment of white folks. For a man who loved swimming and who had gloried in the free use of the parks in Chicago and Washington, D.C., the idea that a marvelous oak-lined public beach was forbidden territory was just too much to abide.

The 1959 wade-in was no fluke or accident. It was premeditated. I had been thinking and talking about such a move from the first time I saw that long, wonderful beach. The intense beauty of the Mississippi Gulf Coast had been one of its attractions for me. When I joined the Gulfport branch of the NAACP in 1955, one of the first suggestions I made was that we set the goal of opening up use of the beach to all citizens. I was already committed to the cause of civil rights when I first returned to Mississippi. I had shocked Dr. W. P. Kyle, Biloxi's elderly retired black doctor, in 1955 when I had told him that I intended to see Biloxi's schools desegregated within seven years. Dr. Kyle said, "You might as well leave now." Dr. Kyle had little faith in Mississippi or the U.S. Constitution. He and I both knew that white Mississippi contained a mean element which had no qualms about bringing suffering or even death to those who would defy the system. I knew that up in Indianola racists had burned the home of Dr. Clinton Battle, an acquaintance of mine and a Meharry medical graduate. The white community put the economic screws on Clinton Battle and forced him to leave the state in 1958 or 1959. Dr. Battle went into practice in Chicago with Dr. T. R. M. Howard, another black Mississippi physician who had been driven out of the state.

Beyond livelihood, those who even appeared to challenge the racial status quo in Mississippi risked their very lives. Shortly after I set up practice in Biloxi, poor Emmett Till, a teenager, was murdered upstate in Mississippi for so-called "flirting" with a white woman. In 1956, Reverend George Lee, my last pastor at St. James Baptist Church in Jackson, got his head blown off for trying to register to vote in Bolivar County where he also pastored a church. Then, Mack Charles Parker was lynched in Poplarville in 1958. The dangers involved in confronting the devil in his own den were clear. The extremists among our white brothers had proven that they had no respect for the U.S. Constitution, federal law, or the laws of God. Mississippi's white establishment, hearts hardened by years of racist practices, repeatedly ignored racist violence and gross injustice perpetrated upon black citizens.

As a member of the Gulfport branch of the NAACP, I continually asked why the branch didn't do something about access to the beach for black citizens. I never got an answer. In view of the violence that was in the air, I guess I understood why. Racism and racist laws represented a powerful evil. On the other hand, if we failed to take a stand, we acquiesced in a kind of spiritual slavery that denied us our full manhood and womanhood. The words of that old Negro spiritual rang in my young ears: "I'd rather be dead and in my grave than live and be a slave." I wanted to live. I wanted to live a long life, but I wanted the chance for a full and wholesome life for my family and for us as a people. I did a lot of praying, a lot of thinking, and a lot of talking before I took that first step into the water on Biloxi beach in 1959. The time was right. The federal courts were moving in the direction of assuring racial equality. So, we stepped forward in the faith that a merciful God would protect us as we, his black children, claimed our rights under the U.S. Constitution to enjoy his beautiful world along with all of his other children.

The twenty-six-mile-long beach in Harrison County is a man-made or cultivated beach one hundred to one hundred fifty yards wide running along the south side of U.S. Highway 90 from Biloxi to Pass Christian. A chain of mansions and large homes, many of them antebellum, overlook the beach and the Gulf of Mexico on the north side of U.S. 90. Interspersed along this oak-shaded scenic route are occasional hotels, motels, harbors, and shopping centers. Public officials and private citizens routinely denied black people the right to use any portion of this extensive beach except for a few dozen yards opposite the Veterans Administration Hospital in Gulfport or in a designated area called the Rice Fields opposite the Episcopal church in Pass Christian. Of course, black maids or babysitters sometimes brought white children in their care to the beach without objection. However, if Negroes ventured onto the beach to enjoy it for themselves, they generally got cursed, harassed, spat upon, kicked, hit, or run off by white ruffians or property owners from across the highway. Law enforcement officers routinely stood back and watched this harassment and did nothing. More often than not, lawmen themselves acted to remove blacks from the beach. In 1959 when a white nun teaching at a black Catholic school took her students to the beach in Gulfport for a class project, the Gulfport police summarily removed the teacher and her students from the beach. At Biloxi no part of the beach was accessible to Negroes. Along this twenty-six-mile beach, there was inconsistent policy.

Blacks never knew when or where they might encounter embarrassment, intimidation, or removal from the beach. Even in the small areas at the Gulfport V.A. or the Pass Christian Rice Fields where it was customary for blacks to have access, white property owners' complaints prompted local authorities to remove blacks from the beach arbitrarily. At the same time white people, whether property owners or not, were allowed free and unmolested access to any portion of the beach they might want to use along its entire twenty-six-mile extent.

Since public money was invested in the creation and maintenance of the beach, I believed that the local officials would be forced ultimately to grant free use of the beach to both black and white citizens. I talked over the issue with friends. I talked about the beach with the boys in my Scout troop. I vowed repeatedly to go to the beach one day to claim my rights as a citizen. Several adults said, "Doc, when you go to the beach, let us go with you." Some of the boys in the Scout troop expressed the same sentiment. After four years of talk, I decided that Thursday, May 14, 1959, was the day for us to enjoy our rights on the beach in Biloxi where blacks had hitherto had no access whatsoever. That morning, I announced my plan to my neighbors Mr. James Hoze and Mr. Murray Saucier. Murray and James wanted to go, but Murray asked me to wait for a while so that he could run an errand. By that afternoon we were ready.

On the beach just south of the old Biloxi cemetery sometime between 2:00 and 4:00 P.M., nine of us made our move to start the first wade-in and the first public civil rights demonstration in modern Mississippi history. Murray Saucier, Adell Lott, Otha Lee Floyd, James Hoze, Jimmie Hoze, Gloria Hoze, and Jackie Hoze all took that first step with Gilbert, Jr., and me. The youngsters and I went into the water to play. Unfortunately, a lady traveling in the wrong lane of U.S. 90 caused an accident near our place on the beach. The accident brought the police to the scene. One of the officers spotted us and yelled, "You know that you can't swim here. Come on down here. We're going to put you under arrest." I came out of the water and asked, "Why can't I swim here?" The officer said, "Well, the beach is private property." County trash cans were on the beach, and we had often seen county equipment at work there. I knew that something built or maintained with public money could not be private property, so I questioned him. "Why is it private property? It cannot be private," I said. At this the officer ordered me to get into my car and follow him down to Biloxi police headquarters "to find out about it."

At police headquarters Chief Herbert McDonnell was nowhere to be found, so they took me to his assistant chief. To my question "Why is the beach private property?" the assistant chief had no answer. He said, "If you want to know about that you're going to have to come back tomorrow." They did not book me or bind me over for trial at this time. I suppose that I could have just walked away from the confrontation, but I didn't. The next morning, Murray Saucier and I came back to city hall with the same question on our minds. How can this beach be private property? Why are black folks prevented from swimming there? This time the officers ushered us into the august presence of Biloxi's mayor, Laz Quave. Mayor Laz Quave soon impressed me as insensitive and unfeeling. He acted ignorant. Whether he truly was so or not, I cannot say. Over the next several years, I concluded that this mayor huffed and puffed to make a show for the white population while hoping that his posturing would bluff or intimidate the blacks. When the civil rights struggle heated up, Laz Quave was given to making irresponsible and inflammatory remarks like "The communists are behind this." Well, we've long since proven that it wasn't the communists giving him headaches over Jim Crow. No, it was just one big-foot boy from Jackson, Mississippi.

Needless to say, my first encounter with Mayor Quave did not go well. Straight out I asked him why black folks couldn't use the beach. "It's on the book," he said. I demanded, "What about the beach is on the book? I want to see the book. Show me the book." Obviously frustrated, the mayor made an accusation. "You're just trying to get that NAACP down here," he growled. He then gave me the old spiel about how some of his best friends were black folks. Notwithstanding the human degradation and deprivation all around him, Mayor Quave's demeanor and attitude would have you believe that the races had lived in some kind of Jim Crow utopia before I came to Biloxi starting trouble. Now, I was a member of the NAACP, but I had gone to the beach on my own. We had no Biloxi branch of the NAACP at this time, and the Gulfport branch had not shown any interest in the beach problem. Still, I showed my colors. "Yes," I answered. "I belong to the NAACP, and I also belong to the First Missionary Baptist Church in Biloxi. I am a native Mississippian," I asserted. "I was born in Jackson, Mississippi, and my family has roots that go back nearly two hundred years in Mississippi. So, I want to see the book with this statute in it." "Well," he replied, "the book is not here." I asked, "When will it be here so that I can examine it?" He would not say. It became plain that there was no room for negotiation. I wanted to see the book, and he would not or could not produce it. At this point, Mayor Quave cursed and threatened me. He said, "If you go back down there on the beach, *we're going to leave you down there!*" By this time, my wife had arrived with my friend Christopher Rosado, a fellow Scouter. Standing outside the mayor's door, Natalie overheard this threat and later swore to it in an affidavit. I took the mayor's threat seriously, but it did not stop me.[1]

I left Biloxi City Hall and immediately called Dr. Felix Dunn, the president of the Gulfport branch of the NAACP, to ask for help. There seemed to be few options available to us. I had acted on my own without the Gulfport branch voting to get involved. For some unknown reason, the Gulfport branch remained silent about the beach. However, I did ask Felix if he could at least recommend a local attorney who might research the beach issue and all the legal ramifications for us. There were no black attorneys on the Mississippi Gulf Coast at that time, but Dr. Dunn suggested that a white attorney in Gulfport, Mr. Knox Walker, might be helpful. That very same day, May 15, 1959, Dr. Dunn introduced us. Knox Walker was indeed willing to do the research, so I engaged him as my counsel. Over the next few months, Mr. Walker proved himself to be a principled man who was genuinely concerned about all people. It took a lot of guts for a white southern lawyer to take a case like this. At the same time, I was planning to send Knox Walker's work to Dr. James Nabrit at Howard University for an opinion. Dr. Nabrit was a friend of mine and dean of the Howard University School of Law. Nabrit had been one of the attorneys on the *Brown v. the Board of Education* case in 1954. Before I went to Howard University, I had met Dr. Nabrit through a high school friend of mine from Yazoo City. I contacted Nabrit and kept him informed about all developments related to the beach.

Knox Walker delivered some good research. From the minute books of the Harrison County Board of Supervisors going back to 1924, Walker showed that investments of public money in stabilizing the coastline had been going on for decades. In 1924, the county had authorized a 2 percent local gasoline tax, a so-called seawall tax, for the construction of a concrete barrier on the south side of the road that became U.S. Highway 90. The seawall was designed to protect the roadway from erosion. There had apparently been some natural beach and marshlands south of the highway, but wave action made this a shifting shoreline that threatened the highway. The county had built the seawall with no objection from property owners on the north side of the highway. Years later in 1947, a massive hurricane struck the Mississippi Gulf Coast. The resulting shoreline erosion showed that violent wave action could undermine the seawall itself and again threaten the highway. Following the 1947 hurricane, the Harrison County Board of Supervisors asked for and received federal assistance to construct a twenty-six-mile-long sand beach fifty to a hundred yards wide to further protect the seawall and the highway. In exchange for at least $1,300,000 in federal funds, the Harrison County Board of Supervisors signed a contract that guaranteed that the reclaimed beach would be open to the public in perpetuity. (The total taxpayer investment in the construction of the beach was over $3,000,000, including state, local, and federal money.) Walker's research showed that the board of supervisors had not conducted a formal eminent domain process to gain easements south of the seawall. However, publicly funded work on the beach had proceeded without protest from any of the twelve hundred property owners on the north side of U.S. 90, except for one. In Gulfport a man named Henritzy had built a cabin on his property south of the seawall to protest the beach project. The Mississippi courts had ruled that Henritzy had no right to block beach construction. His cabin was torn down and the project was completed. It could be argued that the investment of public money in beach construction and the contractual agreement openly entered into between the United States government and Harrison County gave all citizens, including blacks, the right to use the beach forever. Nonetheless, in the absence of eminent domain proceedings, Walker was uncertain what a court case might produce. In any event, he found no statutory prohibition of blacks using the beach. In theory, when the police had removed us, they were enforcing the rights of the white property owners north of the highway. These property owners were presumed to own the beach south of the highway opposite their homes. It was as if the Henritzy ruling had never occurred. It was clear that the legal questions at issue would revolve around the county's guarantee of public access in perpetuity and the extent to which our paying taxes to build and maintain the beach gave us user rights superseding any private property rights.

These facts gave me a personal sense of certainty that we would eventually gain equity and equal opportunity on the beach. However, facts alone did not change any county or municipal officials' behavior. We were going to have to challenge their practice of systematically excluding blacks from the beach either in a political body, in the courts, or on the streets. Whatever we did, it seemed likely that there would be a long, tough, and potentially expensive struggle. We had to come up with a strategy. The Gulfport branch of the NAACP still chose not to do anything with our information. No existing black organization stepped forward to act. Moreover, it seemed that many of our supporters in the black community felt uncomfortable acting in the name of the NAACP. The NAACP label invited increased white harassment. Therefore, in June of 1959, Dr. Dunn and I decided to organize interested persons into a new county-wide umbrella group, the Harrison County Civic Action Committee. In the city of Biloxi we resurrected a black organization called the Biloxi Civic League. These were true grassroots organizations. Dr. Felix Dunn was elected chairman of the Harrison County Civic Action Committee, Calvin Corley secretary, P. I. Green treasurer, and I was elected the whip. In Biloxi I became president of the reorganized Biloxi Civic League.

We began speaking wherever we could to raise public awareness of our legal rights and to make known our intent to desegregate the entire twenty-six-mile beach. From the beginning we talked about the likelihood that we would have to undertake a wade-in. We spoke to ministerial groups, to clubs, and to churches in Biloxi and Gulfport. I must have spoken personally to at least a dozen groups that summer. It appeared that everyone to whom I spoke endorsed the goal of gaining for black folks full access to the entire beachfront. With the black community behind us we began a voter registration drive, prepared to petition the Harrison County Board of Supervisors, and began planning for a massive county-wide wade-in to be launched if our petition failed. According to my daily diary for 1959, on September 3, I met with Mr. Eulice White, Mr. Joseph Austin, and Dr. Felix Dunn at the 19th Street Community Center in Gulfport to draft the petition. On September 7, we held a mass meeting in an open field in the Soria City neighborhood of Gulfport. At the Soria City meeting, the Harrison County Civic Action Committee voted to adopt this petition and present it to the Harrison County Board of Supervisors with the request that this board enforce our rights to use the beach. I drafted the language of the petition. The petition included a short statement of facts along with a simple request for remedy. The beach was maintained for public use with public funds under the control of the Harrison County Board of Supervisors. The police in some municipalities along the coast denied certain citizens use of the beach. We therefore petitioned the supervisors to end existing municipal police impediments and guarantee all citizens the unrestrained use of the entire beach. The whole group voted to adopt the petition, but it was left to four individuals to sign it in the name of the group. Mr. Joseph Austin, the longtime director of the Negro Division of the City of Gulfport's Recreation Department, Mr. Eulice White, a general repairman privately employed by a white Gulfport family, Dr. Felix Dunn, and I were the ones who signed.

We brought the petition before the five-member Harrison County Board of Supervisors on October 5, 1959. Our original plan was that all four of the signers would appear before the board to support our cause. However, the week of that board meeting, Dr. Dunn went to a World Series game. That left Eulice White, Joseph Austin, and me to appear before the supervisors. Eulice and Joseph decided that it was best for me to do the talking. The three of us went to the supervisors' meeting, and I presented the petition and our supporting research. Things turned hostile. Mr. Dewey Lawrence, Sr., was president of the board. "If you go back down there [to the beach] again," Mr. Lawrence warned, "there's going to be bloodshed." I retorted, "Blood flows in white folks' veins as well as in black folks' veins, but we did not come here to talk about blood. We came to talk about the beach." Mr. Lawrence then asked me, "How much of the beach do you want use of?" My response was quick. I said, "All twenty-six miles, every damn inch of it." This was what I had said to every black group to whom I had spoken all summer. "Wouldn't access to a portion satisfy you?" he asked. Again I said, "No, we want all twenty-six miles." Now, I did not know it at the time, but the Sovereignty Commission papers show that soon thereafter, a handful of black and white folks began talking behind the scenes about a compromise deal for some kind of a separate, protected, all-black beach. I never knew about that until I read the Sovereignty Commission files almost forty years later. The blacks allegedly involved in these talks knew that such a compromise would have been totally unacceptable to me. Since my tax dollars had built and maintained the whole beach, why should I have to drive miles to some special zone, when white taxpayers could go anywhere they wanted? I was uncompromising. I guess that's why I was kept in the dark.

The Harrison County Board of Supervisors took no action on our petition. They took it under advisement. However, the next day the coast newspaper, the *Daily Herald*, ran a front page banner headline story, "Negroes Seek Use of Harrison Beach," which characterized our little petition as "the first significant test of Mississippi segregation laws. . . ."[2] Within forty-eight hours, the board attorney, Senator Stanford Morse, was in Jackson pressing the State Sovereignty Commission to investigate Dr. Dunn and me with the intent of discrediting us. The Sovereignty Commission agents who reported this also stated that local officials believed that they could "handle" Joseph Austin and Eulice White.[3] There were immediate negative repercussions for them. Within twenty-four hours, the city of Gulfport fired Joseph Austin. On the night of October 5–6, the Ku Klux Klan burned a six-foot cross in Mr. Austin's yard in the Handsboro community, and he received threatening phone calls. Though he never said a word to us about it, Joseph Austin came under great pressure to withdraw his name from the petition and to get me to withdraw my name also. However, to my knowledge Joseph Austin never withdrew his name, and he never once even suggested that I withdraw mine. Eulice White and his wife were both fired by their white employers. My diary entry for October 7 notes that Eulice White withdrew his name from the petition. Joseph Austin and Eulice White were both good men. They paid a high price for daring to exercise their First Amendment rights. For many months, the Harrison County Civic Action Committee took donations and placed them in an account in the Hancock Bank for White and Austin, because no local employer would hire them after they took this stand.

As for me and Dr. Dunn, a hail of threats soon erupted on us. Anonymous telephone calls at our homes and at our offices day and night carried hateful messages such as "Nigger, you'd better leave town, because we're going to kill you." Dr. Clay Easterly, one of my white physician friends, responded to the newspaper story about the petition in a friendly way by calling me aside. He said, "I want to congratulate you on your efforts, but I ask you to do one thing. Be careful. Be careful." He wanted me to be aware of forces outside the hospital that would harm me physically, psychologically, and economically if they could. Dr. Easterly meant this as fatherly advice, and I took it that way.

My diary indicates that on October 28 agent Zack Van Landingham of the anti–civil rights State Sovereignty Commission paid me a visit at my office. The State Sovereignty Commission files state that Van Landingham had first tried to talk to Dr. Dunn at his office in Gulfport. However, when Van Landingham arrived, Dr. Dunn had gone on seeing a patient and let Van Landingham cool his heels for fifteen minutes. Offended, this impatient state agent abruptly left Dunn's office and came to my office in Biloxi. I went ahead and saw him. Agent Van Landingham characterized me as "curt and cool" in my deportment toward him. He reported correctly that I was firm in my determination "never to agree to anything except complete integration of the entire beach." After three weeks of threats my position remained unchanged. Before he left town, Van Landingham took this information straight to State Senator Stanford Morse, attorney for the board of supervisors, to Gulfport mayor Billy Meadows, and to the president of the board of supervisors, Dewey Lawrence. According to Van Landingham's memos, these officials believed that they could wait us out, and that eventually a majority of black citizens would accept a separate beach and thus leave Dunn and me isolated. A copy of Van Landingham's memorandum was sent to his director and on to Governor J. P. Coleman.[4]

Along about the same time in the fall of 1959, Attorney Knox Walker shared some frightful information with Felix Dunn and me that showed just how high the human cost of our pressing forward might be. One of Knox's clients had connections to the Klan and had obtained a secret KKK assassination list with twelve names on it. Knox showed it to us. Dr. Felix Dunn and I were on the hit list, along with Aaron Henry, Medgar Evers, C. C. Bryant of McComb, R. L. T. Smith, Jr., and R. L. T. Smith, Sr., in Jackson. I think five other black men around the state were also targeted. Through Medgar Evers, we, of course, warned these men.

The growing number and seriousness of threats to my life caused me to accept organized personal protection from a group of friends who called themselves the Black Angry Men, or BAM for short. My BAM-recruited security detail included Sam Edwards, A. A. Dickey, Marvin Dickey, Clifton Nunley, Joe Kennedy, Arthur Bousqueto, John Elzy, Harold Boglin, A. J. Haynes, Alfred Thomas, Earl Napoleon Moore, Richard Magrone, and Charles Davis, plus the prettiest BAM, Myrtle Davis. They made themselves available to stand guard over me day or night in shifts as needed for about four years. For a solid year of that time in 1960 and 1961, they covered me around the clock. My security accompanied me on hospital rounds. They posted themselves outside each hospital room while I checked my patients. BAMs went with me on house calls. During office hours, they kept a vigil from a gas station across the street. At night the Black Angry Men watched my place from the rooftop of Arthur Bousqueto's house across a vacant lot from my house on Fayard Street. When speeding cars fired gunshots toward my house, the BAMs returned fire, and they checked into anything that looked suspicious.

Toward the end of 1959, my friends foiled an assassination plot in which the would-be paid murderer, a black man, actually gained entry into my home. We were still living in the Nixon Street Apartments at the time. I was at home one evening when this dude knocked on the door wanting to see me. I recognized the man. Though I did not consider him a personal friend, I had treated members of his family. We let him in the door. I noticed that he had a big bulge in his pocket. Before I knew it, my security guards rushed into the apartment. They would not leave me alone with this man. Our would-be assailant started fumbling around aimlessly and talking about needing a house call. When I declined to go with him, he left. Later we were told that some whites had put a black nightclub manager up to hiring this hit man. My guards had learned about the plot but had not told me. They knew exactly what was going on when the man showed up at my door with his pocket bulging. We knew the club manager who had hired him, but we never found out exactly who was ultimately behind this plot.

Meanwhile, I had sent our beach petition with the thick packet of Knox Walker's research to Dr. James Nabrit at Howard University School of Law. Nabrit turned over our material and maps to his law students and professors for further research and argument in Howard University Law School's moot court. The law students picked the case apart, debated it, and rendered a verdict just as if they were before the Supreme Court. Again, all of this was done on my initiative. There was no NAACP involvement at this point. I found out that Dr. Nabrit would be coming to the all-black Louisiana Teachers' Association meeting in New Orleans in November of 1959. I asked him for an audience so that we could discuss his opinion of our case. He agreed to a meeting. On November 23, 1959, I gathered up our petition, maps, and copies of minute book entries and drove over to New Orleans, by myself, to see Nabrit. I met him at the home of Dan Byrd, executive director of the Louisiana Teachers' Association. Here we talked at length about the background of the beach problem in Harrison County. Nabrit asked a lot of questions and finally pointed to the map on which I had redlined the portions of the beach reclaimed with public money. He said, "We find that there's no reason why you can't go anywhere along that beach." Nabrit asked me to bring my attorney and Felix Dunn for a second meeting the next night. It was late when I got back to Biloxi, but I went ahead and called Felix and Knox Walker to ask if they would go back to New Orleans with me the next night. I had given Knox Walker a good fee for his services, and when he heard that Nabrit wanted to talk to him in person, Knox agreed to go. So did Dr. Dunn. I really think that Knox Walker was always proud that we had brought him in on this. Nabrit cross-examined Knox and Dr. Dunn about the facts in the case. Satisfied that he knew all that he needed to know, Nabrit told Knox about Howard University law school's conclusion that the public money spent on seawall and beach construction and the supervisors' agreement to open the beach to the public in perpetuity gave black people the same rights to the beach as anyone else. I was elated with these findings and wanted to implement a mass wade-in right then.

Our petition to the Harrison County Board of Supervisors was still hanging in limbo. With all of the threats flying, it appeared useless to go back to the board of supervisors or to city officials with our problem. A lawsuit looked like the best course of action. However, we believed that we would have to get ourselves arrested in order to move the dispute into court. We suspected that we would lose in the local courts, but we wanted to appeal all the way to the Supreme Court, if necessary. We began talking up a large-scale wade-in for the spring of 1960. At a mass meeting on October 22, 1959, the Harrison County Civic Action Committee had adopted the goal of carrying out a county-wide wade-in. We had named the plan Operation Surf. We knew that getting large numbers of people involved would take time and many additional meetings and rallies. If we were successful, mass arrests in the spring would produce the court challenge we needed.

When Knox Walker told us that he would take our case all the way to the U.S. Supreme Court for ten thousand dollars, we had already started raising money for the fight. Ten thousand dollars was quite a large sum in 1959 and 1960. We touched everybody we could think of for money. We wrote to our friends, classmates, and black organizations statewide and nationwide soliciting support for our cause. In January of 1960, Felix Dunn and I made a trip up to Clarksdale to see if Aaron Henry could point us to some good donors. There was as yet no mention of bringing in the NAACP legal staff. On this same trip we called on Grand Master James Gillam, the top official for Mississippi's black M. W. Stringer Grand Lodge of Prince Hall-Affiliated Masonic lodges. We also tried to see the top state black Elks Lodge officer, Mr. Cochran. These black lodge organizations sent donations. Money started trickling in little by little. A retired black physician in New Jersey sent a letter congratulating me for taking up the fight for the beach and enclosed ten or fifteen dollars. Black lodges and benevolent groups sent ten dollars here and there. Some churches contributed a little. Felix Dunn put some money up, but in the end most of what was paid to Knox Walker for his services came out of my pocket. Of course, I was the one who eventually got into the most trouble with the law, and Knox had to go to trial with me twice in 1960.

While we slowly accumulated financial resources, we promoted and planned the mass wade-in. Our target date for Operation Surf was Easter Sunday, April 17, 1960. We hoped to generate simultaneous challenges to the race restrictions all along the twenty-six-mile shoreline from Biloxi to Pass Christian. Under the auspices of the Harrison County Civic Action Committee and the Biloxi Civic League, we held more rounds of meetings in Gulfport and Biloxi, all pointing toward an April 17 wade-in. With things moving at a slow pace after our October petition, folks in Biloxi seemed especially anxious to carry out this new plan. As a matter of fact, our last meeting in preparation for the April 17 wade-in was held in Biloxi at New Bethel Baptist Church. Everybody said, "Doc, we're right behind you. We'll be there on Sunday at one o'clock." Of course, I assured everybody that I would be there. I knew that I would be arrested, so I arranged for Natalie and our friend Mr. Wilmer McDaniel to be ready to bail me out.

At my church on Easter morning, April 17, 1960, as Dr. John Ware, now professor of music at Xavier University, remembers, I made a final appeal for people to join me on the beach that afternoon. At the appointed hour, 1:00 P.M., I rolled up to the beach and parked my car near the Biloxi lighthouse. The place was practically deserted. No one showed up from my church. In fact, nary another black soul appeared on the scene. If I was going onto the beach, it looked like I would have to go by myself. Still, I was determined that even if no one else went, I was going. I stripped down to my swimming trunks, walked onto the sand beach, and went into the water alone. After about ten minutes, a Biloxi motorcycle cop, Officer Vene Lee, pulled up, dismounted, and walked to the edge of the seawall bordering the beach. He yelled, "Boy, don't you know you can't swim down here?" I ignored him. Soon he said, "Oh, that ain't no boy. That's Dr. Mason." When he called me by name, I responded. "What's the matter, officer?" I asked. He said, "You can't swim here. We've told you that you can't swim here." I said, "Well, why can't I swim here?" He just repeated himself, "Well, we've told you." I asked, "Am I under arrest?" He answered, "Yeah, you're under arrest, but I'll let you drive your car to police headquarters." When I got there they took my name, charged me with disturbing the peace and disorderly conduct, booked me, and fingerprinted me. When Natalie arrived, she heard Biloxi police chief Herbert McDonnell go on a verbal rampage, cursing and threatening to get someone to beat me up if I ever put my "ass on that goddam beach again." Natalie and McDaniel immediately bailed me out. Natalie again swore an affidavit to document the chief's threat. My trial date was set for the next day, Monday, at 6:00 P.M., in city court before Judge Jules Schwan, Sr.

Dr. Dunn reported that he and his wife, Sarah, and their children had attempted to swim at Gulfport that day. As Dr. Dunn told it to me at the time, Mayor R. B. Meadows himself asked the Dunns off the beach. Dr. Dunn complied with the mayor's request. There was some bad talk, but there were no actual arrests or charges filed in Gulfport. This is all that Dr. Dunn reported to me in 1960 as having happened that day. Moreover, Gulfport's restraint in removing but not arresting Dr. Dunn was never represented to me as in any way implying a softening of that city's race-restrictive policy on the beach. To the contrary, the Sovereignty Commission files make it clear that Mayor Meadows intended to continue a segregationist policy of excluding blacks from the beach. In a memorandum dated May 4, 1960, agent Zack Van Landingham summarized a conversation he had with the Gulfport mayor on April 29. Van Landingham reported that Mayor Meadows bragged that he had "run Dr. Dunn and his family off the beach" on April 17. Moreover, Meadows allegedly stated to Van Landingham that he (Meadows) was "through handling the Negroes with kid gloves."[5] According to Mrs. Lola Baker, when she and her family attempted to swim off Thornton Avenue in July of 1959, the Gulfport police removed her family from the beach but did not arrest her.[6] Forcefully removing blacks from the beach without arresting them appeared to be the Gulfport approach to resisting desegregation.

The one-man challenge to Jim Crow on Biloxi beach and the reported small group challenge in Gulfport were all that seemed to have materialized of the Operation Surf mass wade-in plan. The city of Biloxi was the only municipality to actually arrest and charge anyone that day. So, I was the only black arrested anywhere on the twenty-six-mile Mississippi Gulf Coast beachfront on April 17, 1960. The county-wide mass wade-in that we had spent months planning and promoting had all but failed to materialize in Biloxi, and it was inconsequential elsewhere. Just eleven months earlier nine of us had initiated the first wade-in. We had spent almost a year following that event trying to overcome the reticence due to fear which existed in the hearts of our people. We had worked hard to build support for Operation Surf in the black community in Gulfport and Biloxi. We had invested time and personal finances in legal research and petitioning. Joseph Austin and Eulice White had lost their jobs. We had endured Klan threats and cross burnings. We had seen our names on a hit list and had dealt with a would-be murderer in our home. We had written letter after letter to raise money for a lawsuit. Wherever we had spoken, black folks had said they were behind us. They had said they supported our goal of free access to the whole beach. After all of this effort, and after so many had professed confidence in our goals and methods, I was quite surprised when no one showed up in Biloxi to wade in with me.

I was surprised, but I was not defeated. I remained confident in the rightness of going to the beach. Like a good Scout I had done my best. The tenth rule of the Boy Scout Law came to mind at that time. "A Scout is brave. He has the courage to face danger in spite of fear and to stand up under the coaxing and jeers of enemies. And defeat does not down him." I was not down in spirit. At least my second foray onto the beach had gotten the issue into court. If convicted, I still had every intention of appealing all the way to the Supreme Court, even if I had to go it alone. Little did I know that my solitary arrest would inspire a new resolve throughout the black community in Biloxi. Sunday, April 17, 1960, turned out to be the last time I had to go swimming alone. The next Sunday, things were very different.

FIVE

The Bloody Wade-In

The hand of the Lord was upon me, and . . . set me down in a valley which was full of bones, . . . and, lo they were very dry. And He said unto me, "Son of Man, can these bones live?" And I answered, "O Lord God, thou knowest." Again He said unto me, "Prophesy upon these bones, and say unto them, O ye dry bones, hear the word of the Lord. Thus saith the Lord God unto these bones; Behold, I will cause breath to enter into you, and ye shall live: . . . and ye shall know that I am the Lord."

—Ezekiel 37:1–6

I WAS ALONE WHEN I WENT ONTO BILOXI BEACH ON SUN-day, April 17. I was not alone when I went to court the next night. Something was happening to the spirits of people in the back-of-town section where I lived and worked. On the Monday after my arrest, a group of teenagers from Nichols High School stopped by my office to see me between patients. Ethel Rainey, and, I believe, James Black were in this group. Ethel did most of the talking. I think that she summarized a feeling in the black community about my arrest when she said, "We've got a family affair here. Doc, I know you went [to the beach] yesterday by yourself, but if you will organize us, we'll go back [to the beach] next Sunday." There in my office, at the behest of Ethel Rainey and her friends, we began organizing a new wade-in attempt in Biloxi for Sunday, April 24. The circle of willing waders quickly broadened to include adults as well as youth. One of those rare moments of action was developing. You could almost feel the rising tide of sentiment. In the neighborhood people were talking, saying things like, "This is my doctor going down on the beach," or "He's a member of my church. He's my lodge brother. I'm going to support him."

By Monday evening at 6:00 P.M., when my trial came up in municipal court, it felt as if practically the entire black population of Biloxi had enlisted in my cause. The old Biloxi municipal courthouse sat in the middle of Main Street at its intersection with Howard Avenue. Let me tell you, I was so proud to see the turnout of black folks. Now, there were some right-thinking white folks there, too, but I was so proud to see the black community overcoming its fears to show its support. On the way into the courthouse I saw that things were not well with an angry section of the white community. A crowd of white ruffians pushed and pulled on me and on my attorney, Knox Walker. They tried to keep us from entering the building. Somehow we just walked on through the goons and made our way into the courtroom to the defendant's table. Inside, at least two hundred Negroes filled all the seats on the side of the courtroom reserved for blacks and stood around the walls. I felt like Moses watching the children of Israel cross the Red Sea. Some of the faces, white and black, in that room are still influential in the community today. Judge Jules Schwan presided. My case was the last one on the city court docket that evening. Officer Vene Lee took the witness stand to describe my swim at the beach on April 17. The officer reported accurately that he had found me swimming about a hundred feet from shore between the Buena Vista Hotel and the Biloxi lighthouse. The city prosecutor, John Sekul, also called Assistant Police Chief Walter Williams and perhaps Mayor Quave to testify that I was a repeat offender. I had been caught on the beach twice within a year's time. After the first incident, they said correctly, I had been told not to go back, or I would face arrest. They said that I had stated to them that I would go again to the beach, even if arrested. In their view I had been given ample warning after the first offense. My defense was simple. There was no law prohibiting anyone from using the beach. In fact, we argued, the beach was maintained with public money and thus should be open to all members of the public.

When both sides rested, Judge Schwan turned to us and said, "I'll tell you what I am going to do. I'm going to take this case under advisement." I looked at Knox Walker, my attorney, and asked, "What does that mean?" Knox replied, "He wants to think about it." It was a risky case involving the first civil disobedience activity of any kind in Mississippi. Judge Schwan wanted to delay his pronouncement. Well, of course, I knew exactly what I wanted to do. I immediately posted bond to appeal Judge Schwan's ruling, whenever he might release it. As fate would have it though, he never ruled in the case, so it was never sent over to county court. The Sovereignty Commission files show that delaying the ruling was a concerted strategy which Biloxi officials undertook with the blessing of Governor Ross Barnett. Sovereignty Commission agents reported that both Mayor Quave and Governor Barnett thought that I would ultimately win an appeal, but they thought that if they could delay the court decision long enough, they could wear us out.[1]

The following Wednesday evening, Dr. Felix Dunn chaired a meeting of the Harrison County Civic Action Committee in Biloxi. There we reported on the events of April 17 and finalized plans for a new Biloxi wade-in attempt to be made on April 24. The participants would assemble at my office on Division Street and proceed in three groups to three designated areas on the beach. One group would wade-in at the foot of Gill Avenue west of the lighthouse. A second group would hit the beach a few hundred yards down the beach at the lighthouse itself. A third group was assigned an area a mile farther to the east in front of the Biloxi Hospital. We coached our people on nonviolent tactics. Nothing was to be taken to the beach that could in any way be used as or even construed to be a weapon. No pocketknives, no combs, no hair picks or pins were allowed. If attacked, we would cover our heads and tuck if we could. I did not anticipate any violence. During the previous year, both the mayor and the chief of police had yelled at me, cursed me, and threatened me. However, .my actual arrests had been nonviolent, and the arresting officers had been reasonably courteous. I thought that we would be removed from the beach, but that law enforcement would surely protect us from bodily harm. In Biloxi, Mayor Quave and Chief McDonnell had made some rabid statements to me. However, we thought that enough dialogue had gone on with other city and county officials since our October petition that right-thinking white folks would not interfere with our demonstration. Under the impression that county officials had ultimate authority over the beach, Dr. Dunn testified publicly that he had called Sheriff Curtis Dedeaux to inform him of our intentions to carry out a peaceful demonstration on the beach on Sunday, April 24.[2] I have no doubt that Dr. Dunn, like any good citizen, expected protection from the sheriff. No one anticipated what was to transpire. I was certainly naive about the meanness of the Biloxi establishment and the meanness of Biloxi's white rabble.

When Sunday, April 24, finally came, I again attended church and made an appeal for volunteers. That afternoon about 125 people showed up at the assembly point in front of my office on Division Street. We had ample volunteers for three groups. We got them organized and decided to go ahead and send them to their appointed zones on the beach at 1:00 P.M. It soon became obvious that the authorities and a group of white ruffians knew every move that we had planned to make. As we were getting ready to roll we noticed white guys, civilians, with handheld two-way radios on Nixon Street in front of my building and up on Division Street. We heard the sounds of the radios as the white men talked back and forth to each other. As we pulled out for the beach I heard one of these white men speak into his walkie-talkie and say, "They're leaving now."

In my car I cruised down the beach surveying the protest zones. On my first pass down the beach from Gill Avenue going back east to the hospital, everything looked quiet. I noticed dozens of sheriff's deputies already on the beach at two of our three target zones. I mistakenly supposed that they would protect us. Oddly, there were very few Biloxi policemen around. On this first sweep, I saw no evidence of white gangs or any other potential trouble. I turned around and headed back west on Irish Hill and then south to the beach.

By the time I got back to the lighthouse the shit had hit the fan. Hordes of snarling white folks poured onto the beach at the foot of Gill with bricks, baseball bats, pipes, sticks, and chains and attacked our unarmed black protesters. The law enforcement officers were just standing around. I immediately realized that our group was in imminent danger. I did not know it, but back down the beach in front of the hospital a similar violent confrontation was transpiring. Our folks were like lambs being led to the slaughter. I thought, "Lord, what have I gotten these people into." Some of the forty or fifty blacks at the foot of Gill were already in the water with at least four or five hundred whites surrounding them and beating whomever they could lay hands on. It was too late to call it off. When they started whipping on Le' Roy Carney, one of my Boy Scouts, he took off running down the highway and ran through the cemetery and along the railroad to escape his white pursuers. There was no protection for any of us from law enforcement. The dozens of sheriff's deputies on the scene appeared to step back so as not to interfere with the melee on the beach. The sheriff himself was there and did nothing to stop the white mob. Up until this time, I would not have anticipated even the Biloxi police behaving this way, let alone the sheriff. I was later told that FBI agents had observed these beatings from the lighthouse, and they apparently did not do anything to stop them either.

Seeing these developments from the highway, I immediately wheeled my car back around through the cutoff in the Highway 90 median west of Gill and headed back east to the scene of the riot. In the neutral ground, five white men with cue sticks were beating two black youths, Joe Lomberger and Gilmore Fielder. A deputy sheriff stood nearby letting the beating proceed and doing nothing to protect the boys. I halted my car in the middle of the eastbound lane and jumped out to stop these guys from beating on Joe and Gilmore. One of the whites hit me with his cue stick. I grabbed the stick, took it from him, and started working on him with his own stick. When he reached down to try to tackle me, I jammed the sharp end of the cue stick down on his back. Another white thug hit me and grabbed me. I bit him—something I surely wouldn't do today, given what we have learned about blood-borne diseases. At about this time, the deputy sheriff, Merritt Brunies, finally intervened. He grasped my collar and took the two black boys into custody but allowed our white assailants to run away. "You're under arrest," the deputy said to me. "You'll have to come on downtown." I looked over at the beach where several persons were down injured, pleading for help in the midst of the white mob. I said, "I've got more to do than be under arrest." With the cue stick still in my hand, I hurried across the highway to the beach to help the injured. I left my blue '59 Buick sitting in the middle of the highway. The deputy made no move to stop me. The sheriff himself was there with his hands on his hips doing nothing but posturing as if to say, "Boy, you're in a heap of trouble now." We were indeed in a heap of trouble.

When I stepped across the seawall, cue stick still in hand, the hoodlum mob just melted away. As I walked, they parted like it was the Red Sea. Mr. James McGowan, Sr., was down bleeding with his teeth knocked out, sand and blood mixed all over his face. Miss Burnell Burney summoned me there. Mr. Dorothy Galloway had been beaten across his knees with a cue stick and lay on the ground crippled. Across the highway, a Negro airman lay knocked out cold on the ground from a beating that was so brutal that a white lady had rushed from her house with a gun to scare his attackers away. A State Sovereignty Commission agent reported that an ambulance was called for, but none arrived during the twenty minutes that the agent was there.[3] As far as I could see, none of the sheriff's men made any effort to assist those being beaten or those injured. One officer even stated that we (the blacks) were getting what we deserved. On the beach a white airman from Keesler tried to help Mr. Galloway to his feet. Other blacks heroically helped the wounded off the beach. We carried Galloway and McGowan off the beach to my car. Deputy Brunies met us at the car. I told him that I couldn't go to jail right then, because I had to go sew people up. I promised to turn myself in when I finished. Surprisingly, the deputy accepted my promise and let me go on to work. Marvin Dickey drove us in my car on to the hospital, so that I could see whether I would be needed there. The same type of mob violence was producing casualties on the beach in front of the hospital. The lawmen there also just stood by and watched. As black people ran from the beach, white gangs pursued them. Thus, the violence spread across the Biloxi peninsula and continued into the night. Our April 24 demonstration had become "the bloody wade-in." The Jackson *Clarion-Ledger* and the *Jackson Daily News* quickly labeled it the worst and bloodiest race riot in Mississippi history.[4]

At the hospital several people had come into the emergency room. I got their names and their employers' names from the hospital admission forms. Curiously, the white nurse, Mrs. Spiers, had written the word "integrational" as the cause of injury on each admission. Sovereignty Commission files show that their agent dutifully took down the names for his purposes, whatever they might be, and the press reported them, too. Kenneth Thames, age eighteen, Marzine Thames, age twenty-one, Luzell Bullock, age thirty-eight, Sanford Williams, age unknown, and my undertaker friend and longtime patient, Wilmer B. McDaniel, age thirty-five, all had been admitted to the Biloxi Hospital. When I got there, Dr. Eugene Trudeau was sewing up McDaniel, who had received ugly gashes on his chin and head, as well as an eye injury, in the fighting in front of the hospital. Baseball bats and chains had delivered these injuries to McDaniel. I stuck my head into the room to see about my friend. I asked Dr. Trudeau how things were going. Dr. Trudeau said only, "Yeah." McDaniel said, "It's okay, Doc, I don't care who sews me up. Just go ahead and let him [Dr. Trudeau] do it." I left the hospital for my office where others who had been injured were heading. However, the next day, Dr. Trudeau filed a complaint with the hospital staff that I had interfered with the doctor-patient relationship when I had checked on McDaniel. At my office, Ellis Brown and two or three others were awaiting treatment when I got there. I bandaged or stitched folks up and gave tetanus shots as needed. Eight others were said to have been admitted to the hospital at Keesler Air Force Base.[5] In my opinion, the newspaper estimates of injuries in the riot were way too low. They reported only emergency room treatments at Biloxi Hospital or Keesler Air Force Base hospital. The newspapers did not count those injured who were treated at my office or at the veterans' hospital or who took care of their wounds at home.

Large crowds gathered in the streets around my office and down at my apartment on Nixon Street that afternoon. Several hundred people milled around telling Natalie that they were there to protect me from arrest. A white merchant who owned a general store that sold groceries and hardware in our neighborhood started walking up the crowded street shooting a pistol into the air, I guess trying to scare people off. Natalie remembers

Biloxi police cruisers roaming around with loudspeakers broadcasting threatening messages. "If there is any trouble," they blared out to the crowds, "Dr. Mason will be held personally responsible!"

At some point during that tumultuous afternoon, Dr. Dunn showed up at my office. He had not been present in the beach demonstration that day. Dr. Dunn and I knew that Roy Wilkins and Clarence Mitchell, our top national NAACP officials, were in Meridian, Mississippi, that day for an NAACP regional conclave of some sort. From my office, we telephoned their meeting place in Meridian. We talked personally to Roy Wilkins and Clarence Mitchell. We reported our beatings and the apparent complicity of the authorities. This was our first effort to get the national NAACP involved in the Biloxi beach desegregation struggle. Wilkins and Mitchell suggested that Medgar Evers investigate the situation.

Later on in the afternoon, when people stopped coming to me for treatment, I went over and turned myself in at the city courthouse and jail, where deputy Brunies happened to be hanging around. When I presented myself, the deputy looked surprised and said, "Well, he promised he would come back, and he did." The authorities charged me with fighting in a public place and obstructing traffic. They also charged Joe Lomberger and Gilmore Fielder. Our attackers were never arrested. I made bail immediately. My second beach-related trial within a week was set for Monday afternoon.

Dr. Dunn and I attended a meeting at New Bethel Baptist Church late that afternoon. New Bethel was the largest African American church in Biloxi at that time. The house was packed. Folks were feeling angry and betrayed, and they spoke out freely. Many expressed the belief that the police and the hoodlum mobs that attacked us were in cahoots with each other. Forty years later, after reading the Sovereignty Commission files and listening to their tapes, I can say with certainty that powerful people had indeed prompted the white hooligan mob to go after us on the beach. In good faith, Dr. Dunn had informed the sheriff of our peaceful intention. Citizens have the right to expect protection in the exercise of their basic rights. The sheriff chose to break faith with the citizenry, as did officials of the city of Biloxi.

The moral fault, the blame before God for the evil done in the 1960 Biloxi riot lies with the authorities who decided to use public safety information for diabolic ends. The Sovereignty Commission files make clear that days before the Sunday wade-in, an array of state, city, and county authorities and police agencies knew about our plan, and they knew about the white mobs that would be waiting for us. In collusion, and with malice aforethought, a broad spectrum of morally corrupt state and local officials and police agents all abused and misused the information entrusted to them. And what evil did they do? Rather than using their knowledge to protect us, as was their sworn duty, the authorities themselves recklessly passed along their information about our plans to the meanest and most virulently prejudiced and irresponsible elements in the white community. The mob of white thugs who met us on the beach west of the lighthouse had first assembled around the law enforcement vehicles that were parked nearby. When some of these law enforcement officers pulled away, it seemed to be a signal for the white thugs to move onto the beach. When the white gang made their move, the Biloxi police had purposefully made themselves scarce, and the scores of sheriff's deputies and Mississippi highway patrolmen on the scene did nothing. The riot proceeded with the police viewing it from the sidelines. The ruffians appeared to have coordinated everything they did on the beach with the sheriff's men and with Biloxi city officials.

I would not have believed such a thing possible before I saw it on April 24, 1960. At the time, I was one of those who strongly suspected collusion between the authorities and the white gangs. Now, almost forty years later, I have found independent, hard proof that a racist violent intent existed in the Biloxi Police Department long before April 24, 1960. The Sovereignty Commission files reveal that as early as October 15, 1959, Assistant Chief Walter Williams told a Sovereignty Commission agent that the only way to end the beach controversy was to "go out and beat the hell out of any Negro found on the beach."[6] The Sovereignty Commission agent did nothing but record Williams's heinous pronouncement without even a hint of any concern for the legal or moral implications of such a statement coming from the mouth of a high police official.

Further, there is now hard evidence of police complicity in the white gang's assault on the beach. This is seen in Sovereignty Commission investigator Bob Thomas's memorandum on the riot. After local officials tipped him off to our wade-in plan, Thomas made a flying trip to the coast on April 22, the Friday before the riot. On that Friday afternoon, Biloxi's police chief, Herbert McDonnell, and Assistant Chief Walter Williams told agent Thomas that they expected a march on the beach on Sunday. McDonnell said that rather than beef up his force to protect the public, he intended to "operate on a skeleton crew," and that neither the chief nor the assistant chief would be on duty. The chief said that "a lot of people had notified him that they would be around the beach in case Mason showed up." In short, state agents knew that Biloxi authorities had decided to let vigilante violence reign down on us, and the state agents did nothing to stop it. In the same interview, Chief McDonnell lamented the fact that the white Citizens' Council was weak around Biloxi. He thought the white Citizens' Council was "badly needed" to "coordinate the activities of citizens against" civil rights demonstrations.[7] This same state agent was present on the beach during the riot and reported that Sheriff Dedeaux told his deputies not to make any arrests on the beach.[8] In short, there was official foreknowledge and complicity in the violence. Whether they consciously solicited and coordinated white hooliganism on the beach or merely turned their heads once it erupted, Biloxi city officials, State Sovereignty Commission agents, the sheriff of Harrison County, and the Mississippi Highway Patrol all shared guilt in promoting a bloody confrontation where none was intended, needed, or wanted. In this sordid affair, it was these white public officials alone who had the power to decide how to use the notification they had received for good or ill. The white authorities chose to render harm instead of help. They decided to direct or to permit the direction of a mob assault on peaceful demonstrators. In so doing, they bear full and complete responsibility for the blood that flowed over the next two days in Biloxi.

The Dunns and the Masons had a long-standing custom of taking our Sunday evening meal together. Because our Nixon Street apartment was so small, when we hosted the Dunns in Biloxi, we usually went to the Blue Note, which at the time was a first-rate black cafe. When the Dunns had us to Gulfport, we often ate at Dr. Dunn's spacious house. After our meeting at New Bethel Baptist Church in the late afternoon following the bloody wade-in, Dr. Dunn invited us to his home in Gulfport for dinner. As we started to leave the Nixon Street apartment, two Biloxi policemen came to the door. The officer doing the talking said that they had a message for me from the mayor. He said, "The mayor sent us to tell you that if anybody's killed tonight, we're going to hold you responsible." Threats of this type were getting to be a habit with Biloxi officials. I was concerned, but I went on to Gulfport to Dr. Dunn's home. As it turned out, Dr. Dunn's dinner invitation probably saved my life and the lives of my family that night.

The violence that the authorities had allowed to be unleashed on the beach in the afternoon continued and intensified in Biloxi's streets throughout the night. After dark, vicious white mobs roamed Howard Avenue between Lemeuse and Main streets and milled around at the police station and the bus station assaulting black passers-by. Two airmen were beaten up downtown in the vicinity of the old courthouse. White hoodlums stopped Reverend John Ferdinand, the black associate pastor of New Bethel Baptist Church, and slapped him around. This gray-headed reverend told them, "I'm old enough. You can beat me up if you want to, but it's not going to stop us." Louis Johnson, a black air force master sergeant, was coming home from an Elks meeting in Moss Point. Sergeant Johnson always carried a .45 caliber pistol in his car. Johnson made the mistake of turning up Howard Avenue coming north off Highway 90. Near the old courthouse a bunch of white ruffians jumped in front of his car and started banging on it. One brandished a pistol and rapped on the sergeant's car window with it, saying, "Roll the window down." Johnson pulled his .45 out and rapped right back on the window with it. The white guy dropped his pistol and took off running. A white eyewitness reported seeing another black man stopped, dragged from his car, and thrown through the plate-glass window of a furniture store. During the night, armed white hooligans invaded the African American section of Biloxi that we called "back-of-town." Some white gangs traveled on foot and beat any black they came upon, or they stopped cars carrying blacks and attempted to beat the riders. Other trouble came in white-driven automobiles and pickups that attempted to run down blacks in the streets. Gunshots rang out from cars loaded with white men and teenagers. They raked black businesses, clubs, and cafes with shotgun blasts. The Twilight, the Kitty-Cat, and the Little Apple cafes were shot up. Mrs. Myrtle Davis witnessed the shots fired into the Kitty-Cat, where two people received buckshot wounds. When Mrs. Davis reported it to the police chief, he promptly arrested her for making the report. The chief asked Mrs. Davis if she knew "that Dr. Mason." She said, "No, but I'm going to make his acquaintance as soon as I can." Myrtle had seen enough. She later became a local NAACP officer.

A black-owned Standard station across the street from my office on Division Street lost three windows to shotgun blasts. Some whites attacked a truck owned by Wilmer McDaniel. They broke out the windshield and attempted to get at the black driver inside the truck, but he managed to drive away. Some blacks who worked late shifts in white sections of town on that Sunday evening found their places of work surrounded by white mobs. Many were so alarmed by the mayhem in the streets that they were afraid to go home after getting off work. This kind of intimidation of black workers continued for days. One evening later in the week, I personally drove through a threatening white crowd to a po' boy cafe in an east Biloxi white neighborhood to bring home Mrs. Ella Cotton, a fearful black cook who, along with her husband, was blockaded in the cafe. During

Sunday night alone, according to the *Clarion-Ledger*, at least eight blacks and two whites suffered gunshot wounds.[9] The press reported that, in all, more than twenty blacks were injured in the riot.[10] Many others sustained unreported injuries. Worst of all, later that week, after the newspapers quit counting, two young black men were tragically murdered in a continuing racist crime wave on the coast.

The vast majority of riot-related violent assaults and the only deaths in this frenzied week came down on blacks. Almost all of the reported victims were black. However, our story would be incomplete if we did not acknowledge that a handful of blacks were guilty of carrying out reprisals on innocent whites. A white physician friend of mine, Dr. John B. O'Keefe, was coming back from Pascagoula and made the mistake of turning down Division Street in the black section of town. Black folks brick-batted the doctor's car and pelted it with rocks. White taxi drivers running through the area also reported their cars being pelted or stopped and rocked. The newspaper reported that a white teenager, Andrew Parker, was riding in a car near Main Street when some blacks yelled at him to stop. He got out of the car and was shot in the back. Luckily, the wound was only superficial.[11]

Sometime after I arrived at Dr. Dunn's house in Gulfport that night, my brother called from New Orleans. The news from Biloxi about road-blocks, shootings, and uncontrolled mob action had reached New Orleans. At my brother's urging, I decided to spend the night at Felix Dunn's house. With this reign of terror going on in the streets of Biloxi, Chief McDonnell slapped on a curfew at 10:00 P.M. that night and ordered all bars closed. Having in effect unleashed this thing, the chief now went on radio to appeal to everyone, white and black, to get off the streets.

On Monday morning, black folks started going early to hardware stores to buy guns and ammunition. When word got out that blacks were arming themselves, whites also started buying ammunition. The local newspaper reported that, by Monday afternoon, stores in Biloxi were sold out of ammunition. Sheriff Curtis Dedeaux issued a notice, carried on the front page of the afternoon paper, decreeing registration of all firearms with the sheriff's office.[12] Sporadic episodes of white gang activity continued in Biloxi for several days. Before business hours on Monday morning, unknown perpetrators tossed two firebombs at my office at 439½ East Division Street. One of these kerosene-filled pop bottles, stuffed with rags, crashed through a window into the examining room and burned itself out, doing little damage. The other smashed up against the outside wall of the building and burst into flames. Asariah Taylor and another man visiting a neighbor jumped a fence and put the fire out. Someone called me. I immediately drove to the office and called the police. The police officers made only the most superficial and unenthusiastic inquiry. They did not even take fingerprints from the surviving bottle and fragments. They never gave me a report.

That afternoon, I was scheduled to be back in court before Justice of the Peace Anthony Anglado. I was charged with public fighting and obstructing traffic on Highway 90. Before leaving my office for court, I was made aware that we had become a national news item. A New York area radio station called me and recorded an interview. There were many newspaper interviews. By this time the press was saying that the authorities had identified me as "the instigator" of the wade-in.[13] "Instigator" is a label that I have since been proud to wear in the campaign for equal rights, equal justice, and equal opportunity. Later in the week, the *Jackson Advocate* quoted me in response to a provocative question as saying, "Anyone who says that I touched off the riot is an unmitigated, calculated and pathological liar."[14] I never tried to hide my role as a leader. I took the heat willingly. However, I did not cause this riot. I had led peaceful demonstrators who were unarmed and thoroughly coached in nonviolent tactics. Others chose to attack us. Others had decided to touch off a riot.

After the radio interview, I drove to court and parked my car nearby. Two police officers met me at the car as if they were going to have to bring me in. They walked with me down the street to the courthouse. I mention this police escort in order to refute the caption beneath an AP wirephoto of me walking down the street beside the officers. I did not request this escort. And I was certainly already on my way to court voluntarily when the officers appeared. Yet the newspaper caption falsely states that the officers "escorted" me to court after I allegedly "expressed fear" for my safety.[15] Through the grace of God, I really felt no fear that day. However, even if I had felt fear, the Biloxi police would have been the last people on earth that I would have let know about it. I was absolutely not going to do anything that would reward or encourage their ongoing efforts to intimidate blacks. So, the news photo caption completely misrepresented my mood.

At the courthouse I met my attorney, Knox Walker. A large black turnout for the trial again buoyed our spirits. Judge Anglado issued a warning about disturbances in open court and then for some reason took me, Joe Lomberger, and Gilmore Fielder into his private office for the trial. To charges of disturbing the peace, we all pled not guilty. Deputy Brunies stated that we had all been fighting, and that I had parked my car in the middle of Highway 90, blocking traffic. Lomberger and Fielder argued that they were merely fighting to defend themselves from a group of whites who had attacked them. I argued that I had abandoned my car to try to break up the fight and render first aid to the injured on the beach. Notwithstanding the deputy's admission that a group of whites had run away when he arrested us, we were all three found guilty and fined twenty-five dollars for disturbing the peace. I got an additional twenty-five-dollar fine for blocking traffic. Truly here was a case in which the victims of crime were blamed and fined. Several other cases stemming from the Sunday afternoon and Sunday night fighting were heard in city and county courts Monday afternoon and evening. It is important to remember that African Americans made up the vast majority of those injured in the riots. However, according to the *Clarion-Ledger*, while twenty-two Negroes were found guilty of riot-related offenses that Monday, only one white man was similarly convicted.[16] There was no such thing as evenhanded law enforcement or evenhanded justice in this affair. Of course, I filed to appeal my conviction.

The most tragic and horrible events associated with the hateful week of the bloody wade-in were the murders of two young black men, Bud Strong and Malcomb "Papa" Jackson. Today we would call these hate crimes. The loss of each one of these boys was heartbreaking, but the murder of Bud Strong especially touched the black community, because he was mentally retarded and could not have helped himself. Bud Strong's murder touched the members of my church in a special way, because Bud's sister, Miss Coreen Strong, was a member of First Missionary Baptist Church in Biloxi. Miss Coreen taught Sunday school at our church and was extremely dedicated and really good at what she did. She was a public school teacher with an excellent reputation in Biloxi's segregated school system. Her brother, Bud, was retarded but not institutionalized. Bud Strong would come up to you on the street and say innocently, "Give me a nickel, mister. Give me a nickel." A couple of nights after the riot, someone took poor, helpless Bud Strong and cut his throat, all but decapitating him, then left him dead in the neutral ground on Highway 90 in front of Beauvoir facing the beach. Of all the places in our community to kill a black man, none could have sent a more sinister or a more powerful symbolic message than Beauvoir, the antebellum mansion that served as the post–Civil War home of Jefferson Davis. Although he could not have understood what was happening around him, Bud Strong was a victim of race hatred. I went to McDaniel's Funeral Home and examined Bud Strong's body. The only thing holding his head onto his torso was the skin of the neck and the *ligamentum nuchae* that runs down the neck. Bud Strong was a lamb led to the slaughter, a victim and a martyr in the struggle for the desegregation of Biloxi beach. No one was arrested for his murder.

Because of the riot, the Mississippi Highway Patrol and other police agencies beefed up their presence on the coast. In this awful mood of hate and bigotry, with racial passions running wild in the state and with local all-white police forces, unwarranted police assaults killed teenager Malcomb "Papa" Jackson. Jackson, age eighteen, was a former member of my Scout troop. Police in the neighboring coast town of Pascagoula beat "Papa" Jackson to death in custody. I examined photographs of this boy's beaten and bruised body. There is no doubt in my mind that these boys would be alive today were it not for the racist rancor and hate-filled atmosphere which the authorities unleashed over the wade-in. One of the first projects of the new Biloxi branch of the NAACP was to press for investigations of the murders of these boys. On private retainers, Howard Andre McDonnell, one of the finest criminal attorneys on the coast, investigated the murders of Bud Strong and Malcomb "Papa" Jackson. However, as with many other cases of racial murder in Mississippi, no one has yet found out who killed Bud Strong or who beat "Papa" Jackson to death in the Pascagoula jail.

Anyone who ever doubts the virulence or viciousness of the passions which the Jim Crow system nurtured in people need only review the events of the last week of April 1960 in Biloxi, Mississippi. Jim Crowism was a wild, mad-dog system in its effects. How else could you explain how the simple desire of 125 people to use a few yards of a twenty-six-mile-long beach could trigger such rage, mayhem, and murder? Jim Crowism caused a certain segment of the white population of the South, at times, to behave like surgically decerebrated cats—as if they had somehow lost all touch with the part of the brain which adds the learning-based thought, judgment, and inhibitory messages that normally restrain the raw reflex rage reactions promoted from the hypothalamus. Surgically decerebrated laboratory animals will literally rage themselves to death in reaction to the slightest noise or irregular stimulation. Like the phenomena seen in surgically decerebrated animals, racism is man-made. In an environment filled with mean and dehumanizing practices that equated status with skin color, madness could be set in motion if anything threatened, or could be made out to threaten, the status of the least privileged of the privileged group. When they had ignored or blessed the vicious, wild, mad-dog reactions that had been bred up in the perverted union of hateful racist dogma and sinful segregationist practices, Biloxi's so-called city fathers had decerebrated the community. As a result, Bud Strong and Malcomb "Papa" Jackson died, and dozens of others were hurt.

Having sown to the wind, Biloxi's white establishment tried through disinformation to deflect blame for the resulting whirlwind of violence onto imaginary "outside agitators." In a UPI interview, Mayor Laz Quave claimed, "We've got Negroes here from Alabama, Louisiana, all parts of Mississippi and everywhere else. It has to be an organized move."[17] Here and now, I say without hesitation that the mayor's statement was an absolute bald-faced, vicious, pathological, and unmitigated lie. None of the blacks arrested were from out of state. In an Associated Press interview, Anthony Ragusin of the Biloxi Chamber of Commerce accused the NAACP of being behind the trouble. This was another deliberate lie. There had been no NAACP involvement in the beach demonstrations up to that point. Even more outrageously, Ragusin falsely appealed to McCarthy-era paranoia when he told the reporter that the demonstrations were "financed with overseas money." The Associated Press quoted Roy Wilkins, executive secretary of the NAACP, who said in a statement from New York, "When Anthony Ragusin . . . implies . . . that the NAACP is acting as an agent of the 'enemies of the United States' by inspiring demonstrations 'financed by money from overseas' he is telling a deliberate, premeditated and vicious falsehood."[18]

I suppose the establishment resorted to this false line about outsiders because they thought it would be believed in the white community. A lot of white folks at that time, even some well-meaning whites, had a strange psychology about the Mississippi blacks that they knew. They assumed that the native black folks didn't have sense nor guts enough to do anything to change the status quo. Their racism led them to underestimate us. Some whites probably believed that it must be foreigners or outsiders stirring things up. Even Governor Barnett and Mayor Quave seemed to believe that we had no gumption or staying power and that the movement would burn itself out. Filled with racial hubris, they were stupid enough to live under the illusion that black folks didn't have the power to think or the guts to act. Well, they met a different breed of Negro when they met me and other young blacks of the same mind-set.

Whereas an unthinking bunch of lower-class whites did the violent dirty work of the Biloxi riot, a segment of Biloxi's elite white establishment almost immediately set out to intimidate an aroused black community through economic pressure. The A&P food store fired Mr. Marvin Dickey, who had driven my car from the beach to the hospital during the riot.

However, Marvin found another job right away. Mr. Bill Bradford, just about the best brick mason and cement finisher in the country, lost his job for going with me to the beach. Bill was never again able to find work with a white contractor in Mississippi. In retaliation for the wade-in, one of the big drugstores on Howard Avenue fired six employees, including short order cooks Mrs. Lorea Barnes Wright, Mrs. Eleanor Shelby, and Mrs. Ola Mae Odom and handyman Mr. Willie Wiggins, who was a deacon at my church. None of the six discharged drugstore employees had even gone near the beach. The firings of innocents were apparently meant as a message to the whole black community back-of-town. In a similar move, Borden's Milk Company fired Mr. A. A. Dickey, who was never involved in any wade-in.

All through the week following the riot, local and state authorities attempted to discourage any thoughts that we might have had about going back to the beach the next Sunday. There were many questions about our intentions. I decided to keep them guessing. I might return to the beach, I said. There was no law forbidding it, and there could be no law forbidding it. In Jackson that week, the Mississippi State Legislature hurriedly passed, and Governor Barnett quickly signed into law, a special bill designed to seriously discourage any further civil rights demonstrations on the beach. In the civil rights community they took to calling this bill the "Mason Bill," a weapon specially designed to corral me. The "Mason Bill" made breach of peace a felony punishable by up to ten years in the penitentiary, if anyone was hurt or killed in a riot construed to stem from the breach of peace. Moreover, the bill made the specific act of "breach of peace *on a coastal beach*" a special crime subject to a two-hundred-dollar fine and a four-month jail term, even if no injury or deaths were involved. In explaining the bill, Senator W. B. Alexander of Boyle maintained that "the bill was most urgently needed on the Coast and may be needed this weekend." It passed quickly. As soon as Governor Barnett had signed the "Mason Bill" into law, the news reports said, copies "were rushed to Gulf Coast officials . . . in anticipation that another flare-up of racial violence may occur in the next several days." There could be no doubt that the bill was aimed at one man—me. I had been charged with breaching the peace and disorderly conduct when I went to the beach on April 17 and April 24. Besides the prison time, the law had other potentially serious ramifications. Some in the segregationist establishment tried to lay the blame for the riot on me. With these new laws on the books, a felony conviction associated with any future demonstrations could easily lead to the loss of my Mississippi medical license. Several other pieces of legislation were debated that week which, through stiff fines and jail time, aimed to discourage sit-ins and other types of civil disobedience activities that had not yet been seen in Mississippi. The "Mason Bill" led the way.[19]

Our adversaries also applied a variety of other pressures to Dr. Dunn and me. Again, during the week following the riot, I received innumerable threats on my life in the mail and by telephone. Knox Walker obtained another Klan hit list with our names on it. We took note and increased our personal vigilance. However, Dr. Dunn and I also got plenty of direct economic bullying aimed at us. In those days, Dr. Dunn was quite a businessman. I admired Felix Dunn's entrepreneurial spirit. To me, he was a good example of Garveyism and the new spirit of black pride in taking up business activity. Over the years, Dr. Dunn had invested in a number of businesses. For example, he bought the Standard service station at the corner of Nixon and Division streets across from my office. In 1959, Felix Dunn had started Top Flight Amusement Company, a jukebox and vending machine company that placed machines in thirty-two black-owned bars and cafes in Harrison and Hancock counties. However, the bigger you are, the bigger the target you offer your enemies.

On the night of April 24–25, 1960, while the riot raged in Biloxi, Harrison County constables Hudson Puckett and Clyde Collins carried out a series of provocative raids on black bars in the Gulfport area. These establishments just happened to do business with Dr. Dunn's new Top Flight Amusement Company. In a sworn affidavit published in the *Daily Herald,* the constables admitted that when they "heard about the racial battles going on in the City of Biloxi . . . ," they immediately "took steps against places in the City of Gulfport where crowds of Negroes were known to be gathering and which were selling intoxicating liquors." Six black-owned Gulfport establishments were raided the night of the riot, and the newspaper reported that over the next forty-eight hours, the two constables hit another fifteen joints.[20] The black bar operators were officially charged with possessing and selling intoxicating liquor. In 1960, Mississippi still had its prohibition laws on the books. Selling liquor was technically a misdemeanor offense. In Harrison County, however, local officials, with state connivance, routinely overlooked liquor sales in bars, whether black or white owned, so long as the state's "official" black market liquor tax was paid on the whiskey sold. Sovereignty Commission files and tapes indicate that the black bar operators believed that the April 24–26 constables' raids sought to pressure them to change their vending and jukebox contracts in order to break Dr. Dunn's new company.[21] Extortion charges were filed against the two constables but were later dropped due to insufficient evidence.[22]

The pressure came down on me in the form of threats that my hospital privileges would be withdrawn. The first hint that this weapon might be used came in the police station after my arrest. Natalie came in with my bail and heard Biloxi police chief Herbert McDonnell ranting and raving to the effect that I was ruining the hospital. Natalie was a quick retort specialist. (I used to call her a retort transcendentalist after Emerson's work by that name.) Natalie told the chief he had better calm down since he had suffered a recent heart attack, and besides, she said, "If one doctor could do that much damage to a hospital with thirty other doctors, I just wonder, what kind of doctor could that be?" Later that week, at about eight o'clock one night, I was still working at the office when the phone rang and the person on the other end said, "Gilbert." I hung up. Back in those days, if you did not address me by my proper title, Dr. Mason, I hung up. The phone rang again, and this time a member of the hospital staff executive committee identified himself and said, "We [the staff executive committee] want to see you at the conference room of the Biloxi Hospital as soon as possible." I closed the office and went straight to the hospital.

There I found the conference room packed with people. "We have been reading about your activities and the wade-in," a prominent physician and staff officer said, "and we don't appreciate it." He threatened, "If it continues, we're going to put you off the staff." He implied that I could be held guilty of conduct unbecoming a physician, a charge that not only threatened my hospital privileges but could also threaten my Mississippi medical license. However, I discovered once again that I had friends. I will always remember the courage of Dr. Frank Gruich, a Christian gentleman and my ob-gyn preceptor, who, on this difficult night, rose once again to my defense, just as he had at the medical society meeting the year before. Dr. Gruich said, "Dr. Mason is guilty only of exercising his rights as a citizen. He has as much right to go to the beach as anyone else. What he has done [regarding the wade-in] is within the law. Beyond this, he has done no more than anyone else would do to defend himself or to obtain his rights." Thanks to Frank Gruich, nothing came of the charges. They did not put me off the staff, but the threat remained.

Beyond the hospital Natalie heard talk at church that some of my patients' white employers were encouraging them to change doctors. Some domestic workers seemed to have expressed concern that they would have to stop seeing me, but if anyone thought that they could use black people to drive me out of private practice because I was standing up for people's rights under the U.S. Constitution, they were mistaken. Our community would not let it happen. After the bloody wade-in the old scare tactics just didn't work very well anymore. When they needed a doctor, folks kept coming to me. There were other little signs of the white business community's displeasure, though. Natalie and I suddenly got some unfriendly pressure from our white landlord about the rent for our drugstore. Then, when the court maneuvers started later in the year, a white contractor with whom we had reached an agreement suddenly refused to install an aluminum carport for me on the house I was buying on Fayard Street.

With the economic screws or the threat of them being put to our people, it was time for back-of-town to respond. We did not return to the beach on Sunday, May 1. Instead we organized a targeted boycott and announced it in a meeting at the United Benevolence Association Hall on Division Street on Sunday. The Sovereignty Commission files show that both police and state agents were there listening. We did not see anything to be gained by a general boycott of white businesses. We believed we could be successful and make an important point about black economic power if we focused our boycott mainly on three establishments. We selected the white-owned general food and variety hardware store at the corner of Nixon and Division streets. This store did a brisk business with black folks. It sold everything from nuts and bolts to ham hocks and collard greens. This business was targeted because pipe and chain from that particular store was used to beat up our people on the beach, and because the owner himself was seen among those rioting against black folks on the beach on April 24. Borden's Milk Company was also targeted for boycott. Borden's had fired Mr. A. A. Dickey, who had taken no part in the beach demonstrations. As a matter of principle, we refused to buy any more Borden's milk products either from home deliverymen or in grocery stores. Our third main boycott target was the large drugstore on Howard Avenue which had fired six black employees, four of whom had never been to the beach.

Before we had been at work on the boycott for even a good week, the Sovereignty Commission agents were writing memos labeling our boycott as "a complete failure."[23] However, Borden's Milk Company was soon out of business in back-of-town in Biloxi. For many years thereafter, no Borden's milk was sold in Biloxi. We negotiated with a competing company called Dairy Fresh. Dairy Fresh hired A. A. Dickey and bought out the Borden's facilities. Dairy Fresh thrived. We put the general store at the corner of Division and Nixon streets totally out of business—lock, stock, and barrel. For many long days a cadre of ladies, often including Mrs. Vashti Tanner, stood across the street from that store keeping vigil and educating any black who looked to be headed there. Of course, if you failed to learn the lesson and headed on toward the store, these ladies educated everybody else about your failings in this matter. The proprietor soon gave it up and closed the store. I should say, those ladies closed him up. He eventually sold the store property to a group of black investors who hoped to open a new black-owned supermarket. I think that we made an important point with these two successes. However, we were never able to exert enough business pressure on the offending downtown drugstore on Howard Avenue to bring its owners to repentance. They never hired back the employees they had let go. They had enough white customers to see them through. Still, I think that by any objective standard our targeted boycott was highly successful. All sorts of inaccurate reports on our intentions made it into the press. One should not measure the boycott by what the press or Sovereignty Commission agents said it was trying to do. They were misinformed and passed on misinformation. Measure the boycott instead by its own aims and results. We never pursued a general boycott. Our targets were narrow and thoughtfully selected because of the special connection of particular businesses to the violence on the beach or to reprisals against innocent people in the aftermath of the bloody wade-in.

In this atmosphere, in the throes of unprecedented violence and intimidation, the black community back-of-town in Biloxi, Mississippi, held up its head and found a new identity, a new pride, and a new spirit. The dry bones of lost hope suddenly reconnected and came to life. In the fires of adversity new leadership came forth—leadership fitted to the times and tasks at hand. Those revived hopes and that new leadership gave birth to the Biloxi branch of the NAACP. By my count there were three NAACP members in the whole town of Biloxi before our heads were smashed on the day of the bloody wade-in. Except for those who belonged to my Masonic Lodge and the Elks Lodge, I could hardly get Biloxi's black community notables—not even the Scout leaders—to participate in civil rights activities. Because of the fear of our people that the NAACP label would make them special targets for white reprisals, we had created the Harrison County Civic Action Committee to carry on the campaign for the beach. Because of the fears of our people, the NAACP had nothing to do with the first wade-ins. That all changed overnight on April 24, 1960. The folks now saw that they needed a really big bad dog to look out for them. I pointed them to the biggest and the baddest one I knew.

In response to our talk with Roy Wilkins and Clarence Mitchell,

Medgar Evers, the field secretary of the Mississippi Conference of the NAACP, drove down and met Dr. Dunn and me at my office on the Monday after the riot. Right away Medgar Evers began soliciting memberships to see if there would be enough interest and commitment to organize a separate new local NAACP branch in Biloxi. Sometime that week we had an organizing meeting at the United Benevolence Association (UBA) hall. It was a memorable gathering. We were talking up a storm. Talk, talk, talk, talk, talk. We were going to do this, and we were going to do that. Soon Reverend John Ferdinand, the associate minister at New Bethel—he got full. He grew very impatient with the lack of direction. He stood up with that gray hair, looking like Frederick Douglass, and said, "Talk don't buy no land. Let's do something." Reverend Ferdinand had been beaten in the street the previous Sunday. He went on, "What are you going to do now? You've had your wade-in, and you've gotten beat up, and you've been arrested. But talk don't buy no land."

That gave me an opening. I said, "Our man Medgar Evers is here." Then and there, with Medgar Evers's guidance, we got serious about a new strategy. We decided to accept NAACP legal assistance. We decided to gather affidavits from persons beaten on the beach or who had otherwise been deprived of their right to use the beach. As Medgar Evers used to put it, we decided to see who "duly deposes, avers, and says" they are aggrieved. In short, it was time for a showing of faces behind NAACP leadership back-of-town in Biloxi, Mississippi. Now, downtown city officials were saying, "They're just a bunch of Negroes who went and got arrested. They can't do nothing." Back-of-town we were out in the open working with Medgar Evers and looking to the big dogs of the NAACP to help us carry on the struggle. Segregationists might frame a law to keep us from demonstrating, but they couldn't frame a law to keep us from suing them. Before the week was out in back-of-town, seventy-two courageous persons had signed sworn affidavits. There would have been more affidavits if there had been more time to gather and type them. We also collected photographs of the riot to be placed in evidence with the affidavits. An inquiry was made as to who of the seventy-two people who had signed sworn affidavits would be willing to stand up in court and become a plaintiff in a federal suit. All seventy-two wanted to go to court. All seventy-two were ready for such a showing of faces.

At the end of the week, city and county officials tried to appease us with the appointment of an all-white, nine-man committee to study the beach problem. The clear implication was that their nine men would recommend a separate beach for blacks in each municipality. After all the scars inflicted during the previous week, I had no intentions of accepting a segregated beach. I stated this publicly at the UBA hall on Sunday, May 1. It amused Medgar Evers greatly when I added that I had a nine-man committee of my own to review this problem—the U.S. Supreme Court. Both the press and Sovereignty Commission agents reported this statement.[24] Of course, we were already well down the road toward a suit demanding total and unrestricted access for all citizens to any part of the beach. We were about to deliver a punch that no one in the white power structure thought we could deliver from that little black section back-of-town in Biloxi.

And the showing of faces continued. Before the week was out, ninety-two people had become charter members of the new Biloxi branch of the NAACP. Ninety-two folks signed on to bring the big dog to town and feed him. At thirty-one years of age, I was elected the first president of the Biloxi branch, and Mrs. Ruby Tyler was elected secretary. Reverend M. C. Easily became our treasurer, and Mr. Rehofus Esters, Mr. Luzell Bullock, Sr., and Mrs. Ossie Seymour filled out our initial slate of local officers as first, second, and third vice presidents. Over the next week, we attended to the business of organizing the new branch. Heavy police patrols prowled the beach and the neighborhood back-of-town. Things got a lot quieter—so quiet, in fact, that just three days after I had made my statement about having my own "nine-man committee," Sovereignty Commission informant David McDavid of the *Jackson Daily News* speculated to Zack Van Landingham that "someone had gotten to Mason . . . and quieted him down."[25] White folks were still underestimating the strength that we had gained when those dry bones of suppressed black hope and pride had come back to life. Our spirits were high. Our resolve was unchanged. Nobody had gotten to me.

Those who underestimated us got a wake-up call on Sunday, May 8, when, from Atlanta, Roy Wilkins, executive secretary of the NAACP, announced plans for a national "wade-in" campaign in response to events in Biloxi. Biloxi gave the lexicon of the civil rights movement the term "wade-in."[26] This was good, but we had something better in the works.

Medgar Evers and the NAACP legal defense team had delivered our affidavits, and the Civil Rights Division of President Eisenhower's Justice Department answered our call for justice. On May 17, from the halls of the U.S. Justice Department, our own Big Bertha roared. The U.S. Justice Department filed suit in federal district court in our behalf against Harrison County, the board of supervisors, Sheriff Curtis Dedeaux, the city of Biloxi, Mayor Laz Quave, and Biloxi police chief Herbert McDonnell for denying Negroes use of the beach. Local officials on the coast were stunned. One newspaper report said that the president of the board of supervisors and Mayor Laz Quave looked as if they were about to have a heart attack when they first got word of the suit. They'd been fooling themselves, thinking they would wear us out or that they would appease us with their nine-man committee. They had boasted, "Ain't nothing going to come of this." The Jim Crow establishment told themselves, "Those blacks ain't got no gumption. The money's coming from overseas." No, the money came from Division and Nixon streets. The gumption was also homegrown.

Looking back in 1978, and thinking about the crisis of these great days in Biloxi, I wrote lines that to me still ring true: "Born in the month of April 1960, amidst the turbulent, ominous temperament of a vicious, unfeeling, rabid segregationist South, propelled into a discordant maze of a confused America which could not stop the change to a new equality, the Biloxi branch came forth squalling a clarion call for justice, which was, then and now, at a fervent pitch—so fervent that virtually every significant forward step was a cadence of the Biloxi branch."

In a press interview in 1960, I credited divine providence for the turn of events that brought federal intervention in our behalf. What I had been through between April 17 and May 17, 1960, seemed nothing short of miraculous. One Sunday, I was arrested in a lone protest on the beach. Not even one person from my own church would go with me. The next Sunday, 125 volunteers had shown up and taken a beating with me on that same beach. But the things that hate had designed to defeat us had made us stronger. Fear left our hearts, when it should have overwhelmed us. Instead, we found the courage to come together to create a proper local instrument for our struggle for freedom and equality. At the beginning of every meeting we had attended that year, whether we were outdoors in a field or inside a lodge hall, we had prayed. When the police wouldn't let me go onto the beach freely by day, I had gone secretly to the beach at night to pray. In the darkness, on that beach, I had prayed for God to protect us and give us salvation. I had prayed for wisdom, for guidance, and for success in gaining freedom. I had prayed for brotherhood and for us not to lose sight that we are all brothers under the fatherhood of God. I had no doubt that God was the architect of our fledgling success, the reliever of our fears, our protector from danger. "Providence has ways and means of salvation for all people," I told the press.[27] I still believe that. However, in May of 1960, the struggle in Biloxi had barely begun.

SIX

Harassment, Lies, and Sovereignty Commission Spies

The Lord is my light and my salvation; whom shall I fear? The Lord is the strength of my life; of whom shall I be afraid? —Psalms 27:1

I met my brother the other day.
I gave him my right hand.
And just as soon as ever my back was turned,
He scandalized my name.
Do you call that a brother? No, no!
You call that a brother? No, no!
Call that a brother? No, no!
Scandalize my name.
—African American spiritual, "Scandalize My Name"

AFTER THE WEEK OF THE BLOODY WADE-IN OF APRIL 1960, my volunteer security group guarded me around the clock for twelve straight months. Natalie and I started sending our child to Mrs. Blanche Elzy's house to sleep at times when the threats increased or were particularly intense. Mr. Elzy was one of my guards. Gilbert, Jr., never knew why he got to sleep over at Mrs. Elzy's so often. He just knew that he liked her, she liked him, he loved the food, and he had great fun playing with her grandchildren. For those who love their family, threatening calls are difficult. Sometimes there were male voices on these anonymous calls. At other times they were females. I could handle it in the daytime, but at night when I was fatigued the calls disturbed me. Natalie, however, became very good at retorting those middle-of-the-night telephone terrorists. They'd call her "bitch," and she would say, "Well, your mother ought to know." If they said, "We're going to run you out of town," Natalie might say, "Well, if you come by here trying to do it, they might find you in the street." If they asked her if we were going to the beach again, she told them, "Sure, we plan to be there next Sunday." If they bragged about the number of guns they were going to use on us, Natalie would tell them, "You better come by and check our house first. You ought to see how many guns we have." Saying things like that felt good, but it was just propaganda. The fact was that we were committed to nonviolent methods, and we were essentially unarmed in our home. Anytime my name appeared in the paper, we came to expect an increase in harassing and threatening telephone calls or letters delivered in the mail. This was true for thirty years up until the early 1990s.

Sometimes the harassment went beyond threats. Cars would sometimes slow down near our house, get off a gunshot or two, and speed away. On many occasions, I was working late at the office or the hospital when these drive-by shooters appeared. Natalie would call me to report it. Of course, my guardsmen were always outside. They sometimes returned fire. One of them, Joe Kennedy, became so concerned that he brought us a .30-06 rifle to keep in the house. We used to joke about Natalie sitting in the rocking chair all night with the .30-06 across her lap so that we could get some sleep. The truth is that she never learned to use the rifle at all. She was scared of guns. I once took the rifle to a Boy Scout camp, Camp Attawah, and shot it a few times on the rifle range, but we knew that our lives were really in God's hands at all times. By the grace of God, despite many episodes of gunfire, we knew of only two bullets that actually struck the house. When this happened, we heard gunfire and found the bullet holes in the brick beside the front door frame. I left the bullet holes unfilled as a reminder of the need for vigilance. We suffered a small amount of property damage compared to others in the civil rights movement who lost homes or churches to firebombs, but in 1963 hooligans burned out the interior of my blue Buick, and, again in the 1970s, when I came out of a Biloxi restaurant I discovered that my car had been doused in gasoline and that a number of burned-out matches were lying nearby that had been thrown at the car but not gotten close enough to ignite it. It was the 1970s before police investigations of these incidents satisfied me as to their seriousness and thoroughness.

The psychological warfare aimed at driving me out of town or shutting me up in 1960 also included the malevolent southern tradition of cross burning. One evening in 1960, after we had moved to Fayard Street, the neighbors called to tell us that there were two crosses burning in our yard. Our house was on a double lot, which gave us a large yard on the north side. There we found the two crosses burning on that north yard near the willow tree. Our guardsmen could not be everywhere or see everything. In the darkness we were vulnerable. Yet, we were more annoyed and inconvenienced by these threats than we were fearful. Gunshots and burned crosses and telephone threats made us more aware, more vigilant, and more security conscious. Beyond being aimed directly at us, much of this meanness, no doubt, also represented attempts to intimidate our friends. The enemies of our freedom thought that they would make an example of that Mason fellow in order to show everybody what happens to black folks who don't stay in their place. If intimidation was the aim, it did not change us or discourage our friendships. We prayed for God's protection, put our faith in Jesus Christ, and rested in the assurance that God would not fail us if we continually sought his guidance. Somehow, neither Natalie nor I harbored any great fear. Fear never paralyzed us and never stopped us from doing what we thought was the right thing or the best thing at the time.

In addition to the cross burnings and verbal threats, harassment also came in the form of weird sounds from the telephone—clicking noises, mysterious interruptions, or sounds like those created when there is an open line or an extension in use. These anomalies made us believe that the authorities had wiretapped us. Too often, the content of private telephone conversations between two people became public knowledge. Information was passed on that could not have been obtained except through wiretap. On the other hand, some of the clicks and noises on the line were probably deliberately created in order to try to intimidate us with the knowledge that our enemies were able to listen in on us at will. There is no direct wiretap information on me in my Sovereignty Commission file. However, these papers do shed some light on segregationist uses of wiretaps. Sovereignty Commission agent Bob Thomas reported in the summer of 1960 that Sheriff Gerald Price in neighboring Hancock County had "tapped the phones of several Negroes suspected of being agitators. . . ."[1] This statement does not surprise me in the least. Agent Thomas reported it without any comment or sign of surprise. I suspect that use of wiretaps was routine all over the coast and all over Mississippi. However, I would caution future researchers about trusting reports from surviving wiretap files. Since we knew or believed that we were wiretapped, we came to be very cautious in telephone conversations, and we did a lot of "jivin' and shuckin' " for the benefit of any unwanted secret listeners. We would say one thing when we meant another, give out purposeful misinformation or disinformation, and use a lot of jive talk or black street lingo as a kind of coded language for hiding things from white wiretap listeners.

We could not trust our telephones, nor could we trust the U.S. mail. Local post office clerks in Mississippi tampered with my mail and with the mail of other civil rights leaders. The week following the bloody wade-in, I got my first inkling of how insecure and unreliable postal communications could be for someone in my position. *Jet* magazine, the *Amsterdam News*, the *Chicago Defender* and several other mainstream and black-oriented national news organizations had given the Biloxi riots coverage across the country. *Jet* was the only one of these publications usually available on newsstands in Biloxi. When the issue of *Jet* that covered the riot arrived in Biloxi we saw white folks going to the newsstands and buying up every issue of *Jet* that they could lay their hands on. White folks said, "Don't let those darkies know what's going on. Don't let 'em know what the national press is saying." Of course, keeping black folks ignorant and in the dark about events that affect their destiny was a control tactic going all the way back to slavery days in the South. When I saw what was going on, I determined to find a way to get some copies of *Jet* distributed outside the newsstands. Alex Poinsett of *Jet* was down covering developments in Biloxi. At my asking, Poinsett wired Chicago to get a big package of *Jets* put into the mail to me. In a day or two, the parcel arrived. The local post office sent me a notice to come in and pick it up. When I got to the post office to claim it, the package had been torn open. Nothing remained of the shipment except its outer shell. I took the matter up with the postmaster. He claimed that it was just a torn package that had lost its contents. Having seen the white folks making quick work of buying up *Jet* just days before, I could not believe the postmaster. I immediately called Alex Poinsett to get another batch sent, but this time I had the package sent to Mrs. Blanche Elzy. This time the package and contents arrived safely and intact. We distributed those *Jets*.

When it came to dealing with the civil rights movement, local postal clerks, in cahoots with the Citizens' Council or the KKK, were ready to defy federal law and tamper with the mail. Our local NAACP branch meeting announcements were often mishandled in the postal system, or were mysteriously returned to me, as if to let me know that the postal service had my number. Occasionally a branch notice was returned with derogatory comments scrawled across it. One returned notice came with this statement: "I saw your old dilapidated, run-down office. What do you do with your money, give it to the NAACP?" Another memorable returned-mail message smeared my race with the remark that black people "ain't worth nothing with them big rumps." This type of stuff was designed to intimidate us by creating the impression that the Klan and Citizens' Council were in every powerful organization and that they were watching us legally and illegally.

With this kind of interference going on with our mail, I was not at all surprised to find one of our branch notices that had been mailed to Marvin Dickey in my Sovereignty Commission file. Sovereignty agent Robert Thomas claimed that Mr. Louis Hollis of the Citizens' Council had obtained our notice from one of his "new members" to whom it had been delivered "by mistake." This poor Citizens' Council member had supposedly "opened the letter" rather than return it to the postal service for a proper delivery.[2] From my experience in those days, I think it more likely that a postal worker helped the Citizens' Council get this notice, knowing that it would be forwarded on to state agents. For this reason I did not trust the U.S. mail, and neither did Medgar Evers or most other civil rights leaders around the state. Our experience was that too many things related to civil rights—far more than the usual—got "lost," were "misdelivered," or were mysteriously slow in arriving. Being unable to trust either the telephones or the mail meant that packages or sensitive messages had to be carried personally. Medgar and his driver, Sam Bailey, spent a lot of needless time on the road because the mails and telephones could not be trusted. Driving that old '58 Oldsmobile, one or both of them might start the day driving from Jackson to Vicksburg, come back to Jackson, head to Meridian, and then go back to Jackson or on to the coast doing things that today we would handle by fax, e-mail, UPS, FedEx, or the U.S. mail. It is a shame that the black citizenry back in those days had to forbear with such an ignorant, virulent, racist society. The world's meanness cost all us a lot of time that could have been used to accomplish so much, if it had been available for other projects to benefit humanity.

Of all the harassments or punishments that came down on me personally for my civil rights stand in 1960, none hurt more than the punishment fellow Scouters inflicted on me. Scouting was and still is dear to my heart, and a part of my very soul. I had believed in the principles and values taught in Scouting and had taken them to heart as a boy. To me there was a perfect congruency between the ideals of Scouting and my civil rights activities. Some folks on the Mississippi Gulf Coast did not see it that way.

When I arrived in Biloxi in 1955, I immediately became active in the Boy Scouts as an assistant scoutmaster. The boys in Biloxi had never seen a first class badge or a black Eagle Scout before I came. One evening I awed them by wearing my old merit badge sash with sixty-one merit badges affixed. Two of the next four black Eagle Scouts in Mississippi came from my troop. In January of 1960, I was promoted from assistant scoutmaster to scoutmaster for Troop 416, which my Masonic Lodge sponsored in Biloxi. As was the custom, white Boy Scout troops were organized into districts separate from the black divisions. My troop was one of the largest, white or black, on the Mississippi Gulf Coast. We were very active in the so-called coast division, composed of black troops from Long Beach east to Pascagoula and Moss Point. My boys won just about every banner and every trophy at every camporee or jamboree or summer camp. My troop always heard a lot about freedom. Several members of my troop and several boys from neighboring Troop 419 sponsored by St. Paul's United Methodist Church in Biloxi participated in wade-ins with me.

In 1960, the Boy Scout National Jamboree was to meet in Colorado Springs in July or August to celebrate the fiftieth anniversary of Scouting in the United States. In my teenage years, I had longed to go to a national jamboree, but World War II caused the national jamborees to be cancelled. To my great delight the Pine Burr Council chose me and James Harris, the scoutmaster for Troop 419 in Biloxi, as assistant scoutmasters for our division to attend the national jamboree in Colorado Springs with our boys under a scoutmaster from Mobile. We undertook training meetings in February and early March at Camp Attawah, the black Scout camp in south Mississippi. Scouting in Mississippi was segregated like everything else, so black and white Scouts from the same town might never meet each other except at the national jamborees, which were integrated. The white scoutmasters from our area did their local preparation for the jamboree twenty-one miles away from Camp Attawah at Camp Tiak. At these meetings, we met and got to know the thirty-six boys who were to attend the jamboree. We got acquainted with the program, inventoried and signed out equipment, and made the logistical preparations necessary to be successful with thirty-six boys on a trip from Mississippi to Colorado. All that was done in February and March.

Then arose the matter of the wade-ins on April 17 and April 24 and my commitment to desegregate the beach. I had suddenly became a noted, some would say a notorious, public figure and a spokesman for African American rights. That was too much for some white folks, and they complained loudly to the Pine Burr Council. The council voted to withdraw their invitation for me to attend the jamboree. They sent the chief Scout executive, Mr. Tolbert, a white man, and a black Scout executive, Mr. P. V. McMillen, to break the news to me. Tolbert called and said they had something important to share with me in person. They asked me to suggest a neutral meeting place. I suggested Dr. Dunn's office in Gulfport. When I got there, Tolbert began telling me how many complaints about my activities they had received from white people on the coast. "Well," I said, "there ain't no white boys in my troop." Nonetheless, Tolbert quickly made it clear that they didn't want me to go to the jamboree. The Pine Burr Council had already written the letter stating, "Due to the choice that we now make, you will not be able to go to the national jamboree." So they bumped me, and my lifelong ambition to go to the national jamboree seemed lost. I loved Scouting. Scouting had been so good to me as a boy. That fellow Scouters, keepers of the legacy of such a noble institution, would fail in their idealism hurt me. So Scouting has been both bitter and sweet for me.

Well, they bumped me, but I did not retreat quietly into the background. I gave the letter to a higher-ranking fellow black Scouter, hoping that the black scoutmasters would raise a hue and cry and come to my rescue. In the weeks after the Biloxi riot, that was just one battle too many for the black scoutmasters to take up. Nobody came to my rescue. That my fellow black Scouters would not carry on a principled fight for me was my second disappointment. I thought that some people were playing it safe, trying not to offend the establishment so that they could maintain whatever status they might have had. In the end, however, the Pine Burr Council could not keep me from going to the jamboree at my own expense, and this I did. And I kept being engaged in Scouting. I am still involved on the executive committee. In 1962, I took twelve Scouts from Biloxi, Moss Point, and Pascagoula to Philmont Scout Ranch in New Mexico. If Scouting was sometimes bitter, it was also sweet. One of my life's great ironical turns came when I, who had been denied the honor of taking a Scout troop to the national jamboree, was named a 1962 winner of Scouting's coveted Silver Beaver Award. To this day, the Silver Beaver Award is one of the most valued honors ever bestowed upon me. I have always believed that suffering without justification is redemptive. Perhaps God has sent me honors like this as reminders that human beings and human institutions are redeemable. In two short years, I went from being an unwanted victim of local Boy Scout harassment to being a Scouting honoree. The same Mississippi Pine Burr Council which had deprived me of the honor of attending the 1960 Jamboree nominated me for the Silver Beaver Award two years later.

I have no way of knowing what degree of coordination existed among the persons who made threatening phone calls, sent harassing mail, or shot up the street I lived on. At the time, the police gave us the distinct impression that they were not displeased that these things were happening to one who stood up for freedom in Biloxi. I do know that much political power and influence is exercised informally outside the formal structures laid out in constitutions and bylaws of institutions and organizations. I do not know whether the many harassments and threats that I received in the 1960s were merely spontaneous individual expressions of racial hatred or if state or local governmental officials coordinated or prompted them in some way. I do know that the state of Mississippi, through the state legislature and governor, contributed to an atmosphere of permissiveness toward racial intimidation and hate crimes in 1956 when it created an official state spy agency, the State Sovereignty Commission, with the sole mission of maintaining segregationist laws and customs. And we do know that the State Sovereignty Commission made substantial donations of tax dollars to the white Citizens' Council,[3] an organization that in turn often supplied information to Sovereignty Commission agents. The very existence of such an agency with overt connections to a bitterly racist group like the Citizens' Council sent an approving message to all those who practiced racial humiliation, harassment, and intimidation in the name of upholding segregation.

Psychological lynchings precede real ones. It takes a kind of psychological slander and libel for a racist to convince himself that he is justified in harassing or threatening another person or in taking reprisals on another person who merely asks to be accorded an equal opportunity for life, liberty, and the pursuit of happiness. As a system of lies, racist dehumanizaton begins with the lie that racists tell themselves when they say in their minds that blacks, or some other target group, do not possess the same aspirations, needs, ambitions, hopes, and feelings as white folk, or some other would-be perpetrator group. Lies are at the root of much of this world's evil, but those lies which deny their victim's humanity have been most accursed in our times. Such lies have provided the deadly psychological foundations necessary for mass murder and genocide in some places in this unfriendly world. In the American South, lying self-deceit justified every kind of racial evil from the humiliations of Jim Crow to lynchings, beatings, harassments, and the economic sanctions which I have described. In the long run, though, truth is more powerful than untruth. In order to maintain itself, untruth must weave an ever more complex web of lies. In self-deceiving racist minds, not only were blacks less than fully human, but, the truth of the Thirteenth, Fourteenth and Fifteenth Amendments notwithstanding, in segregationist minds, blacks could not possibly be a part of the "We the people . . ." envisioned in the Constitution's preamble, nor in the racist mind could the "truths [that are] self-evident, that all men are created equal," of which Jefferson wrote in the Declaration of Independence, apply to blacks. In the mental illness called racism, lies compound upon lies.

As federal court decisions and federal civil rights legislation swept away the legal underpinnings of racist laws, the strength of the truth showed itself. As racist laws entered their death throes, the racist lie gasped and grasped for artificial life support. In a desperate attempt to give its unconstitutional Jim Crow practices artificial life support, the state of Mississippi had unleashed the Mississippi State Sovereignty Commission. To maintain segregation the Mississippi State Sovereignty Commission had to create new lies to justify and bolster Jim Crow. Racism itself dehumanized and scandalized a whole people. Sovereignty Commission lies and spies set out to scandalize black leaders, sow dissension in the civil rights cadres, and thus demoralize those whose passionate fight for freedom was itself a veritable living repudiation of the great racist lie.

Like the racism that brought the agency into the world, the Mississippi State Sovereignty Commission files are filled with untruth. Some of the untruth in these files is untruth of the type that might be found in the raw files of any police investigatory agency that collects rumors of criminal activity and seeks corroboration. However, the fact that a so-called free society would set in motion criminal-like investigations of advocates of freedom certainly puts the records of the Sovereignty Commission into an unusually immoral and hypocritical category. Moreover, in a free society we test police-generated information in the courts before juries where witnesses can be confronted, cross-examined, and refuted. There was never any such winnowing process in the secret workings which produced the Sovereignty Commission files. Raw police files represent unproven suspicions at best, and libelous destructive rumormongering at worst.

In the case of the Mississippi State Sovereignty Commission and similar agencies created to defend segregation and racism in other states, the lies go beyond the collection of unproven rumors or uncorroborated assertions. Sovereignty Commission untruth includes distortions that reflect both the overt racism of investigators and their desire to discredit and defame black leaders in the eyes of their own people and in the eyes of potentially sympathetic white moderates. Other untruth in these files derives from the agency's efforts to control black leaders. The files are filled with groundless and misleading speculation about stalwart black men and women who, white agents theorized, might be used to counter emerging local civil rights leaders. Most of the time the agents making such reports had no acquaintance or firsthand knowledge of the black notables about whom they wrote. Moreover, these state agents passed on the imaginative theories of white informants about black communities that the whites little understood. Strikingly, because there are so few black informants, the files I have examined pile rumor upon speculation and flavor the product with racist assumptions, all of which combine to compound untruth.

Because they begin with a racist stance and contain so many bald-faced, unmitigated lies and baseless assertions about individuals, I do not trust the Sovereignty Commission files. Especially their racist speculations and interpretations of Negro intentions and character must be taken with a pound of salt. Racists ran that agency intending to protect segregation. Its sole purpose was to block or frustrate movements of the type we were leading in Biloxi. If there was a way to put a negative interpretation on a black person's motives or to defame a black leader, their agents were likely to try to do so, according to my examination of the Sovereignty Commission files. Where facts were sparse or incomplete, Sovereignty Commission investigators' negative imaginations were rich.

Nonetheless, when given the opportunity to redact information or delete any reference to my name from these files before they were opened, I declined to withhold anything in the Sovereignty Commission files from public scrutiny. However, this decision should not be taken as an indication of any acceptance of these files as truth. It most emphatically is not. These files are in fact full of gossip and untruth. Still, just as surviving gestapo files show us something important about the Nazi era, the Sovereignty Commission files illustrate a part of the history of racism and the civil rights struggle in this country. Just as no one would argue that raw gestapo files should be taken at face value, no one should be fooled into taking the Sovereignty Commission files at face value. The Sovereignty Commission files show the abuses of state power and the stupid nature of many of the agency's investigations more than they provide any real understanding of the motives, methods, goals, or internal problems of the civil rights movement in Mississippi. Any lay reader of the files is likely to be amazed at how much time and public money was wasted on ridiculous activities and rumor reporting. God only knows how many hours were wasted typing up gossip. Lay readers will also be astonished at the time agents apparently spent in duplicating and cross-indexing various reports and newspaper clippings in order to file them under multiple headings. There are 250 pages of documents in my Sovereignty Commission file. Many of them are duplicate or triplicate copies of the same materials from different agency file groups.

While the factual content of the files cannot be trusted, these files are an important illustration of the nefarious means which a dying segregationist order used to defend itself. Beyond their illustration of racist perversions, the files show examples of sloppy, unprofessional, and incompetent investigatory work. For example, I am astonished at how little progress the agency actually made in cultivating sources of information in the black community. There are almost no black agents or informers. Most of the information about me came from press clippings or from pure speculation and rumor reported by white police or white public officials on the coast. Little or none of the information gathered on me came directly from black informants. Only Percy Greene, the notorious black editor of the *Jackson Advocate* who has long been reported to have been in the Sovereignty Commission's pay, attempted to aid the agency in discrediting me. Now, there could have been things about this agency that the files do not let us know about. It is widely known that Erle Johnston, the agency's director in the post-Barnett era, destroyed some of the Sovereignty Commission files.[4] What concerns were uppermost in his mind when he selected documents to burn are not known, so perhaps at one time there were more than 250 pages of documents related to my activities. It is also noteworthy that my file grows very thin after Governor Barnett left office. Although materials were added as late as 1968, the vast majority of reports and documents on me had been collected by 1963. Most of them have to do with the effort to desegregate the beaches. I had hardly begun to fight when they slowed down their file-making on me. I was surprised to find so little in the files on the desegregation of the schools, an activity in which the Biloxi branch took special pride as a leader in the state.

So, how did this ramshackle racist agency operate? First of all, they made lists. The earliest documents in my file represent an effort to gather the names of all NAACP members in Biloxi in 1959 before we organized the Biloxi branch. Their source for the local list was the Biloxi Police Department, whose chief, Herbert McDonnell, duly reported that Dr. Gilbert Mason and W. B. McDaniel were NAACP members. The chief also reported that we had no branch in Biloxi. Interestingly enough, the same document contains information from Harrison County sheriff J. J. Whitman, who reportedly "was sure there was an active NAACP operating in Gulfport," but he could not identify the leaders because "they kept their movements and activities secret." On the other hand, chief of police G. E. Mullins in Gulfport was able to identify Dr. Dunn as president of the Gulfport branch, but could not identify other members of the branch.[5] In my file I found a handwritten list of persons connected with civil rights organizations around the state that was apparently compiled by Percy Greene. Sovereignty agents also collected license tag numbers of automobiles seen near civil rights demonstrations or civil rights meetings in order to identify the owners. Their list-making included lists of black pharmacies across the state. I qualified for this list because Natalie and I had organized the Modern Drug Store in 1960.[6] Why in the world would they collect a list of black pharmacies and pharmacists? I can only speculate that pharmacists represented an economically independent class of black businessmen who might have been thought difficult for the white establishment to control. In many cases, the black-owned pharmacy was itself a nexus in black communities. Aaron Henry's name is on this list. Aaron's Fourth Street Drug Store was legendary and served as a one-stop NAACP information and voter registration service center in Clarksdale. My medical office on Division Street in Biloxi played the same role in the Biloxi civil rights struggle.

The papers in my file show that when Sovereignty Commission agents came from their Jackson headquarters to the coast, they typically made rounds to local elected officials, the police, and the sheriff. Mostly, these trips involved routine checks to see if white officials had any news or rumors of civil rights activities in the area. At other times Sovereignty Commission agents came to the coast because local officials requested investigative assistance. The first Sovereignty Commission investigation of me personally was launched in October of 1959, after I presented the petition to desegregate the beach to the Harrison County Board of Supervisors. I found a copy of the petition in my Sovereignty Commission file. The main purpose of the investigation was to develop material that could be used to discredit me as an emerging black leader. The file alleges that this investigation was undertaken at the specific request of state senator Stanford Morse of Gulfport, who was acting as attorney for the board of supervisors. According to agent Zack Van Landingham's account, Morse's main interest was in me, because local officials claimed they had already developed allegations to be used to discredit Dr. Dunn.[7]

To aid the board of supervisors' attorney's effort to destroy my credibility, Van Landingham verified my birth records with the State Bureau of

Vital Statistics in Jackson and checked papers relating to my medical licensure in the Mississippi Medical Library. Agent Van Landingham checked my educational credentials from high school through college and medical school. He ran a credit check on me and on my father with the Retail Credit Bureau in Jackson and "found nothing derogatory" to report. Locally, the Harrison County Credit Bureau records reflected that "Dr. Mason paid his bills promptly." They checked both Jackson and coast police books to find that I had no arrest record. (That would soon change.) Van Landingham checked on me with the Selective Service Headquarters in Jackson, and he interviewed Dr. Kirby Walker, Jackson's superintendent of schools, who reported that I had been a straight-A student at Lanier High with no disciplinary action recorded in the school file. Van Landingham's only information about my civil rights activities to that point came from law enforcement officials in Biloxi. Similar investigations were run on all four of the signers of the 1959 beach petition.[8]

On the surface this may look like a competent check, but Van Landingham apparently had no references or informers in the *black* community in Biloxi from whom he could get information on me. The little information being passed on from the black community came through white local officials or newspaper reporters, and it appears to have been second- or thirdhand by the time Sovereignty agents recorded it. I am sure that Van Landingham was disappointed to find nothing that could be used against me. After receiving this first report, Senator Morse observed to Van Landingham that I seemed to be "a very smart and educated Negro who apparently had been well informed by some attorney with reference to legal rights."[9]

Ironically, while the files complement my understanding of the legal basis for demanding our rights on the beach, they contain disparaging innuendos about my local white attorney, Knox Walker, who had done the basic research for me. I must say that my admiration for the courage, competence, and commitment of Knox Walker is high. This white attorney suffered for the cause of civil rights in Harrison County right along with the black leadership. In addition, Knox Walker probably did more pro bono work on charity cases than any other lawyer in the county. He had a good heart. His activities on behalf of civil rights and labor put a strain on his marriage, which I understand ended in a sad divorce. Knox Walker's law practice suffered because of his willingness to represent the cause of "that agitator Gilbert Mason" in our efforts to desegregate the beach. His colleagues in the legal profession ostracized him. Suffering from a kind of white economic boycott, Knox Walker became economi-

Gilbert R. Mason, M.D., 1997

All photographs courtesy of Dr. Gilbert R. Mason, unless otherwise noted.

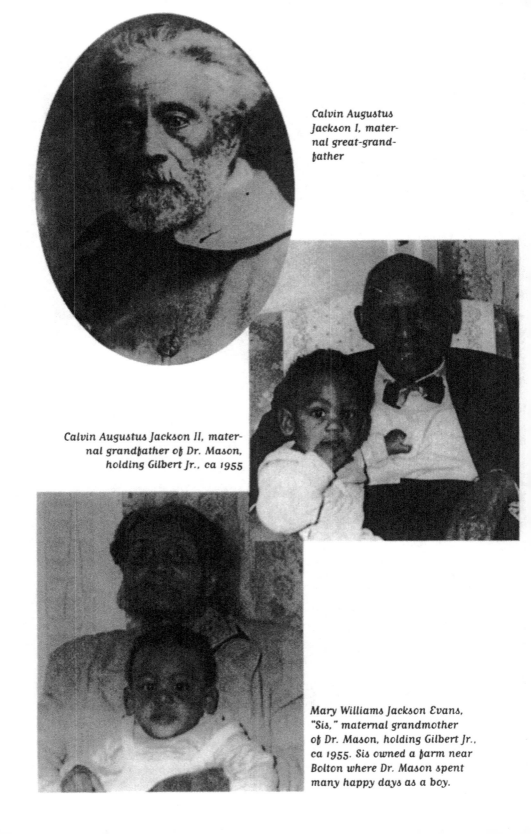

Calvin Augustus Jackson I, maternal great-grandfather

Calvin Augustus Jackson II, maternal grandfather of Dr. Mason, holding Gilbert Jr., ca 1955

Mary Williams Jackson Evans, "Sis," maternal grandmother of Dr. Mason, holding Gilbert Jr., ca 1955. Sis owned a farm near Bolton where Dr. Mason spent many happy days as a boy.

Effie Trotter Mason, "Little Mama," paternal grandmother of Dr. Mason, ca 1940. Dr. Mason spent summers with Little Mama in Chicago to work and earn extra money during his college years at Tennessee State.

Walter Harrison Mason, paternal grandfather of Dr. Mason, ca 1930. Walter was a barber and a Baptist minister.

Dr. Mason's parents, Willie Atwood and Alean Jackson Mason with Gilbert Jr., 1955

Gilbert R. Mason with Natalie Hamlar in Washington, D.C., just before their wedding in 1950 and just before Mason began study at Howard University School of Medicine

The 25 April 1960 headline on the bloody wade-in. Reprinted by permission of The Sun Herald.

Dr. Felix Dunn (left) with journalist Alex Poinsett of Jet magazine in a Biloxi service station at the corner of Division and Nixon Streets after the 24 April 1960 wade-in

NATIONAL ASSOCIATION FOR THE ADVANCEMENT OF COLORED PEOPLE

TWENTY WEST FORTIETH STREET • NEW YORK 18, N.Y. • LOngacre 3-6890

Please direct reply to:

Mr. Medgar W. Evers
1072 Lynch Street, Room 7
Jackson 3, Mississippi

FLeetwood 3-6906

October 18, 1960

Dr. Gilbert Mason
742 Nixon Street, Apt J
Biloxi, Mississippi

Dear Dr. Mason:

      Relative to our conversation the last time I was in your city of Biloxi, I have written the enclosed letter to the persons whose names appear thereon. I am anxious to get something going here in Jackson to the point that I am willing to risk even life itself.

      We have procrastinated long enough in the state and the treatment from the whites has not lessened rather increased. My feeling is, if we are to receive a beating, lets receive it because we have done something, not because we have done nothing. Let me hear from you on this right away.

      Sincerely yours,

      Medgar W. Evers
      Field Secretary

MWE:ll
Encls

A letter from Medgar W. Evers to Dr. Mason, 18 October 1960, showing Evers's willingness to "risk even life itself" in the wake of the 1960 wade-in and Biloxi school desegregation initiative

Evers, NAACP field secretary for Mississippi, in a Biloxi service station at the corner of Division and Nixon Streets after the 1960 wade-in and riot

October 11, 1960

Mr. Robert L. Carter
20 West 40th Street
New York 18, New York

Dear Bob:

I am calling about two things, number one, there is a group of Citizens in Biloxi, Mississippi who would like to file suit to desegregate the schools for the second semester term, 1960-61; these individuals asked me to get in touch with you and find out if we can get the organization to take charge of the case.

Secondly, as you know I am a paid worker with the NAACP, and at the same time I have two school age children who are presently going to private school (segregated). Now it is rather difficult for me to reconcile to the general public the fact that I believe in what I preach, while at the same time practice something to the contrary. To be very candid I would like to be one of three or four Plaintiffs to initiate legal action to destroy the segregated system here in Jackson, either my wife or I, or both, are ready and willing to affix our signatures authorizing such action in our behalf. I would like an immediate answer to these questions.

Sincerely yours,

Medgar W. Evers
Field Secretary

MWE:ll
cc: Mrs. Ruby Hurley
    Mr. Roy Wilkins
    Mr. Gloster B. Current

A letter from Evers to Robert L. Carter, 11 October 1960, regarding the start of school desegregation legal maneuvering in Biloxi, enclosed in Evers's letter to Dr. Mason

Reporter James Hicks of The Amsterdam News (New York) standing outside Dr. Mason's apartment in Biloxi after the 1960 wade-in

Blood-stained victims, Mr. Ellis Brown (left) and Mr. Dorothy Galloway (right), outside Dr. Mason's Biloxi office after the 1960 wade-in. Beaten with chains and pipes, Brown received a wound above his left ear, and Galloway suffered fractured knee caps in the violence that day. Photograph courtesy of Mr. Leo Russell.

Dr. Mason (middle row, second from the left) with Gulf Coast Boy Scouts at Philmont Scout Ranch in Cimarron, New Mexico, 1962

The headline from the 24 June 1963 wade-in. Reprinted with permission by The Sun Herald.

Massive traffic jam on U.S. 90 in Biloxi during the 1963 wade-in. The van in the background was used for arrests. Photo courtesy of Mr. Leo Russell.

Helmeted police officers escort the first in a line of seventy-one arrested demonstrators off Biloxi beach, following the 1963 wade-in. Photo courtesy of Mr. Leo Russell.

The white crowd overturns the car of a black protester at the 1963 wade-in. Photo courtesy of Mr. Leo Russell.

The crowded beach scene at the 1963 wade-in. Photo courtesy of Mr. Leo Russell.

A police officer extinguishes a fire in Dr. Mason's 1959 Buick during the 1963 wade-in. Photo courtesy of Mr. Leo Russell.

The painted moving van used to remove the demonstrators from Biloxi beach in the 1963 wade-in. Dr. Mason vigorously protested crowded conditions in the hot, unventilated van when the protesters arrived at the police station. Photo courtesy of Mr. Leo Russell.

Dr. Mason pushes open the van doors to allow the protesters to disembark. The black flags were carried as a memorial to Medgar Evers who had helped plan the demonstration and who had been assassinated the previous week. Photo courtesy of Mr. Leo Russell.

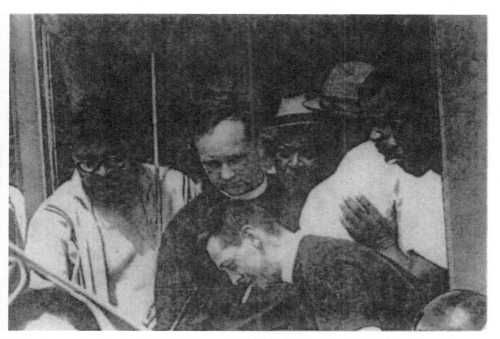

Protesters are unloaded from the van at the Biloxi police station in the aftermath of the 1963 wade-in. Mr. Charlie Avery (far left) and Reverends Roger Gallagher and John Aregood of the Back Bay Mission are in the center foreground.

Dr. Mason (left) with Roy Wilkins, executive secretary of the national NAACP at the COFO voter registration rally at New Bethel Baptist Church in Biloxi during the summer of 1964

Dr. Mason on the south lawn of the White House in November 1964 at the end of an invitational White House Conference, listening to President Johnson's commitment to the Head Start initiative. Charles Evers stands on the front row with his foot on the stage to Johnson's left. Dr. Mason and Dr. Felix Dunn stand in the third row directly behind Evers. Aaron Henry stands in the back row, fourth from the left.

Dr. Mason and President Nixon at the White House in 1970 after Mason's appointment to the Mississippi Advisory Committee to the Cabinet Committee on Education

A meeting of the State Advisory Committee officers with the Cabinet Committee on Education in Atlanta in 1970. Seated left to right, Dr. Kirby Walker; U.S. Secretary of Health, Education, and Welfare Eliot Richardson; Dr. Mason; Warren Hood; Postmaster-General Red Blount; unidentified; unidentified; and U.S. Secretary of Labor George Schultz.

The legendary Mrs. Fannie Lou Hamer gives her support to Mr. Charles Young, a fellow member of the Mississippi delegation, during a long session of the 1972 Democratic National Convention in Miami, Florida.

Dr. Mason and President Carter in 1978, during one of four White House Conferences Mason attended

The Mason siblings: Willie Louis Mason, Rozelia Mason Stamps, and Dr. Mason at a family gathering in Jackson, Mississippi, ca 1981

cally strangled and financially overextended to the point that lenders cut off his credit. In this bind, to keep his airplane from being repossessed, he sold it to me. I had good credit and could assume the note. Knox then bought the plane back from me, and I would use his payments to me to make my payments to the lenders in Dallas. He needed the plane to tend to his far-flung clients, and I was happy to help him find a way to keep it. He eventually fully redeemed the plane.

A man like Knox Walker with fortitude, courage, and devotion to the principle of equal justice for all did not deserve to be smeared by police agencies, but Sovereignty spies recorded negative aspersions whenever they thought it might be useful. Knox Walker also received some overt threats aimed at discouraging his association with me. He took the shoves and pulls of the white ruffians outside the courthouse right along with me. The Monday night after he first appeared at trial as my defense attorney, the Biloxi police followed Knox Walker from the courthouse down to Highway 90, where they arrested him for "failing to signal a turn and having an improper car tag."[10] Knox Walker, a white southerner, suffered with us for our stand in gaining freedom for our people to use the beach. I remember asking another white Biloxi lawyer why he would not join in the civil rights movement. He laid it all out bluntly. "I want to eat and I want to feed my family," he said. This reticence in the white legal establishment illustrates the intimidation and fear that segregationist craziness created in the right-thinking portion of the white community. Lawyers like Knox Walker knew that they would have a tough go of it if they took our cases. Local authorities depended on the fears white lawyers harbored about taking civil rights cases as a tool to keep the lid on local civil rights activities. However, fear did not control Knox Walker. He is an unsung local hero of human rights.

The Sovereignty Commission undertook some big, albeit incompetent and unsuccessful, attempts to smear and discredit Dr. Felix Dunn and me. So far as I know, they never used the derogatory rumors about Dr. Dunn which they recorded in the file, but they did lie to Felix Dunn, and they did lie about him and about the role he tried to play in attempting to resolve the beach issue in April of 1960. Dr. Felix Dunn and I never disagreed on anything. We both wanted the schools desegregated unconditionally, and we both wanted the beach desegregated unconditionally. I was loud and adamant. Felix was soft-spoken and firm. In old football running-back parlance, he was Mr. Inside. I was Mr. Outside. We were a team. In the aftermath of the rioting and killing associated with the bloody wade-in of April 1960, Felix Dunn and Knox Walker made a trip to Jackson to try to get state help in resolving the issue of black access to the beach. They marched straight into the devil's den, the Sovereignty Commission headquarters in Jackson, where they had a long conversation which they did not know was being taped. Ironically, the tape that was probably made in hopes that it could be used against Dr. Dunn now is a good example of the Sovereignty Commission's strategy of lying and deceit. Now, what is of interest here is the difference between what Dr. Dunn said, which was recorded on tape, and what the Sovereignty agents wrote in his file and later released to the press about this meeting. The authorities lied and scandalized Felix Dunn. The agents' own tape demonstrates their agency lies.

The week of the riot, when this recorded conversation took place, Felix and I had been "through the mill." We had seen what had been planned as a peaceful demonstration turn into a bloody white-led riot which had resulted in eight shootings, two deaths, and dozens of injuries. Felix was with me in the office when we decided to call Roy Wilkins to ask for national NAACP help. During that week, Felix Dunn met with Medgar Evers. I do not recall Felix telling me he was going to Jackson that week. However, we were good citizens and were still ready to negotiate with local authorities, provided that the starting point of any negotiation was a recognition of our unquestioned right to use any part of the twenty-six-mile beach that we might wish. Sovereignty Commission tapes show that this was the basic message, secretly taped by state agents, that Felix Dunn took to Jackson on April 28, four days after the riots.

Now, anyone who is well acquainted with Dr. Dunn will know what I mean when I say that when it came to dealing with white officials, he was one of the best "shuck and jive" men around. In this mode Felix tried to persuade these Sovereignty Commission dudes that so-called "integration" shouldn't even be a concern on a twenty-six-mile beach that was big enough for people to find a place to themselves almost anywhere along its entire extent. The issue, Felix told them, was free access, not "mixing" on the beach. Felix tried to disarm these seg enforcers by saying that not many local folks used the beach anyway, because the water was usually muddy. They tried to twist his words and find some contradiction between his statement that access to the beach did not necessarily mean mixing with white folks and his statement that he favored integration of the public schools. On tape, right there in the devil's den, Dunn can be heard making a strong case for desegregation of the schools with these agents in his face telling him that any form of integration was against Mississippi law and out of the question. Again and again Felix stated on tape that we had a legal right to use the beach. He jived some by telling them that until recently blacks pretty much used the beach when they wanted to most anywhere but in Biloxi. He told them that we just needed a uniform and predictable policy. The agents would not buy that jive. Felix specifically rejected the idea of a legally segregated beach, and told them a special beach fixed up for blacks on the west pier at Gulfport was absolutely not acceptable.

Dr. Dunn argued that the board of supervisors should stop municipal police forces along the coast from interfering with blacks using the beach. He tried to approach things in a practical way. Felix stated that there was no mechanism for talking to local authorities or for getting the municipal and county officials into the same room to come up with a common policy. He solicited Sovereignty Commission help in getting local authorities to discuss a common county-wide policy to resolve the crisis. But these agents persisted in twisting his words and demanding that Dr. Dunn propose a definite plan then and there. Felix said repeatedly that he was there to get talks going, and that he had no authority to present a plan. He asserted that any plan would have to win approval with the Harrison County Civic Action Committee. One agent asked Felix what he would do if the local officials denied blacks any use of the beach at all. Felix would not say what he would do, but he and his attorney carefully pointed out that the NAACP had not been involved as of yet, and that continued trouble on the beach could affect the tourist trade. He was quite open about being president of the Gulfport branch, and he laid it out before these good ole boys that he could keep the NAACP from intervening legally if the local folks would deal with him.

When the Sovereignty agents claimed that Mason might oppose a negotiated solution, Dunn jived them some about how he could influence the black community and "control" me, if necessary. Now I must say that, in reality, Felix Dunn never ever gave the slightest hint to me that he was even thinking about trying to control me. We shared the same civil rights goals. However, on this control jive, Felix faked the agents out of position and got the ole boys with their noses wide open. They bought Felix's line on this control thing. You find them repeating this control disinformation to themselves in the files whenever they get disturbed about my activities. They did this even though they never had another conversation with Felix, and Felix certainly never tried to control me.

After they kept pushing on Felix for some sort of a plan, and after he repeatedly told them that he had no authority to make a deal, Felix wound up speculating. Hypothetically, would a stated policy that ended police harassment and ended all specific prohibitions of black use of the beach be compatible with informally agreeing that certain places on the beach in each municipality would be viewed as primarily available to blacks? In the talk around this point Felix specifically ruled out any formal prohibition of blacks using any beach area they might choose, but he did not rule out the possiblilty that blacks might voluntarily limit themselves to certain areas. Now we in Biloxi would have absolutely rejected any such informal agreement to direct our beach use to a particular area, even if it meant that we would not be prohibited from going elsewhere, and Dr. Dunn knew this. However, in these speculations, Dr. Dunn never said anyone would agree. He was trying to get discussions going between local officials and black leadership on the coast. He was not trying to come up with an acceptable hypothetical end product. He said this repeatedly.[11]

This was a long meeting. The tapes run for more than two hours. I have here laid out so much of the taped record in order to show the distortion in agents' summaries and uses of these records. Toward the end of the meeting, someone, not Dr. Dunn, brought up the reprisals taken on black bars doing business with Dr. Dunn's jukebox company the night of the Biloxi riots. Dunn acknowledged the raids and stated his belief that they had been undertaken in order to try to break him. He stated that he had worked to try to resolve racial conflict in the community and did not deserve such treatment. This discussion, which took up perhaps the last twelve or fifteen minutes of the 130-minute meeting, became the main event according to the agent's written summary of the meeting. In agent Zack Van Landingham's racist interpretation, a medical doctor took a day off work in a crisis week that had seen riots, shootings, and death in his community to come to Jackson for the "primary purpose" of protecting his vending machine company. The long, drawn-out discussion of "Negro use of the beach" which took nearly two hours appeared to the cynical white agent to be "of secondary importance." The agent's negative assumptions kicked in as he wrote, "Without coming outright and saying so, both he (Dr. Dunn) and his attorney (Knox Walker) desired the Sovereignty Commission to take some action in having the local authorities ease up the pressure on Dr. Dunn with reference to his juke boxes and cigarette vending machines' being placed in certain places run by Negroes." Just to set the facts straight, the day before Dr. Dunn's trip to Jackson, the sheriff of Harrison County served arrest warrants on the constables involved in the raids on black bars. The constables had already been arrested on charges of extortion connected with those raids before Dr. Dunn went to Jackson. Dunn had no need nor likely expectation of state help in this matter. Yet, in the biased written summaries of this meeting, selfish, petty business worries were interpreted as the main concerns of a dedicated physician,[12] whom I knew to be a genuine humanitarian and a long-time benefactor to his community. Tapes of the meeting belie the agent's biased view, and I reject the one-sided racist interpretation of my friend's motives.

Moreover, Dr. Dunn's carefully worded statements that specifically rejected any de jure segregation of the beach and repeatedly upheld the principle of unrestricted black access to the beach were twisted in the agent's notes to say falsely that Dr. Dunn believed that certain sections of the beach "should" be set aside for black use in each of the municipalities. This misleading summary totally disregarded Dr. Dunn's repeated advocacy of negotiations, his statements that he had no authority to propose a plan, and his repeated resistance to stating ideas about a plan. Agent Zack Van Landingham heard what he wanted to hear. When I first read Van Landingham's memo, I could not reconcile what was written there with what I knew about Felix Dunn's commitment to our cause. I suspected that the agent had greatly distorted things. In comparing the secret tape of this meeting to the written summary, I found out how correct my suspicions were. There is a clear editorial gap between what actually was stated and what agent Van Landingham wrote.[13] Researchers beware!

The tapes indicate that, when this meeting between Dr. Dunn and the Sovereignty agents ended, reporters were gathered outside the office. The parties to the meeting agreed that since they were trying to get negotiations started, they should make no statements to the press about the substance of their talks. There were news stories the next day reporting that the meeting took place at the State Sovereignty Commission offices, but none of the substance of the talk was revealed—that is, nothing was revealed until it served the mean purposes of the Sovereignty Commission to discredit Dr. Dunn.

On May 17 the U.S. Justice Department intervened in the beach case. On May 19, the *Jackson Daily News*, some of whose reporters fed information to the Sovereignty Commission,[14] ran a front-page story beneath a huge lying headline: "NAACP Requested Segregated Beach, Asked Sovereignty Commission for Facilities Three Weeks Ago." The story presented a gross distortion of the April 28 conversation between Dr. Dunn and the Sovereignty Commission agents. The newspaper used this lying headline as a lead-in to report the Justice Department's beach desegregation suit.[15] I believe that the Sovereignty Commission released an inaccurate account of a supposedly privileged conversation at a time calculated to demoralize efforts under way to build NAACP membership. The timing of this lie was, I believe, also aimed at discouraging petitioners in the beach desegregation suit. The lie in the *Daily News* headline made it appear that the local NAACP leadership was unprincipled, and might be such low scoundrels as to lead poor black folks out onto a limb in this beach lawsuit and then saw it off behind them. None of it was true. The release of this false account of the April 28 meeting was designed to embarrass the NAACP and undercut its leadership. This news article offers just one small sample of the dirty tricks this agency pulled all over the state in its attempts to discredit black leadership.

I never had a direct conversation with a Sovereignty Commission agent that was twisted or misrepresented in the manner of Dr. Dunn's April 28 conversation, but the Sovereignty Commission spread a false rumor about me in the press in an effort to discredit me as a physician. It seems that on April 29, 1960, the Sovereignty Commission's paramount paid black informant, Percy Greene of the *Jackson Advocate*, planted the idea with agent Zack Van Landingham that I could be discredited as a physician. Now, the press was already quoting me as saying we were going to file a lawsuit over the beach. Greene told Van Landingham the false story that at the convention of the black Mississippi Medical and Surgical Association in Jackson during the week following the bloody wade-in, the president of the National Medical Association, I believe it was Dr. W. Montague Cobb, had "bawled Dr. Gilbert Mason out for the manner he had assumed in the Biloxi race riot."[16] This alleged incident never happened. It was either a deliberate bald-faced lie or a Percy Greene hallucination. No one who knew of Dr. Cobb's civil rights activities, or who knew of the spirit of Howard University or of my personal relationship with Cobb as one of his students at Howard University's medical school, could have placed any credence in such a report. Dr. Cobb later served as national president of the NAACP. Notwithstanding the utter falsity of Percy Greene's report, Van Landingham was confident that this fictitious episode would quiet me down. What happened next demonstrates the close cooperation of the Jackson newspapers with Sovereignty Commission efforts to libel and discredit black leaders. Percy Greene gave Van Landingham the idea on April 29. On April 30, the *Jackson Advocate* editorialized against me, saying, "It appears to us that the great discoveries yet to be made regarding the cure of cancer, heart disease . . . and the broad field of medical research, would leave little time to the really dedicated doctor for leadership in political action." Greene's editorial went on to accuse me of a lack of "diplomacy and statesmanship and goodwill," which Percy

Greene said served only to confirm the statement of Edmund Burke, concerning the French Revolution, that the "sides of sick beds and the arms of dentists' chairs are not the places to train statesmen and the leaders of the people."[17] On May 4, the *Jackson Daily News* ran an editorial accusing me of neglecting my patients in order to gain the notoriety associated with leading civil rights activities. The white editorialist somehow thought I enjoyed having my life constantly threatened and my office firebombed. Still, this Sovereignty Commission-inspired *Daily News* editorial charged that the Harrison County Public Health Department was covered up in patients because my services were no longer readily available. "While he pursues a business of integration and socializing on the beaches," the paper alleged, "the State of Mississippi continues to carry out its efficient, beneficial and much-needed health work through its clinics supported by the taxpayers of this state."[18] Thus the Sovereignty Commission turned a fictitious incident into a press attack on my leadership and my professional dedication. I hasten to add that the premise of the editorial was false. I kept just as busy with my medical practice as always, and the public health nurses in Harrison County had nothing added to their chores due to my civil rights activities. It should also be pointed out that the national NAACP office had just launched an investigation of racial discrimination in state health department services in the South. Moreover, when representatives of the NAACP's Medical Committee on Civil Rights visited my office, they complimented me on the community ombudsman activity that my medical office had undertaken.

There is other direct evidence of the cozy relationship between certain sections of the press and the Mississippi State Sovereignty Commission. On May 4, 1960, chief Sovereignty Commission investigator Zack Van Landingham reported that "Mr. McDavid of the *Jackson Daily News*" had telephoned to inform Van Landingham that the newspaper had "a number of listening posts on the Gulf Coast."[19] The information passed on in this phone call was false, but the fact that the reporter felt free to make such a call is indicative of the special relationship between sections of the press and the Sovereignty Commission. In his report on racial tensions surrounding a Fourth of July picnic undertaken by my church, First Missionary Baptist, at the DeSoto National Forest recreation area, Sovereignty Commission agent Bob Thomas noted that reporter Tom Cook of the *Daily Herald* stated that he (Cook) had tried to "keep this story quieted down as much as possible." The same Tom Cook years later remembered his meeting with Medgar Evers in Dr. Dunn's office as being most pleasant. How strange, complex, and hypocritical were the relationships that

Jim Crow imposed upon us all. I think when Tom Cook spoke of keeping the DeSoto National Forest picnic story "quieted down," he was probably referring to the self-censorship policy of his bosses at the *Daily Herald*, rather than some intiative of his own. This would be consistent with other things that I was personally told about the *Daily Herald*. At about this time in 1960, I asked reporter Billie Ray Quave of the *Daily Herald* why the local paper was not more fair in reporting the news of the civil rights struggle. I told him that I did not feel that our side of these controversies was being adequately explained. His reply was revealing. "Doctor," he said, "I must tell you that I have a boss that I must answer to." Newspaper self-censorship aided and abetted the aims of the State Sovereignty Commission, whether undertaken with that intent or merely practiced out of fear of the wrath of white advertisers or subscribers. For other newspaper publishers, a misguided allegiance to the racial status quo led them far away from the journalistic ideal of pursuing the truth to become themselves purveyors of destructive rumors and lies in active league with Sovereignty Commission enemies of truth.

I cannot leave the subject of lies and distortions in the Sovereignty Commission files without a forthright effort to set the record straight for innocent people, many now dead, about whom Sovereignty agents' records leave misleading or distorted impressions. I take this endeavor very seriously, because most of the people the agents wrote about were not known personally to the agents. Regarding my friend Dr. Felix Dunn, whose motives and life are so unfairly characterized in the Sovereignty Commission files, I would say this: Felix Dunn was a genius. He went beyond taking the heat, the threats, and attempted bombings of his clinic that came with being a known state and local NAACP officer; he pioneered many things that have for years benefited black people and poor people in Gulfport. I want to acknowledge that Dr. Dunn's early success in getting federal funds to build the Bell Apartments inspired me in some of my later housing initiatives as chairman of the Harrison County Community Action Agency. When I finished medical school, I came home to Mississippi hoping to make a difference, knowing that decent housing for the poor was a way of promoting long-term gains in public health. Dr. Dunn was the pioneer who showed us the way. Our TurnKey low income housing project drew its inspiration from the William E. Bell Apartments, which were named for the longtime president of Dr. Dunn's alma mater, Alcorn State University. Dr. Dunn was also personally responsible for the construction of the Saraland low income retirement complex in North Gulfport. Beyond these contributions to the life of the community at large, it is almost impossible to calculate the amount of his own personal financial resources that Dr. Dunn invested in the cause of civil rights. He paid large sums to get documents copied, bought a life membership in the NAACP, and supported the cause of civil rights through political donations. Dr. Dunn freely gave of his know-how in any worthy project, and he gave substantially to student scholarships at Alcorn State University. All of these things and more define Felix Dunn as a man who put the welfare of his people above his business interests. He was an example of black entrepreneurship and black civic devotion. In their rush to smear and discredit a good man, the Sovereignty agents missed all of this about Dr. Felix Dunn.

The racist mind is so intently busy looking for the negative that it misses the positive in so many people and situations. In their rush to judgment, without knowing anything meaningful about the personal pilgrimages through life that had led me or Felix to take up the fight for freedom, they dismissed us, they dismissed the depths of our longings, they dismissed our capacity to suffer to gain freedom, and they wrongly assumed that we could be "controlled." Without ever really knowing me, and without inquiring very deeply about me in the black community, the Sovereignty Commission agents assumed in 1959 that some black community leader would easily pursuade me to remove my name from the first beach desegregation petition presented to the Harrison County Board of Supervisors. How presumptuous! No one ever approached me with such a proposal, and no one in the black community in Gulfport or Biloxi would have had the audacity to approach me with such a proposal. Anyone who knew me, including Felix Dunn, knew that it was downright foolishness, utter stupidity, to try to control me. As a matter of fact, contrary to the assumptions of Sovereignty agents, the vast majority of the comments I heard in the African American community were from people seeking to thank me for my role in drafting the beach petition. Similarly, those who knew Felix from his days as a quarterback at Alcorn University behind Charles Evers, who was his center, knew that Felix was tough, resilient, streetwise, smart, and an unrelenting competitor. The Sovereignty Commission agents never really knew us. Their racism kept them from giving black leaders enough respect to really get to know them. White investigators dismissed us. They expected some negative stereotype of the Negro to kick in, kill the movement, and take their problems away. We reacted to hardship and threats in ways that were absolutely opposite to what the Sovereignty Commission agents expected. Such are the perpetrator's delusions in the racist dream that created for us the nightmare world of segregation. Contrary to the deformed stereotypes of white racist imaginings, we proved to be real people, fully human, with hearts courageous and hopeful and willing to suffer for justice for ourselves and for our children.

Since no agents spent the effort to really know anyone whose skin was black, the picture of the black community that emerges from the Sovereignty Commission files reduces complex and vibrant African American communities to simple dichotomies of characters: the controllers and the controlled. Agents obsessed and speculated about who could control whom, and in this speculation now enshrined in their files, they besmirch the good names of those whose lives were filled with hopes and dreams and determination and faith that far transcended the paltry impressions of black people left in these prejudiced agents' writings. Many of the people so foolishly thought to be potentially useful as controllers of others were in fact just the opposite. Reverend Famous McIlheney and Mrs. Fannie Nichols had no interest in controlling forward-thinking, aggressive, liberty-loving black folks. Anyone attending a PTA meeting at Nichols High School when Mrs. Nichols was principal would have thought they had mistakenly dropped in on an NAACP meeting, so vigorous was her advocacy and concern for freedom. The Sovereignty Commission agent who speculated about her potential as a controller admits that he never met this fine lady.

Like Mrs. Nichols, Reverend Famous McIlheney was an intractable and eloquent advocate of freedom. At a time when some black ministers were afraid to host civil rights meetings in their churches for fear of reprisals, Reverend Famous McIlheney freely invited us to his two churches, Little Rock and Morning Star Baptist churches in Gulfport. Reverend McIlheney openly aided and abetted the Harrison County Civic Action Committee. McIlheney's eloquence and consistency in talking liberty was like pouring gasoline on the fires of freedom that were burning in our hearts. I guess no white men ever heard Reverend Famous McIlheney pour out his heart before God for liberty. The agents freely speculated about this revered man of God, but they never bothered to make personal contact with him. What sloppy work! Reverend Famous McIlheney was an emollient greasing the freedom movement and making things roll faster and better. He never acted as a break or a damper on anything. How ridiculous that without knowing him, without even being in a meeting with him, white agents could speculate about whether they could use such a man as Reverend Famous McIlheney to control others. Had they inquired beyond the white folks' rumor mill, they would have been quickly disabused of this idea. It is not only the prejudice but the utter ignorance of the Sovereignty Commission agents that makes these files so misleading and so frustrating for me to read.

In setting the record straight about Reverend Famous McIlheney, I do not mean to leave the impression that Reverend McIlheney was the only black minister taking a stand for civil rights. Certainly from the very start of our movement Reverend E. H. Potter opened New Bethel Baptist Church in Biloxi to us, and that church became a bastion of civil rights under his leadership. Reverend W. T. Guice at Mount Bethel Baptist Church in Gulfport, Reverend Fox at First Missionary Baptist in Handsboro, Reverend Orange Harris at St. John AME in Biloxi, and Reverend Davis at St. Paul's United Methodist in Biloxi all stood out as men of God and men for God, and all became champions of liberty. Let me also never forget that there were white ministers in this Mississippi who, under the inspiration of God Almighty, tried to put into practice the teachings of Jesus Christ that all of us are brothers. Reverend Orlo Kaufman and his associate, Reverend Harold Regier, at the Camp Landon Mennonite Mission in Gulfport took their stand openly with us, and triggered a Sovereignty Commission investigation of their activities.[20] Moreover, I can never forget Reverend John Aregood and Reverend Roger Gallagher of the Back Bay Mission, who opened their building to welcome the ministers' session of the first state NAACP meeting on the Mississippi Gulf Coast, only to find the meeting besieged by an angry white mob throwing stones and smashing the windows of that sanctuary of good works. The sound of breaking glass provided the devil's accompaniment to our singing of "Lift Every Voice" that night, and still these white men of God stood with us. Scandalized and oppressed by those who knew them not, these men, too, paid a price for walking in the footsteps of Jesus in those hard days of the early 1960s on the Mississippi Gulf Coast.

SEVEN

Ballots, Beaches, and Bullets

And did those feet in ancient time,
Walk upon Englands mountain green:
And was the holy Lamb of God,
On Englands pleasant pastures seen!

And did the Countenance Divine,
Shine forth upon our clouded hills?
And was Jerusalem builded here,
Among these dark Satanic Mills?

Bring me my Bow of burning gold:
Bring me my Arrows of desire:
Bring me my Spear: O clouds unfold!
Bring me my Chariot of fire!

I will not cease from Mental Fight,
Nor shall my Sword sleep in my hand:
Till we have built Jerusalem,
In Englands green & pleasant Land.
—William Blake, from *Milton, a Poem in 2 Books*

NOTHING WORTHWHILE COMES WITHOUT A STRUGGLE.
Some struggles are physical. Some struggles are moral. Some struggles are
legal and political. Every struggle is a spiritual struggle, a test of faith and

will. Recently, a white friend twenty years younger than I heard me speak of the sad events of the bloody wade-in and of the simultaneous struggle we undertook for voter registration and school desegregation in Biloxi. Somewhat taken aback to learn how broad an assault we had launched against segregation in 1960, this white gentleman probed to understand why it was that we had been prepared to risk so much, to suffer so much and endure so long. It took eight years for the courts to settle the issue of our right to free access to the beach. After responding to several of my friend's questions about the source of our motivation and strength without seeming to convey to him a satisfying understanding, I quoted from William Blake's poem *Milton*, ending with these lines:

> I will not cease from Mental Fight,
> Nor shall my Sword sleep in my hand:
> Till we have built Jerusalem,
> In Englands green & pleasant Land.

Then, I smiled and said, "We were building the new Jerusalem right here in Biloxi." That there was a larger meaning, a larger inspiration for our work seemed to satisfy this inquirer. We did believe in a transcendent and redemptive purpose in our work. We believed that our unjustified suffering could awaken slumbering moral sensitivities in the majority white community that surrounded us. With Dr. Martin Luther King, Jr., we held the strong belief that we could wear out hatred with love. That may be why I was moved to tears when, in the fall of 1960, I heard for the first time the song "We Shall Overcome," which was being sung by children from a Laurel, Mississippi, youth choir at a state NAACP youth meeting. That song still moves me. The tears, I think, represented then and still represent the depths of my hopes and prayers for the redemption of all of us, white and black together.

Along about the same time late in 1960, Dr. Clay Easterly, my white surgeon friend, reminded me that such a hope might not be in vain. In the darkest hours of that time, when most white folks in Biloxi were still blazing mad about the civil rights activities erupting in their backyards, Dr. Clay Easterly reached out to relate to me as a man and a fellow physician. Dr. Easterly was a big man. He had been a professor at the LSU Medical School, and he was truly a skilled surgeon. He was also an army reserve colonel and did a lot of weight training. Dr. Easterly had an impressive upper body build and tremendous strength, so much so that people said that he looked like "Mr. Clean," the muscleman mascot of a

1960s floor-cleaning product. One evening in 1960, after Dr. Easterly and I finished a late surgery together, this white man turned to me as a fellow physician and said innocently, "Let's go have a drink together." Now this was long before the Civil Rights Act of 1964 opened public accommodations to people of my complexion, so I was a little surprised at the suggestion. I responded with a question: "Where?" Easterly said, "Let's go to Baricev's on the beach." I knew the racial tension in Biloxi was running high after the riots, so I answered, "You don't want to go in there with me, they'd have me lynched." The look on Dr. Easterly's face turned dead serious, and he curled his lip and replied, "I wish to hell the bastards would bother us." Given his robust build, I had no doubt that, if attacked, Dr. Easterly could have taken good care of himself. Given his principles, I rather suspected that he might just as soon try to clear a barroom as to be forced to disassociate with a friend.

Clearing a barroom might have been satisfying for a moment, but it would have been a strategic error. It would have gotten no one registered to vote. It would have changed nothing in the political power base in Biloxi. We needed people challenging things at the ballot boxes and in the courtrooms much more than we needed folks challenging drunks in barrooms. So, for strategic reasons, I declined Clay Easterly's interesting invitation. However, I have never forgotten the spirit of this white Biloxian's gesture to a black man who had become a pariah to the white establishment. Was not this a sign that Jerusalem could be built here on Mississippi's green and pleasant shore?

During the summer of 1960, Medgar Evers and I also grew close to each other, both as a direct result of the legal action over the beach, and because we in Biloxi began exploring the possibility of filing a lawsuit to desegregate the public schools. My son, Gilbert, Jr., turned six years old in 1960. Therefore, for the first time, I had the proper legal standing necessary to file suit on his behalf to desegregate the Biloxi Municipal School District. If Clay Easterly showed me something about redemption, Medgar Evers showed me something about commitment.

Two of the most treasured papers in my possession are letters that Medgar wrote to me and Robert Carter, the NAACP legal counsel, in October of 1960, regarding my request for the NAACP to file suit to desegregate the Biloxi schools. This was the first such request to come out of Mississippi. Medgar wanted to join the prospective suit on behalf of his own children in Jackson. Because he was an NAACP employee, his desire to become a plaintiff put Medgar in a somewhat awkward position. He wrote these words to Robert Carter at NAACP headquarters in New York:

"I have two school age children who are presently going to private school (segregated). Now it is rather difficult for me to reconcile to the general public the fact that I believe in what I preach, while at the same time [I] practice something to the contrary. . . . I would like to be one of three or four Plaintiffs to initiate legal action to destroy the segregated system here in Jackson. . . ." Medgar followed this letter to NAACP headquarters with a personal letter to me. "I am anxious to get something going here in Jackson," he wrote, "*to the point that I am willing to risk even life itself*" (emphasis added). He went on to say, "We have procrastinated long enough in the state and the [ill] treatment from the whites has not lessened, [but] rather increased. My feeling is, if we are to receive a beating, lets [*sic*] receive it because we have done something, not because we have done nothing." Medgar Evers wound up giving his life practicing what he preached. His words and deeds laid out an example of leadership and devotion which has served as a continuing source of inspiration in my life.

Biloxi was a busy place for me in the summer of 1960. While we began our initial stages of planning for the battle for school desegregation, the question of access to the beach had begun its long journey through a maze of court maneuvers—county, state, and federal. Simultaneously, we got very serious about voter registration. We were determined to have a say over the character of Biloxi's municipal leadership. Mayor Laz Quave's threats and thugs had no place in the Biloxi that we envisioned for our children. We had to register people to vote, and we had to find a political alternative to the rabid segregationists who had hitherto come to the top in Biloxi politics.

The commission form of city government, under which Biloxi operated, made it difficult for minority voices to be heard. The mayor and two commissioners ran for office at large. In office, the mayor-commissioners triumvirate acted as both executive and legislative branches of city government. The mayor and two commissioners oversaw different departments and came together to make ordinances. There was no city council. Since the mayor and two commissioners were elected at large, there was no hope of someone with a black face winning office, and the minority vote carried less weight in elections and at city hall than it should have. Still, the only way to change or moderate the political climate of the city was to elect a new mayor and new commissioners. With at-large elections and no black majority districts, the political challenge was twofold. First, we had to find and ally with moderate white politicians who might have difficulty being elected without our support. And second, we needed to register more black voters. The more black folks voting, the smaller the number of white votes needed to elect a moderate white candidate.

Voter registration as a conscious civil rights strategy came to Biloxi and the Mississippi Gulf Coast several years before the famous long hot summer of 1964, when the Student Nonviolent Coordinating Committee (SNCC) and the Council of Federated Organizations (COFO) ran freedom schools and voter registration drives in over forty Mississippi communities. We were ahead of the curve in Biloxi and on the rest of the coast. On the Mississippi Gulf Coast we had conducted the first civil disobedience campaign in the state. With the May 17, 1960, Justice Department beach access suit, we launched the first federal court challenge to any of Mississippi's Jim Crow laws. For our audacity in standing up for our rights, we had gotten our heads beaten in before it happened to anyone else in the state. Therefore, we got serious about trying to chain up the segregationist mad dog through the ballot box several years earlier than black folks in some other places in Mississippi.

The Jim Crow system of de jure segregation in Mississippi relied on the disenfranchisement of black voters. Mississippi's 1890 constitution engineered black disenfranchisement after the Civil War through the use of devices such as lengthy residence requirements, literacy tests, and the poll tax. All of these devices were outlawed in the mid-1960s, but we had to contend with them in our early efforts at voter registration on the Mississippi Gulf Coast. Overcoming the poll tax obstacle involved persuading our people to pay a tax that had been made optional in an effort to discourage voting, or it meant raising the money to pay the tax for those without resources. It also meant educating people as to the necessity of keeping poll tax receipts handy for three years for presentation at the polls at election time.

The literacy test was a more formidable obstacle. An applicant for registration as a voter was required to appear in person before the county circuit clerk and give an interpretation of a section of the Mississippi constitution. This could be very intimidating in the atmosphere which segregationists cultivated. The law instructed the clerk to evaluate each person's answers and approve only those applicants who could, in the clerk's estimation, correctly interpret the selected passages. The horror stories about the literacy tests and local clerks' arbitrary and capricious evaluations are legion. Most often, clerks assisted whites in making acceptable interpretations or even waived the literacy requirement altogether. On the other hand, even college-educated blacks were often failed for the smallest error on an application form or the least deviation from a clerk's peculiar notion of a correct interpretation of the selected passage. The clerk's decision could be appealed, but the appeal was to the all-white county election commission. If blacks successfully navigated these barriers, in some areas of the state they could expect economic reprisals, loss of their jobs, and physical threats if they exercised the resulting voting privilege. The masses of black people in Mississippi were disenfranchised as a result. One authority estimates that only 5 percent of Mississippi's African American citizens were registered to vote in the early 1960s.[1]

As we prepared folks for the wade-in campaign in 1959 and 1960, the Harrison County Civic Action Committee and especially the Biloxi Civic League, of which I was president, strongly emphasized the need to increase local black voter registration. Personally, I had been a registered voter from the time I turned twenty-one years old. I had registered to vote, and my father had paid my poll tax for me in Hinds County while I was in medical school. When I arrived in Biloxi to set up my medical practice, I immediately registered to vote and paid the poll tax. I was aware of the Southern Voter Institute operating out of Atlanta, which was headed first by Vernon Jordan and later by Wiley Branton. The NAACP was also placing emphasis on voter registration as a vehicle for long-term solutions to many of the problems of the South and the nation. By the time of the bloody wade-in at Biloxi, the NAACP's W. C. Patton was working out of Memphis as a voter registration field representative. Tools were at hand to help us take these steps.

In November of 1960, there was a generational changing of the guard in the Mississippi Conference of the NAACP. Following the bloody wade-in, my old scoutmaster and an early NAACP activist from Jackson, James A. White, wrote to me urging me to make myself available to become more involved in the civil rights movement beyond Biloxi. I was committed, and there was no turning back for me, so I allowed myself to be put forward as a candidate for state NAACP office in 1960. That fall, Dr. Aaron Henry was elected state president. I was elected his first vice president, Dr. Felix Dunn was elected second vice president, and Mr. C. C. Bryant of McComb became the third vice president. Following the leadership of the national NAACP, we young turks on the state level placed a new and heavy emphasis on voter registration as a prime weapon in the battle for human rights in Mississippi. Thus, immediate voter registration projects got under way in the towns where these new state NAACP officers resided. We were determined to change the power base of local government in the state, and we were determined to set an example for other groups across the state.

On the coast in Gulfport and Biloxi, we followed through with a massive voter registration effort. In the Biloxi branch of the NAACP, Mrs. Ruby Tyler was the chairperson of our voter registration campaign in 1960. We invited W. C. Patton to come to Biloxi to help us get better organized for this effort. Because of the unusually congenial disposition of the Harrison County circuit clerk, Mr. E. G. Lindsey, voter registration proved to be far less intimidating on the Mississippi Gulf Coast than it was elsewhere in the state. Mr. Lindsey threw no capricious obstacles into our path. The main problem we encountered was in transporting people the distance from Biloxi to the county courthouse in Gulfport for their state and county registration and then back to Biloxi City Hall for a municipal registration. The law at the time required these two appearances in person for completion of registration. For success in overcoming transportation problems, great laud and honor is due especially to Mr. John Henry Beck. John Henry Beck was an unlettered man, but a natural-born leader. At one time Mr. Beck had been the Worshipful Master of my Masonic Lodge, Acme Lodge Number 307, Prince Hall Affiliation, Scottish Rite. We later renamed the lodge and a small park on Division Street in John Henry Beck's honor. He was on our local troop committee for the Boy Scouts. John Henry Beck burned gasoline in his car at his own expense and wore the tread off his tires hauling people over to Gulfport to register and then back to Biloxi City Hall to complete the process. He hauled people to register anytime, not just in the heat of a political campaign.

Once we got people to the courthouse in Gulfport, things were very predictable in the office of Mr. E. G. Lindsey. Mr. Lindsey actively aided the registration process by always asking the same question, an easy one, to allow people to demonstrate so-called "literacy." Mr. Lindsey would say, "One of the things I must ask you to do is read and interpret a portion of the constitution of the state of Mississippi." He would then say, "Now write this down," and proceed to read aloud the same predictable phrase from the state constitution: "There shall be no imprisonment for debt." Then, Mr. Lindsey would explain it to you and ask you what it meant. Voter registration in all three of the Mississippi coast counties took place in front of similarly fair-minded clerks in the early 1960s. This was certainly advantageous, and by 1968, it meant that in the Fifth Congressional District covering the Mississippi Gulf Coast, I could get elected as a delegate to the Democratic National Convention through the regular delegate selection process. Others from inland counties found the barriers which racists threw into their paths to be insurmountable such that a successful credentials challenge was launched against the Mississippi delegation in Chicago that year. However, if voter registration on the Mississippi Gulf Coast took place in a comparatively friendly atmosphere, it was still inconvenient. The registration books were never taken out of the courthouse. So we had to make many automobile trips to build our voter base. In 1960, we knew that the rest of Mississippi was not so friendly to black voter registration, and we were quick to grasp the significance of the opportunity which trouble-free voter registration presented. We saw our chance to change the power equation in Biloxi through the ballot box.

The racist cohorts at the State Sovereignty Commission also understood the implications of larger numbers of black citizens exercising their right to vote. As early as February of 1959, they were inquiring about the number of Negroes registered to vote in Gulfport, and they were worried that the Negroes in Harrison County might block vote. White folks block voting in the South didn't scare the segregationists, but black folks block voting bothered them mightily, even though there were very few of us registered. Of course, on our side it was apparent that survival demanded political solidarity, especially after the 1960 riot. The 1950 census had shown the total population of Harrison County to be 84,073, of which 13,421 were Negroes. In 1959 the sheriff of Harrison County estimated that as many as 1,400 Negroes were registered to vote locally. Whatever the actual count, we knew in 1959 and 1960 that we had tremendous untapped political potential in unregistered African American citizens.

The agents of darkness were right to be concerned about our activities in the voter registration arena. The events surrounding the bloody wade-in and the frustrating court maneuvers that followed helped stir enthusiasm for voter registration campaigns in both Gulfport and Biloxi in 1960. In the Biloxi branch, we received assistance from the Long Island (New York) NAACP branch in the form of a donated twelve-hundred-pound printing machine, which we installed in my office. We therefore harnessed the power of the printed word in our cause. We made a massive voter registration push in the latter part of 1960. Rallies and voter registration schools were held at the United Benevolence Association Hall on Division Street. There were meetings at McDaniel's Funeral Home and at New Bethel Baptist Church. All aimed to impart the notion that it was a citizen's duty to register and vote and to educate himself or herself on the issues to be decided at election time. Our home and my office were headquarters for these types of activities. In one three-month period in 1960, we registered as many as 350 new black voters in Biloxi alone. A similar number were registered in Gulfport, where the Gulfport branch and the

North Gulfport Civic Association under Robert Cook's leadership carried on an organized voter registration campaign in 1960 and 1961.

I estimated that as many as one thousand new black voters registered in Harrison County in 1960, and our efforts were continuous thereafter. We felt that our 1960 voter project had been a great success. From the Sovereignty Commission files, I have learned that Harrison County elected officials' estimates of increased black voter registration in 1960 and 1961 exceeded our own. After these substantial voter registration efforts on our part, Harrison County officials told Sovereignty Commission agents in 1961 that countywide there were between twenty-five hundred and four thousand Negroes on the Harrison County voter rolls. This compares to local officials' estimates of fourteen hundred Negro voters in the same county in 1959.[2] The significance of our 1960–61 achievement should be judged against the impact of the "long hot summer of 1964." In 1964, COFO and SNCC set up freedom schools and voter registration projects in over forty Mississippi counties, but managed to register only two thousand to three thousand new black voters over the entire state.[3]

1960 was a federal election year. We were aware of and appreciative of the civil rights legislation that President Eisenhower had signed into law in 1957 and 1960. The 1957 Civil Rights Act made possible the May 17, 1960, federal intervention in the beach desegregation case. Nonetheless, I and most other politically sensitive black leaders determined to cast our lot in presidential politics with John F. Kennedy and the Democrats, rather than with Richard Nixon. Black political activities in Harrison County gained sufficient momentum that year that I was elected to the Harrison County Democratic Committee. I remained a member of that committee for thirty-eight years. Bidwell Adams was the county Democratic chairman in 1960, and Tommy Thompson was secretary. Bidwell Adams, a former Mississippi lieutenant governor, won my respect when he spoke out against Governor Barnett's bid for Mississippians to vote for an independent slate of presidential electors as a means of protesting John F. Kennedy's and the national Democratic Party's pro-civil rights stance. Barnett's demagoguery easily stampeded the white majority to abandon its manifest economic interest in the programs of the Democratic Party and waste the state's presidential electoral votes, but men like Bidwell Adams reminded me that this old Jim Crow Mississippi had its corners of sanity and hope even in 1960.

In Biloxi our voter registration efforts were aimed at political targets closer to home. In the wake of apparent official complicity in the white mob action on the beach on April 24, 1960, we looked to change the mayor and city commissioners. Municipal elections were scheduled for the spring of 1961. Mayor Laz Quave and incumbent city commissioners Pete Elder and Dominic Fallo presented themselves as a ticket in the Democratic primary on May 9, and ran on their "record in office." Mayor Quave touted his police background. He reminded the voters that he had served as the city's police chief and as sheriff of Harrison County before being elected mayor in 1957. Dominic Fallo, Quave's running mate for public works commissioner, was also a former detective in the city police department. Fallo and Elder seemed benign enough. However, the influence and repressive attitudes of the Biloxi police establishment hung heavily in the air around Mayor Quave. The mayor's ticket presented itself as standing for principles: "honesty, integrity, efficient and courteous service, and full devotion" to their duties.[4] Of course, these words had a new meaning in the black community. Given that the mayor had cursed me and verbally threatened my life, it was clear that his record of courtesy was one that had been reserved for white folks. The integrity and devotion to duty of which Mayor Quave spoke must have been the special segregationist notions of integrity and devotion to duty involved in keeping black folks in their place.

Mayor Quave had three opponents in the Democratic primary that year, attorney Daniel D. Guice, Lawrence Semski and Paul Skrmetti. They all opposed the Quave record in one way or another.[5] Because a number of us in back-of-town had registered to vote, several candidates, including Mayor Quave, made meetings in our neighborhood. The campaign produced direct and bitter public confrontations between Mayor Quave and black citizens over his behavior in the bloody wade-in and the rioting which followed. At the Elks Hall I stood up in public and on behalf of the black community of Biloxi demanded of Quave, "Where were you when they were breaking our heads on the beach last year with pipes and chains? Where were you when our neighborhood was being shot up by out-of-control white mobs? Where were you when our cars were being stoned? Where were you when they were firing our people from their jobs in downtown stores? Where were you, Mayor Quave, when Bud Strong was murdered? Where were you when our streets needed fixing and our ditches needed cleaning? Where were you, Mr. Mayor?" No amount of hemming and hawing could supply a satisfactory answer for this crowd. Mrs. Vashti Tanner took up the cry and followed the mayor around with these questions whenever he appeared before a black audience. She never let him forget his many failings in the black community. Things had changed back-of-town, and Mayor Quave had clearly misjudged the reception he would receive if he came to meet with us.

In back-of-town we rather liked the more reflective, temperate, scholarly, and judicial approach of the Tulane-educated lawyer, Daniel Guice, who was running against Quave. The more respectful attitudes of those on Guice's ticket made us believe that our voices would finally be heard in city hall. We believed that we would get a fairer shake out of commissioner candidates William Dukate and J. A. "Tony" Creel, who ticketed with Guice in the primary. Daniel Guice was a gentleman by any standards. He was a young man about my own age when he ran for mayor, but he had already served a term in the state legislature. Biloxi had a choice for both a generational change and an atmospheric change in the mayor's office. Young lawyer Guice was polite and respectful to all citizens, and unlike Mayor Quave, he never once let an uncouth word or threatening remark pass his lips in public. The same was true of Tony Creel, Guice's much older and more experienced running mate for commissioner of public works. Creel expected polite address from everyone, and he gave it in return. He showed respect by addressing black folks as "Mr." and "Mrs." just as he did with white people of every class, and he strongly insisted that everyone observe the same standard of public respect in addressing him. He understood the importance of proper decorum in creating an atmosphere conducive to problem solving. Creel had served as a city commissioner for several terms in the past. He had a reputation for getting things done. If Creel told you that he was going to repair a street, it soon got repaired. William Dukate, Guice's running mate for commissioner of finance, was a native Biloxian and a graduate of Spring Hill College with a master's degree from Harvard. This ticket had polish and class and none of the obvious roughness of the incumbents. Moreover, the Guice ticket pointedly promised to "promote the best welfare of all the citizens of Biloxi."[6] In back-of-town, we took this to be an important nuance carrying a carefully veiled promise of a new spirit of inclusion. In back-of-town, the Guice, Creel, and Dukate ticket seemed a much better choice than the insensitive, cursing, threatening, and head-bashing approach of Laz Quave.

The first primary did not produce a majority for any mayoral or commission candidates. With 5,773 total votes cast in the first primary, Laz Quave led the four-candidate field, but fell 336 votes short of the majority required for outright election. This number coincided with the approximate number of new black voters registered in our voter registration drive. Our new political power was felt. Votes in the black community back-of-town were sufficient to deny the bullying Quave an outright victory. We succeeded in forcing a runoff election pitting Mayor Quave with his team against lawyer Daniel Guice and his ticket.[7]

Guice had polled 2,078 votes in the first primary and had to find at least 809 new votes to defeat the incumbent mayor. The main focus of the runoff campaign was on the obvious temperamental differences between Guice and Quave and the importance of that difference for the city's image. I am told that political professionals generally expect lighter turn-outs in runoff elections, because once the field of candidates has been narrowed, the number of persons actively working to draw friends and family to the polls is greatly reduced. The usual effect is a decreased turn-out. This did not happen in the May 16, 1961, runoff between Laz Quave and Daniel Guice. One hundred and twenty-three more votes were cast in the runoff election than had been cast in the first primary. Daniel Guice won a narrow 50.6 percent victory. His margin of victory was a mere 74 votes out of the 5,830 cast in the mayor's race. The rest of the Guice ticket won more handily,[8] but the results in each race were close enough that any analysis would show that the black vote back-of-town had produced the margin of victory for the entire Guice ticket.

The 1961 municipal election was a watershed in Biloxi politics. Mayor Daniel Guice became the first mayor in Biloxi's history to seek out and appoint qualified black citizens to city boards and commissions. Under Mayor Guice, Biloxi's first black police officers, Bernard Seymour and Florian Tichell, began walking the beats back-of-town. A vibrant black community in Biloxi, Mississippi, had awakened to the opportunity to empower itself through voter registration. A new level of civic involve-ment and influence came as a result. The power we found in the ballot box had cracked open the doors of city hall. Since that municipal election of 1961, every mayor of Biloxi has sought the formal advice and involve-ment of the black citizens in governing the community. The message had been sent clearly to all of the potential Laz Quave-type old-style segrega-tionists that black folks' votes added up in Biloxi. Black citizens took their first steps toward political power in Biloxi, Mississippi, in 1961, three years before the Civil Rights Act of 1964 destroyed Jim Crow in public accom-modations, three years before the Twenty-fourth Amendment to the U.S. Constitution ended the poll tax, and four years before the federal Voting Rights Act of 1965 swept away literacy tests.

From 1961 onward, we heard friendlier, more reasonable voices in Bi-loxi City Hall, but we still had our differences with city officials. Court battles over beach and school desegregation remained to be fought and won. Like all of the other public school districts in Mississippi, the Biloxi

Municipal School District was strictly segregated. Despite a friendlier public demeanor in city hall, the city's appointed school board continued to stall on our request for negotiations to integrate the schools. This stall tactic necessitated an expensive court challenge. Then, there was the ongoing matter of black access to the beach. In fairness, it must be pointed out that Mayor Guice inherited the beach controversy from Laz Quave's administration. The 1960 wade-in had sent the issue forward in a confusing array of court actions in county, state, and federal jurisdictions. The May 17, 1960, Justice Department civil rights suit had named the city of Biloxi and Mayor Quave personally as defendants, along with the Harrison County Board of Supervisors and Sheriff Curtis Dedeaux. We held hopes that since Mayor Guice was not a personal party to the suit, something might be worked out locally at an early date that would save the time and trouble of all of these court cases. However, local politics and local family relationships frustrated this hope.

Robert Carter, the NAACP legal counsel, had cautioned us in April of 1960 that if we chose to undertake legal action with NAACP assistance it would probably be a long and drawn-out proceeding. The question at issue as to whether the beaches were publicly owned or were essentially the private property of the homeowners and business owners on the north side of Highway 90 could go either way, Carter had warned. We knew that we were in for a tough fight, and Carter had cautioned us to carefully gauge the mood and determination of the people in the community. The local people, after all, would be the ones who would have to live with the side effects of a long legal struggle. The decision to proceed was thus left in our hands. The local people decided to proceed. We were therefore elated when the U.S. Justice Department filed suit in federal court on our behalf on May 17, 1960, the sixth anniversary of the landmark U.S. Supreme Court decision in *Brown v. the Board of Education of Topeka.*

We still had the option of filing another suit that would go through the federal courts independently of the government's case. We initially decided that an independent suit would be a waste of money. There were advantages, however, to be gained if we petitioned the federal court to allow us to intervene in the government's case. If the court recognized us as an active party to the government's suit, we would have some say about the terms of any decision to settle out of court, and if a lower court decision went against us, we would have a say in decisions about appeal. Therefore, the NAACP filed a motion asking to intervene on our behalf in the government's case. We knew there would be long delays, but we were still surprised at the variety and time-consuming nature of the maneuvers that unfolded over the next three years.

On May 18, 1960, Mississippi's frothy-mouthed segregationist governor, Ross Barnett, pledged to Harrison County officials that the state would provide "aid in every way possible" to keep the beach segregated.[9] The governor and the state's attorney general, Joe Patterson, characterized the Justice Department suit on our behalf as the "sternest" legal test yet for the state's Jim Crow laws. The state feared that our case would undermine the segregated status of any public park or facility in Mississippi in which any federal funds were invested. The state legislature had just funded a new assistant attorney general's post especially to fight desegregation cases.[10] Mississippi's two United States senators, James O. Eastland and John Stennis, echoed state officials in a joint press release claiming that Harrison County had fulfilled all of its obligations under the 1948 federal contract which had funded the construction of the beach. In these gentlemen's minds, since segregation was the law of the land before 1954, Negroes had not been included in the "public use" which Harrison County had pledged for the beach. Stennis and Eastland predicted that "when the heat" of the 1960 presidential election year "dies down, the action of the Justice Department will die with it." They labeled the Justice Department suit "a travesty on justice," and bemoaned the "use of official processes for such a nefarious purpose."[11]

On May 19, 1960, a Biloxi beachfront property owner for thirty-seven years, Mrs. Lee Dicks Guice, through her attorney husband, W. L. Guice, filed suit against the Harrison County Board of Supervisors in the county's chancery court asserting a claim to private ownership of the beach section located directly across Highway 90 in front of her residence. Interestingly, Mrs. Guice's suit sought to have the courts nullify the assertions made in a personal letter to her from the board of supervisors in which the board claimed for itself ownership of the land south of the seawall. Mrs. Guice also asked that her complaint be ruled a class action suit encompassing the claims of perhaps two thousand property owners along the twenty-six-mile sand beach.[12] A group called the Biloxi Beach Property Owners Protective Association quickly formed to support the Guice suit.[13]

Now, the Guice filing took place one year before the Biloxi mayoral election, but Mrs. Lee Dicks Guice just happened to be the mother of Daniel Guice. Both our federal suit and Mrs. Guice's local suit were still in litigation when municipal elections were held the next year. If the new mayor, elected in 1961, had taken any step to change the city's beach use policy, he would have alienated the powerful Biloxi Beach Property Owners Protective Association and clouded seriously the legal claims put forward by his own family members. Thus, while we got a much better tone of voice from city hall after the 1961 municipal elections, we got no new beach use policy. Our fate was to remain strictly in the hands of the courts and the slow-moving wheels of justice.

The federal case got its first hearing before Judge Sidney C. Mize in Biloxi on June 6, 1960, when attorneys for the county and city officials named as defendants moved for additional time to consider their plea. This was to be the first in a long series of delaying motions employed by the state that succeeded in putting off the ultimate day of reckoning for eight years. Judge Mize's eagerness to accommodate the state's delaying tactics revealed him to be a judge with no sympathy for our cause. Many of the conservative judges who sat on the federal bench in Mississippi in the early 1960s, in effect, became accomplices in the state's overt efforts to subvert or block implementation of federal civil rights mandates. Federal trial judges' rulings in Mississippi in the 1960s were repeatedly overturned on appeal, albeit at great pain to those seeking justice and great expense to the taxpayers who wound up paying court costs. Judge Mize fit right into the segregationist mold. If we were going to get justice, Judge Mize seemed determined to make it very slow in coming.

A sampling of the repeated delays which Judge Mize imposed on the beach court proceedings demonstrates his spirit and also helps convey an understanding of the frustrations that built up in the black community over the next several years and ultimately led to a new major wade-in effort. On June 9, 1960, assistant U. S. attorney general Joseph M. F. Ryan filed a motion on our behalf seeking a preliminary injunction to enjoin Harrison County and the city of Biloxi from preventing Negroes from using the beach under the Fifth and Fourteenth Amendments to the U.S. Constitution.[14] Judge Mize refused to grant this injunctive relief. Judge Mize also ruled against the government's motion for an early date to take depositions from the defendants in order to possibly open the beach to plaintiffs' use during that summer. Furthermore, the federal district judge agreed to grant the defendants two months, until August 8, 1960, to prepare to give depositions before government attorneys.[15] With these two rulings, Judge Mize foreclosed any hope that the Harrison County beaches might be open "perpetually for public use" by all citizens during the summer of 1960.

Under these circumstances, the NAACP, through the offices of Robert Carter in New York and A. P. Tureaud in New Orleans, brought forward the motion asking to intervene on the government's side on behalf of thirty-two Biloxi Negro plaintiffs.[16] The granting of this motion would have given the plaintiffs a say in any proposed settlement and a determining voice in any decision to appeal a negative ruling from Judge Mize. Ten days later, and without ruling on our NAACP motion to intervene, Judge Mize granted the state an additional thirty days' time to answer the government's complaint, and allowed an additional forty-five days for these defendants to file their objections to the NAACP motion to intervene.[17] Additional defense delays granted ostensibly so the defendants could prepare their arguments moved the federal trial date back to November 30, 1960, by which time seven months had elapsed since the bloody wade-in.

At the time, we did not feel that our side of the suit was receiving fair treatment in the local press. Nowhere was this more apparent than in the newspaper headlines. We thought that all citizens should be informed about the role that public officials had played, not only in denying us use of the beach but in aiding the white mob in its first assault on us on April 24. The affidavit evidence which the Justice Department introduced in its complaint charged police complicity in the initial violence which spread through our community and resulted in two deaths and dozens of injuries. We reasoned that any question about police misbehavior of this nature should have been of serious concern to all reasonable citizens, black and white. The local newspaper, however, virtually blacked out the Justice Department's claim. Whereas we thought that these accusations ought to have been in the headline captions or lead paragraphs of stories, the local press buried this accusation. The *Daily Herald* treated the case as a cool unfolding of technical legal maneuvers in which the main public interest was in whether the beach was private property. From our perspective, uninformative *Daily Herald* headlines such as "U.S. Cites Cases In Beach Suit," or "32 Negroes File To Intervene in Beach Use Suit," or "Start Taking Depositions In Beach Case"[18] sanitized the case for the white public and controlled the political discomfort which our accusations may have caused the local white establishment. The Jackson papers took the same approach. In the initial coverage of the maneuvers in federal court, only the Memphis *Commercial Appeal* slipped in its normally segregationist stance and led its coverage with the headline "Police Accused of Aiding Mob,"[19] which we considered to be a central complaint that should have been of concern to the whole community. Of course, the *Commercial Appeal* was read by few people on the coast. The local press certainly did not contribute to any community moral self-examination in the wake of the bloody wade-in.

In September, while we yet awaited the movement of the federal wheels of justice, local chancery court judge William G. Hewes brought forward in his court the complaint of Mrs. Lee Dicks Guice against the county board of supervisors in which she claimed the beach as private property. Oddly enough, in Judge Hewes's court, Harrison County officials denied ever making "a public beach, public park, or public playground" on the privately owned property of Mrs. Guice or other beachfront homeowners. Rather, the supervisors held that they had never claimed title to the beach and had never attempted to open the beach to public use. They argued that the only activities which local government was authorized to undertake on the beach were activities directed purely to maintenance of the beach as a protection against erosion of the seawall and the adjacent highway.[20] Notwithstanding their 1948 pledge to the federal government to maintain the beach for public use, the county's strange new logic asserted that no citizen, white or black, had any right to be on the beach if a property owner objected. Given Mrs. Lee Dicks Guice's claims that she was in legal control of the use of the beach in front of her residence, and given the county's response, the government filed a motion with Judge Mize requesting that Mrs. Guice be added to the list of defendants. This maneuver caused repeated delays in the federal case, as defense attorneys were granted additional time until the end of November 1960 to prepare their answer to the government's amended complaint.[21]

Meanwhile, in chancery court Mrs. Guice's case came up for a hearing before Judge Hewes. After three days of preliminary hearings Judge Hewes announced his intention to rule on the case during the September 1960 session or soon thereafter.[22] The speed with which local officials were able to prepare for and bring forward Mrs. Guice's case in chancery court is noteworthy, especially given the fact that haste was so lacking in Judge Mize's federal proceedings due to the same local officials' own delaying tactics. The supervisors and city officials openly asserted that a Guice victory in the local courts would strengthen their defense in federal court.[23] Thus, our adversaries worked to delay Judge Mize's federal proceedings and so delay the day of reckoning about black access to the beach.

On December 19, 1960, the local courts in the person of Chancellor William G. Hewes upheld Mrs. Guice's claim against the Harrison County Board of Supervisors that since there had been no eminent domain proceedings at the time of its construction, the beach in front of her home was indeed Mrs. Guice's private property. However, Judge Hewes also held that the county had a continuing right to maintain the beach as an erosion control barrier. The local paper reported that even though the judge assigned court costs to the county supervisors, the officials "expressed cautious jubilation." Nonetheless, the jubilant losers determined to appeal the decision to the Mississippi Supreme Court in an effort to further bolster their defense in the still-pending federal suit.[24]

Meanwhile, in our federal case, it took Judge Mize an entire six months, from August 9, 1960, to February 20, 1961, to deliver a negative ruling on our NAACP-backed petition to intervene in the Justice Department suit against the supervisors. The lengthy delays in the federal proceedings frustrated us. NAACP general counsel Robert Carter wrote to explain to me that the option of filing a separate federal suit was still available. However, Carter cautioned that, given Judge Mize's slowness in delivering his negative decision on the NAACP motion to intervene, we were not likely to see much movement on any lawsuit to be heard before this particular judge.[25] In February the government filed a motion for a summary judgment in the federal case. With that motion still pending, we focused our energies on the politics of the Biloxi mayor's race and settled in to await further court developments. On May 22, 1961, over one year after the Justice Department originally filed suit, Judge Mize finally got around to hearing preliminary arguments on the government's summary judgment motion. After this hearing the judge gave both parties an additional forty-five days to prepare written briefs.[26] Even though St. John Barrett, the Justice Department Civil Rights Division lawyer handling our case, was optimistic that there would be a favorable ruling on the government's motion for summary judgment, it soon became apparent that Judge Mize would make no definitive ruling until the Mississippi Supreme Court had spoken in the Guice case. Despite strong government arguments that the county's land-reclamation contract with the federal government superseded any claims made by Mrs. Guice, Judge Mize refused to move. Another whole year elapsed before the Mississippi Supreme Court issued its very predictable May 1962 ruling upholding the Guice claim to private ownership of the beach.[27] Only then did Judge Mize restart the federal case.

On July 27, 1962, over two years after the Justice Department had filed suit, Judge Mize denied the government's motion for summary judgment against the supervisors and city officials. Anyone who thought we would now quickly go to trial was mistaken. In September, the defendants brought forth the 119th motion in this case asking Judge Mize to add all of the property owners along the entire twenty-six-mile coastline as defendants in the suit. This request, which Judge Mize granted in December of 1962 and reaffirmed in March, built in an enormous additional delay due to the difficult requirement that the government serve papers, in person, on some two thousand new defendants. This maneuver also guaranteed a long and drawn-out trial, if we were ever able to get to trial given this segregationist judge's propensity to grant the defendants every desired delaying motion.[28] Obviously, the attorney general of the state of Mississippi in 1963, who directed the defense of the local officials, believed that his office could wear out the Justice Department's civil rights lawyers, just as Governor Barnett and Mayor Quave had believed they could use delay to wear me out personally in 1960. Utterly frustrated, we petitioned U.S. attorney general Robert Kennedy requesting that he intervene personally with the U.S. Fifth Circuit Court of Appeals to request it to order Judge Mize to hold an early hearing on the merits of the beach case. Robert Kennedy, however, ignored this petition.

By March of 1963, our patience with both Judge Mize and the Justice Department was exhausted. In the three years since federal court proceedings had begun, we had elected a mayor and two city commissioners, but we now found that the ballot box held little power over ongoing litigation. Direct action was in the air again. We in Biloxi had carried out the first acts of collective civil disobedience in Mississippi in 1959 and 1960. Now, we watched in great frustration as others took up this tool, while we sat waiting through the interminable court delays that continued to deny our use of the beach. In 1961, while we yet waited for justice in the courts, we saw a dozen freedom riders jailed for violation of the Jim Crow laws at the Trailways bus station in Jackson. In 1962, while we yet waited for justice in the courts, students from Tougaloo College staged a sit-in at the Jackson Public Library. While justice was being denied us on the coast, my older sister, Rozelia Stamps, and her daughter, Carolyn, along with Medgar Evers and many more, had dogs set upon them and were then arrested and hauled off to the state fairgrounds and imprisoned for picketing downtown Jackson, Mississippi, merchants. While our access to the Mississippi Gulf Coast beaches was yet being denied, my older brother, Willie, a New Orleans longshoreman, was giving his financial support to the effort to desegregate the New Orleans public schools.

The behavior of demagogic segregationist politicians added to our frustration with the slow-moving courts. In September of 1962, Governor Ross Barnett's irresponsible behavior led to rioting at Ole Miss and made necessary the introduction of thirty thousand federal troops to enforce James Meredith's right to attend the University of Mississippi. It was reported that two Harrison County constables were seen on the Ole Miss campus during the riot. In the spring of 1963, George Wallace prepared to stand in the doorway of the University of Alabama to block Vivian Malone's and James Hood's pathway to learning. At the same time, President Kennedy talked about a new civil rights bill to open public accommodations to all. Still, the Kennedy Justice Department declined to prod Judge Mize into action on our case. However, the chances for passage of any meaningful new federal civil rights legislation seemed dim in view of the maze of legislative obstacles that could be thrown up by long-tenured segregationist southern congressmen and senators. Given these prospects, I concluded that, despite the frustrations associated with litigation, the dismantling of Jim Crow would ultimately have to be consummated judicially.

In this atmosphere, with the feeling growing in the Biloxi branch that "justice too long delayed is justice denied," I and others began thinking creatively about the means by which we might move the court case past the restraining hand of Judge Mize at the district level. Without consulting expert legal advice, I had observed that some cases moved directly to federal appeals courts from the state courts. It seemed to me that if we were again willing to risk all that might come to us in its wake, another wade-in followed by mass arrests on the beach might give us the means to bypass the recalcitrant Judge Mize. If city or county officials arrested and convicted us, we could appeal to the state supreme court and go from there directly to federal appeals court and the U.S. Supreme Court. Federal trial judges in Mississippi need not be a part of the process.

However, another beach demonstration carried obvious risks. The riot that had broken out in the wake of the 1960 bloody wade-in had left two dead, eight wounded in shootings, and dozens of others injured in beatings. Violent resistance to black demands in Mississippi was rising. In Vicksburg in 1963, my friend Wharless Jackson got into his truck, turned the ignition key, and was blown to kingdom come. We knew that this new scheme might cost us some lives and some hardships and losses. Still, the spirit that prevailed among people my age, who were in their twenties and thirties at that time, was one that demanded that we throw off the remaining vestiges of slavery and assert and utilize our full manhood and womanhood. The law itself constricted us as black citizens in ways that other citizens were not constricted. Life mattered to us, but we were willing to take risks to add to life's wholesomeness for ourselves and our children. Of course, we had prayer on our side. We in the Biloxi branch set our faces toward the beach once again in 1963, and began planning a new wade-in that would bring us a new court strategy and the hope for an earlier resolution of this problem.

In preparation for the 1963 wade-in, we had civilized discussions about security with Mayor Guice, who owed his election to the black voters in back-of-town. The mayor listened and seemed to be sympathetic. We actually negotiated the demonstration date with Mayor Guice in order to maximize the protection available from the police department. The city's annual Blessing of the Shrimp Fleet had already been calendared for Sunday, June 9, our first proposed wade-in date. We agreed to delay the wade-in for one week in order to gain whatever protection we could by avoiding a date when police forces would have to be spread between two different events. Various other officials, including District Attorney Boyce Holleman, tried to talk us out of the demonstration for reasons of public safety, but we were determined to try to get to the Supreme Court by this alternate route. We understood that the mayor would have us arrested if there were a complaint from the property owners on the north side of U.S. Highway 90. We needed those property owners to bite at our bait. We needed to be arrested in order to get a new state court suit going.

Medgar Evers and I were working intensely on our Biloxi school desegregation suit in the spring of 1963. Medgar was in town frequently and therefore assisted us in planning the new wade-in. Through Jess Brown, the Jackson-based black attorney who was handling NAACP work, we sent forward a request for ten thousand dollars in bail money from the national NAACP to cover bail for up to a hundred demonstrators. We expected to have to put up a hundred dollars per person to spring our people from jail. Not knowing the disposition of this request, we searched locally for backup bail arrangements that would be available under our control if the national money failed to come through. Dr. J. O. Tate, a black Gulfport dentist and lover of freedom, came to our aid with a pledge to put up his real estate holdings as security for bail bonds. Bishop Robert Nance of the Church of God also agreed to put up his property to help with bail. We did title searches to make sure that some unknown encumbrances wouldn't slow down the bailouts. Like the 1959 and 1960 wade-ins, the 1963 Biloxi wade-in was a grassroots initiative. We knew that we had to be prepared to take full responsibility for our actions.

Medgar Evers spent the night at my house on Fayard Street on Sunday, June 9, 1963. Medgar got up and shaved on Monday morning. News from Jackson called him back to the state capital where a wave of sit-ins and boycotts had started producing arrests. The Jackson police chased demonstrators with dogs and used cattle prods to herd people into paddy wagons and garbage trucks for trips to the jail or the fairgrounds lockups. Lena Horne and Roy Wilkins were coming to Jackson to bolster morale. As state NAACP field director, Medgar Evers had one very predictable aspect:

when people in trouble called him, Medgar went straight to them. When he left my house Monday morning, Medgar told me that he planned to be back with us to handle logistics for the wade-in scheduled for the next weekend. He left in such a hurry that he forgot his razor.

Many of us over the years had expressed concern for Medgar Evers's physical security. His name was always popping up on Klan hit lists. Medgar lived with threats on his life coming in almost every day in the early 1960s. When a wave of threats on my life had arisen in 1959 and 1960, I had accepted friends' offers to organize a group of guards to watch my office and my home and to accompany me on house calls and hospital rounds when needed. Friends had offered Medgar Evers similar organized protective arrangements, but our field director declined. I had heard Medgar Evers talk of his personal faith that the strong arm of God and the breast shield of God had been put around him. He declined offers of protection because he felt the bare and naked revelation that "God is going to protect me." I had been under threat, and I shared Medgar's faith in God's protective mercies. Unlike Medgar, however, I had accepted the protective offers of friends as one of the means by which a benevolent God might throw his arms around me.

Threats against all of us were constant at this time. As a matter of fact, early in the evening of Tuesday, June 11, 1963, Natalie was at the front gate of our house on Fayard Street talking to a neighbor when the telephone rang. She went inside to answer it, and when she returned to the yard she found a suspicious bulging bag hanging on our front fence. Natalie called me, and I called the police and hurried home. The police arrived promptly to investigate. We would not touch the bag. When the investigating officer cut open the bag, a dead cat fell out. Paperwork took me back to the office and kept me late that night. My friend Mr. W. O. Hill, who lived on Main Street in Biloxi, was attending an Elks convention in Jackson. At around midnight, the phone rang at my office, and W. O. Hill blurted these words into my ear: "They just killed Medgar Evers!" The cowardly Klansman Byron De La Beckwith, hidden 150 feet from the front door of Medgar's Jackson, Mississippi, home, fired the rifle shot that snuffed out the life of this young father, husband, and beloved civil rights leader. He was cut down on his doorstep holding NAACP T-shirts in his hands. Medgar Evers was martyred in a holy cause.

Over the next several days there was a whirlwind of activity and confusion. It was rumored that Medgar's murder was part of a Klan plot to take out all of the state-level NAACP officers at once. The dead cat hanging on my fence certainly made me think twice about the possibility. Medgar

Evers's funeral was set for Sunday, June 16, 1963, the date we had agreed upon for our new wade-in. Of course, our wade-in was postponed. National civil rights leaders from every organization were expected to attend the funeral. Dr. Martin Luther King, Jr., sent word that he would be present. The M. W. Stringer Grand Masonic Temple in Jackson was the only building in the black community large enough to hold a sizeable crowd. I served as an active pallbearer for our slain friend, along with Dr. Felix Dunn, Mr. R. L. T. Smith, Jr., Mr. Henry Briggs, Mr. Paul Cooke, Mr. Houston Wells, Mr. Cornelius Turner, and Mr. Nolan Tate. Thousands of black citizens from all corners of Mississippi converged on Jackson to honor the life and work of Medgar W. Evers. Inside during the services, Roy Wilkins, Reverend R. L. T. Smith, Sr., and Reverend G. C. Hunte spoke. The hymns "Be Not Dismayed," "We Shall Overcome," and "God Be with You" were sung. After the funeral the thousands who could not get into the Masonic Temple walked with us behind the hearse through the streets of Jackson. Dr. Martin Luther King walked just a few steps behind me and the other pallbearers. I had met Dr. King a few months before on an airline flight to Atlanta. He had encouraged our work in Biloxi, and, as an Alpha man himself, Dr. King graciously autographed my Alpha card. Now, in Jackson, we mourned together for a fallen comrade.

In Jackson before the funeral, several civil rights activists, including Robert Carter, the NAACP legal counsel, had gathered at attorney Jack Young's home. Someone in the group asked me, "How will this death affect your wade-in?" "Should this death stop us?" I asked. Medgar was such a dynamic person, and he was planning to be there with us. I said, "I believe Medgar would want us to go on." Bob Carter said "No, don't put it off. This should not make you change your plan. If you have the feeling that you should carry out your plan, go on." I mentioned our request to Roy Wilkins for ten thousand dollars for bail money. Jess Brown, the Jackson attorney who handled NAACP work, told me that I should make alternate arrangements in case NAACP money did not get there in time.

Full of sorrow and dismay, we in Biloxi had to decide whether to go ahead with the planned wade-in. We had several meetings during the week following the funeral and decided to undertake the wade-in as a memorial tribute to Medgar Evers. We decided to carry little black flags as a sign of mourning. Several ladies, including Mrs. Clara Ramsey, went to work making the flags. We knew the danger. We had seen the venom of the white rabble in Biloxi in 1960. This time we were assured of police protection, but we could not know whether it would really materialize or be adequate. We prayed for God's protection, and then we went on with what we as men and women had determined to be necessary to gain our rightful use of a public beach.

On Sunday afternoon, June 23, 1963, approximately seventy-five demonstrators, including two white ministers, Reverend John Aregood and Reverend Roger Gallagher from the Back Bay Mission, and a white college-student intern at the mission, assembled outside my office on Division Street. We then drove to the waterfront together, parked our cars, and walked onto the beach at the foot of Gill Avenue between the Biloxi lighthouse and the old Biloxi cemetery. This was the exact site where the worst of the white mob attacks had taken place three years before. Here, we placed a double row of black flags in the sand to honor the martyred Medgar Evers, who had assisted in our planning of the wade-in. The Biloxi police assembled nearby in a force augmented with sheriff's deputies, police from other coastal towns, and Mississippi Highway Patrol units. At the request of the Justice Department, FBI agents were also on the scene as observers. Some federal agents posted themselves in the lighthouse to take pictures. Mayor Guice himself, along with Commissioner Creel and Commissioner Dukate, was standing by personally to direct police activities. The newspaper estimated that two thousand white spectators gathered, but, in contrast to the bloody wade-in of 1960, the police provided us the protection we needed. This time the authorities actively worked to prevent mob violence from developing.

As I got out of the car and prepared to go onto the beach, a white physician colleague on the Biloxi Hospital staff came storming out of his beachfront house seventy-five yards away, ran over to me, and announced in an agitated voice, "You see that house down there? If you go in front of my house, we're going to have you arrested." Of course, we needed an arrest to get a new suit moving in state court, so that we could bypass Judge Mize on our way to the U.S. Supreme Court. I shrugged and said, "Well, whatever. What else is new?" This was my first indication that the beach property owners might take our bait and make the arrests we needed. They were about to swallow, hook, line, and sinker.

Once on the beach, I headed for the water. We swam, played ball, and milled around for forty minutes or so before real-estate agent William Allen appeared with a bullhorn and started barking orders at us. "I represent the ownership of this house you see here on the corner of Gill and Highway 90," he squawked, "and you are now on private property. If you do not move we're going to have the police arrest you." His announcement was exactly what we needed. Therefore, we did not move. A few moments later, a Biloxi police officer, Detective Leslie Montgomery, took the bullhorn and announced, "You are under arrest for trespassing." Mr. Allen signed the complaint as a representative of Mrs. James M. Parker, who was away in Europe. Yes, it was going to be hook, line, and sinker. Old Br'er Rabbit was going to be thrown back into that briar patch. Unfortunately, as the papers were being prepared, the white mob grew rowdy. They turned one parked car over on its side. Through an open window, someone set fire to the interior of my 1959 Buick, destroying one of the seats and damaging the other. The water used to extinguish the blaze ruined what was left. One of our young demonstrators, James Black, who has since become a well-known minister in Biloxi, had driven my car to the beach that day, parked it, and left a window down for ventilation. This good deed gave the vandals their opening. Following our arrests, my fire-damaged car was towed to A & A Wrecker Service, where someone took a drill to the lock on the trunk and reamed it out. Luckily, there was nothing of value inside, because I had removed my medical bag from the trunk before going to the beach that day. The tires were slashed on a third car in our caravan. No blows were exchanged, although I saw the police quickly corral one white who broke through the police cordon and headed toward the demonstrators. We suffered property damage but no violence at the hands of racist ruffians on this day.

On the beach, police officers formed lines on either side of our little group and marched us up through the gathered white crowd to a waiting moving van parked beside the road. The name of the moving company had been covered with a fresh coat of dark blue paint. We were ordered into the back of that van with no ventilation on a hot and humid south Mississippi summer day. I objected. Once on the van, I tried to hold the doors open. I knew that some of the elderly ladies in our group, particularly Mrs. Altease Fairley Magee and Mrs. Aslena Massey, were in frail health and needed air. Nevertheless, the police forced the doors closed, locked us up in the crowded sweltering darkness, and hauled us down to Biloxi City Hall. When the van came to a stop it was in the midst of a mob of white hooligans, who immediately took hold of the vehicle and began rocking it and picking up on the front end as if to try to throw us out the back. Some of us fell to the floor, but when the doors opened, no one was thrown out.

The conditions inside the van surprised and angered me. I had not thought that Mayor Guice would allow something like this to befall citizens peacefully demonstrating for their rights. So, when the doors opened, I jumped down and headed straight for the mayor to object to the severe treatment we had received in the van. "I would have never thought you would have allowed such a travesty," I protested. Christopher Rosado said he had never before seen "a black man shake his finger in a white man's face," the way I did Mayor Guice that day. I told the mayor that I was surprised that a man of his character would even allow these people to be arrested. As was his manner, Mayor Guice responded calmly, "Well, Doctor, I told you ahead of time that if you went to the beach, you would be arrested. I asked you to postpone it for a week for the blessing of the shrimp fleet, and you agreed." Unlike the 1960 arrests, there was no cursing, no threatening, and no vulgarity. It was all just matter of fact. They locked everybody up. We had not yet received the NAACP bail money that we understood to be on the way. This meant that Natalie and Chris Rosado had to bail me out, so that I could go to work on bail money for the others. Without bail money in hand, they were all loaded back into the van for another hot, suffocating thirty-minute ride to the county jail in Gulfport.

I spent the rest of that Sunday afternoon working to get bail money together. It became apparent that it would be impossible to use Dr. Tate's and Bishop Nance's property bonds to bail people out of jail until Monday morning. Hoping that I might get money wired from the NAACP, I decided to telephone Roy Wilkins personally. The conversation did not go well. I was very disappointed that the NAACP money had not already gotten to us. I was distressed that our people would have to spend the night crowded in a hot, unair-conditioned jail. I told Roy that Jess Brown was to have arranged ten thousand dollars in bail money for us from the national office. Roy Wilkins firmly informed me that, whereas the NAACP was a formal organization, Mr. Jess Brown was sometimes an informal person. Roy Wilkins said he had the ten thousand dollars and would send it. On Tuesday morning the ten thousand dollars did arrive from the national office. However, by that time we had already bailed everyone out on the property bonds of Dr. Tate and Bishop Nance. We put the money from the national office in the bank.

I wish that I could say there were no further repercussions from the 1963 wade-in at Biloxi, and that we just went on to court and made our appeals. There is more to the story. I will credit the police with taking the steps necessary to prevent the kind of white gang activity that terrorized the community after the 1960 wade-in. This time, the police actively dispersed the crowds of whites that started gathering at various locations. The police also cordoned off the black neighborhoods and prevented white persons from driving through the area. Our investment in voter registration and political action had yielded a dividend. We got the kind of police protection that citizens have a right to expect from their police forces and public officials. Things had changed greatly in three years.

The NAACP now stepped in to provide the arrested Biloxi waders with legal assistance from R. Jess Brown. As expected, the seventy-one persons arrested on June 23, 1963, were found guilty of trespassing in city court. Judge John Sekul, who presided, had served as city prosecutor in the 1960 beach case. Mr. Lyle Page was now the city prosecutor. Once again, the city courtroom was packed. Every seat in the Negro section was filled, and more than a hundred additional black citizen observers were left standing. Attorney R. Jess Brown asked the judge to allow standing blacks to sit in vacant seats in the white section. "In the interests of peace," Judge Sekul declined.[29] Forty-three adults were tried and found guilty of trespassing. Because I was a repeat offender, Judge Sekul handed me a one-hundred-dollar fine plus a thirty-day jail sentence, the maximum punishments available to a city court judge. Seven others also received the maximum, including the white ministers, Reverend John Aregood and Reverend Roger Gallagher. The judge reasoned that, despite this being their first offense, Aregood and Gallagher were white folks who should have known better than to go onto the beach with blacks. The cases of the twenty-eight teenagers arrested with the group were remanded to youth court.

Jess Brown filed our appeal from city to county court, where Judge Luther W. Maples presided. Our Harrison County court trial opened on November 20, 1963. District Attorney Boyce Holleman and county prosecutor Gaston Hewes joined Biloxi city attorney Lyle Page at the prosecutor's table. Black folks once again packed the house for the trial. A pool of twenty prospective jurors was examined, including eighteen whites and two Negroes. The prosecutors used two of their six allowable challenges to excuse the two Negroes. An all-white twelve-man jury was impaneled to hear the case. Testimony began on Thursday, November 21, with prosecutors attempting to show that we had willfully and knowingly trespassed on Mrs. Parker's property.[30]

In 1963, the Harrison County Courthouse was located just across the street from the Greyhound bus station in Gulfport. When the trial adjourned for lunch, twelve or fifteen of the black defendants went across the street and staged a sit-in in the white section of the bus station's restaurant. The Gulfport police were called to the scene, but they made no arrests. The blacks were served, but, after completing service, the owner closed both the white and colored sections of the eating facility for the duration of the trial.[31]

On the last day of the county court trial, Friday, November 22, when we recessed for lunch, the news broke that President John F. Kennedy had been killed by an assassin in Dallas, Texas. We were all deeply shaken by the news. When court reconvened and the bailiff directed us to be seated, someone in our number refused to sit and announced that "none of us are going to sit until we all stand for a moment of silent prayer for our slain president." A hush fell over the room, and all stood and bowed their heads, prosecutors and defendants, white and black. This shared memorial moment did not change the predictable jury verdict. Jess Brown summed up; the jury got the case and returned a guilty verdict that very evening. The twenty-nine remaining defendants each posted the two-hundred-dollar appeal bonds needed to carry the case on to circuit court. (Several of those arrested on the beach on June 23 did not make the appearance in county court. Therefore, our appeal involved only the twenty-nine remaining defendants.) Of course, we lost in circuit court a year later,[32] appealed to the Mississippi Supreme Court, and then went on to the U.S. Supreme Court, where, after several years, we eventually prevailed.

Meanwhile, the slow speed of the Justice Department case before Judge Mize confirmed our judgment in opening this second legal front through the state courts. Judge Mize did not bring the Justice Department case to trial until December 14, 1964, over four and a half years after the Civil Rights Division of the Justice Department had filed suit. By this time, the 1964 Civil Rights Act had mandated the desegregation of public accommodations in businesses, restaurants, and hotels, but the state of Mississippi continued to spend money to defend an all-white status for its beaches. Judge Mize died, further slowing things down. His replacement, Judge Harold Cox, did not get around to handing down the expected negative ruling against the Justice Department until the spring of 1967.[33] The Justice Department appealed to the Fifth Circuit Court of Appeals.

On August 16, 1968, after over eight years of litigation, we finally got the affirmation that we had sought. Ironically, it was Judge J. P. Coleman who wrote the opinion which opened the beach to us. In 1959, when I undertook my first wade-in, Coleman was the governor of Mississippi. Now, sitting on the Fifth Circuit Court of Appeals, Judge Coleman ruled that in 1948, the state legislature had required that all necessary lands for the construction of the beach be provided to assure "perpetual public ownership of the beach and its administration for public use only." Judge Coleman found that this act of the state legislature effected a grant directly from the owners of beach property to the state.[34] The beach was now open to all citizens. The U.S. Supreme Court confirmed Judge Coleman's ruling by refusing to hear further arguments. It took until 1970 for the federal courts to reverse our trespassing convictions that had arisen from the 1963 wade-in. Direct action on the sandy beaches, along with a determined litigation strategy, finally delivered to us a hard-won piece of the new Jerusalem. Freedom for every citizen to enjoy the sunsets along a twenty-six-mile beach finally came to the Mississippi Gulf Coast.

EIGHT

Desegregation Now!

I believe in Pride of race and lineage and self: in pride of self so deep as to scorn injustice to other selves; in pride of lineage so great as to despise no man's father; in pride of race so chivalrous as neither to offer bastardy to the weak nor beg wedlock of the strong, knowing that men may be brothers in Christ, even though they be not brothers-in-law. . . .

I believe in the Training of Children, black even as white; the leading out of little souls into the green pastures and beside the still waters, not for pelf or peace, but for life lit by some large vision of beauty and goodness and truth; lest we forget, and the sons of the fathers, like Esau, for mere meat barter their birthright in a mighty nation. . . .

—W. E. B. Du Bois, from "Credo"

SOMEONE ONCE ASKED CHARLES EVERS, "WHAT DO YOU black folks want?" Charles answered, "Well, what have you got? We want what you've got without any strings attached." We wanted segregation destroyed so that black folks might enjoy the same opportunities that were available to other Americans. Most of us in the civil rights movement used the word *desegregation* to describe our goals rather than the word *integration.* We wanted to remove those barriers, de facto and de jure, which denied African Americans their full birthright as citizens of these United States. Access to the best that the public schools had to offer became an important part of the struggle for our full birthright in Mississippi. Personally, from the time of the 1954 *Brown* decision, I was determined to gain for my child and for every child an opportunity for the best possible public education to prepare them for successful living in this world. That meant gaining the opportunity for a true college preparatory curriculum and the right to go where the most money was being spent to create a quality environment for learning. In Mississippi's Jim Crow school systems, black students had access to wonderful, caring, and devoted teachers, but the money, sometimes at as much as a five- or ten-to-one ratio, went to the white schools, leaving black children shut out of access to the best facilities, equipment, and courses of study.

Aaron Henry used to tell about being born on the Flowers plantation in the Delta. When Aaron began attending school and noticed differences between provisions for black and white children under Mississippi's separate but unequal system, he asked his mother, "Why don't I go to school nine months a year like the white kids?" His mother said, "Well, you're smarter than a lot of those white folks. You don't need nine months. You can learn as much in four months as they can in nine." Aaron Henry took great pride in remembering his childhood belief that this was true. It may have been true for an extraordinarily gifted individual such as Aaron Henry. Unfortunately, this kind of overt educational deprivation left the vast majority of black kids in Mississippi undereducated and greatly restricted in opportunities for the development of their skills and talents. As I grew up in Jackson, at least we had nine months of school like the white kids, even if our equipment and facilities were inferior. Like any parent, I wanted my child to have the opportunity to develop his abilities to the fullest. This demanded desegregation. Nevertheless, there were those in the black community who did not want to be bothered with desegregation as a remedy to the problem. There was a natural fear of the unknown associated with desegregation. Some preferred to remain isolated and protected from the unknown risks attendant with sending children into the white world for education. Others feared economic reprisals if they lifted their voices to demand change. As for me and my household and those who joined with us in Mississippi's first desegregation suits, by 1960 we were demanding our freedom and demanding it now!

Paradoxically, by the time my child was gaining the long-sought opportunity to attend the school of his choice, frustration with lengthy court battles and disappointment with the seemingly tenuous fruits of the black political alliance with white liberalism was leading new and angry black voices to raise the cry of black separatism. As I saw it then, and still see it now, separatism in America has always relegated minorities, whether black, native American, or Hispanic, to a second-class status at the back of the bus. I despised this and long ago rejected any second-class status in anything. I wanted and still want the whole cup of America, not half a cup. I wanted for all children the right and opportunity under the law to the full benefits of the best education that our taxes made available. Little by little, and through hard work and suffering, the promise of the *Brown* decision became a reality first in Biloxi, then in Carthage and Jackson, and eventually in all of Mississippi.

The Biloxi branch of the NAACP was essential in providing the organizational structure needed to sustain our local effort for school desegregation. In 1961, just a few months after its organization, and while it carried on vigorous voter registration efforts and carried forward the beach desegregation case, the Biloxi branch began petitioning the local school board to desegregate the schools. A good part of my job as president of a local branch involved dissemination of information to members to keep them informed of relevant national and local developments. Another part of my duty in those early days was to work with the branch executive committee to define local problems and devise means by which these problems might be overcome. From the very beginning, we sought to develop a large cadre of capable local leaders within the local branch to oversee in detail the many programs which we undertook. The Biloxi branch always sent plenty of folks to NAACP leadership conferences to learn about issues and strategies for problem solving. By 1965, as I told one interviewer, another group of generals had come forward in our branch, so that no one man dominated, and a number of persons were qualified and capable of taking over the leadership at any time.[1] Only through broad leadership development were we able to attack on so many fronts at once. If a problem arose, we communicated and we complained—to employers, to school authorities, to government officials, and to any other appropriate persons. If the problem could not be resolved through negotiation, we were prepared to go to court, and by the mid-1960s, everyone knew this. Beach desegregation, school desegregation, political action, open public accommodations, fair employment practices, voter registration, youth activities, public health, and public housing all became objects of organized and concerted action from our branch. Because we became predictable players in every arena, and because we were untiring in our efforts, we gained the respect, if not the accolades, of our adversaries.

The schools presented us with a special object of concern. Embodying as they do the hopes we have for our children, schools are especially dear to the hearts of all parents. Almost from the beginning of our life in Biloxi, and long before Gilbert, Jr., started to school, Natalie and I became involved in the PTA at Nichols, the all-black high school, and Perkins, the all-black elementary school, in Biloxi. I was the team physician for the Nichols tigers and president of the boosters club. We saw firsthand the material deficiencies that black children continued to endure in a segregated school system. On the athletic field, Nichols teams wore old and tattered uniforms. The band instruments were old and not in as good condition as they should have been. The lab equipment for teaching science at Nichols was handed down or salvaged from the discards at the white high school. Textbooks in Mississippi were made freely available to the students, but the textbooks at Nichols were noticeably older and more tattered than those at the white schools. Of course, I had seen this very type of discrimination in the Jackson schools as I grew up, but I found it impossible to accept such treatment for my own child once the 1954 *Brown* decision was on the books. I will be the first to tell you that we loved and valued the teachers at Nichols, and we loved and respected the work of Mrs. Fannie Nichols, the principal. Mrs. Nichols and her dedicated staff made valiant efforts to compensate for substandard physical conditions through cultivating close personal relationships with students not only at school but at the churches and in their homes.

No school can be any better than the board or the community power brokers will allow it to be. In Biloxi, the all-white school board physically neglected Nichols and limited its curriculum. The school board placed the emphasis at Nichols on training in the manual arts. Thus many courses in the sciences, foreign languages, and higher math which were available at the all-white Biloxi High School were not available at Nichols. In mathematics, for example, Nichols students were limited to one year of algebra and one course in geometry. Moreover, until the employment of Mrs. Clare Rhodeman, the board failed to provide college-capable students at Nichols with adequate academic counseling to help them prepare a course of study for the professions. Even though the emphasis at Nichols was on the manual arts, courses in office skills and basic typing and certain industrial trades that were regularly available in the white schools were seldom, if ever, offered at Nichols. Such neglect on the part of the Biloxi school board resulted in a far smaller percentage of Negro students entering college than was the norm for graduates of the white high school.

Until our son started to school, we had no legal standing for filing a complaint in court. Once he enrolled in the all-black school, we encountered several practices on the part of the superintendent and the board that infuriated us. We discovered, for example, that one means by which the superintendent and the board covered up a deficient curriculum was to order that our son and every other child at Nichols and Perkins be given grades on their report cards for courses not even taught at the black schools. Our first awareness of this came when our son brought home a grade of "C" or "S" for music, art, and gym. Now, Gilbert, Jr., had shown an early aptitude for music and art. I think he has perfect pitch. He can pick up almost any song and play it by ear or sing it in a short time. We noticed this natural talent and got him into private music lessons with Mrs. Pettus. So he read music, knew the notes, sang well, and was learning to play the piano. He was also gifted in drawing. When that report card came home showing a grade of "C" (satisfactory) in music, art, and gym, Mrs. Natalie Mason wanted to know the reason why. Come to find out, no music, no art, and no gym classes were being taught at all at Perkins Elementary School. These courses were taught at the white elementary schools, and, because the schools shared a common report card form, the central office instructed the black teachers to just put a grade of "C" on black kids' report cards even though the courses were not being taught to them. We were disgusted. This practice was unfair to the child. If the child either excelled or needed improvement in these subjects the parent would never know. Moreover, this administrative grading decree left the false impression with parents that the children were being taught courses that were actually unavailable to them in the black schools. As a PTA officer Natalie raised a vigorous protest and was incensed to find that even some of the black teachers failed to see the wrong in such a practice.

Something similar happened with the teaching of typing at Nichols High School. To impress parents at a PTA meeting at the beginning of one school year, the district central office set up typewriters in one of the Nichols classrooms. This created the clear impression that the students at Nichols would be offered new courses in typing. The impression was misleading. The typewriters were there, but courses in typing were not being taught. The Biloxi school superintendent, Mr. Robert D. Brown, promised black parents that other courses would be added to the Nichols curriculum, but those promised courses were never scheduled. These incidents suggested that the administration was putting in a window dressing of showpieces and promises to cover up for its own unwillingness to invest in teachers and broader course offerings for Nichols students. Some wanted to let the issue die, but Natalie protested vehemently. There was some new construction on the campus at Nichols in the late 1950s and early 1960s as part of the state of Mississippi's effort to placate black complaints with buildings and thus put off the day when someone would file that first desegregation suit. We needed the classrooms that were built in 1957, and the black community needed the new gymnasium built in 1963. Nonetheless, new buildings could not cover up the board's basic failure to provide equal opportunity at the black schools. With the Masons and the

Biloxi branch on their case, this school board might run from their lawful duty to all of the children, but they couldn't hide.

For me, however, desegregation was about more than substandard facilities or the type of curriculum that the board made available in the black schools. Education is more than what's in a book. A good education should provide the opportunity for students to learn from interpersonal relationships and personal interactions with people from all backgrounds, religions, cultures, and races. We live in a multicultural society in a multicultural world. I wanted my son to know little white children, and I strongly believed that it would be good for the white kids to know my child and other black children. To deprive children of the firsthand learning experiences that could help them become more proficient in navigating this multiracial, multicultural America seemed unforgivable to me as a parent. I believed that sound educational principles demanded that the school reflect the society in which we live. I still believe this. I held strongly the dream of one America. My personal philosophy that we are all God's children demanded that we all—red and yellow, black and white—learn to understand and tolerate one another. I abhorred segregation and all that it stood for. The law of the land said Jim Crow had to go. I for one was ready to invoke the law on behalf of my son and others similarly situated to see that they got their lawful opportunity, as the courts had said, "with all deliberate speed." So it was that in 1960, soon after our son started to the first grade in Biloxi's all-black Perkins Elementary School, we began the long process of petitioning and negotiating with the board for our rights under the Fourteenth Amendment as interpreted in the 1954 *Brown* decision. Three years later, the Biloxi Municipal School System became the first school system in Mississippi to send black and white children to school together.

Gilbert Rutledge Mason, Jr., my son and the lead plaintiff in the Biloxi school desegregation suit, actually started to the first grade in the fall of 1959, when he was only five years old. Mrs. Fannie Nichols personally recruited him out of kindergarten because she thought he was near enough to his sixth birthday, to come in January of 1960, to handle the first grade. She had seen him recite Lincoln's Gettysburg Address in front of a PTA meeting that year. Mrs. Nichols was also concerned about the transfer of a large number of families of black airmen away from Keesler Air Force Base, which might leave the all-black Perkins Elementary School short of first-grade pupils that year. Mrs. Nichols may well have been concerned about the need to justify enough teacher units to keep her faculty together that year. Two or three other older five-year-olds were also taken into the first grade that year.

Gilbert, Jr., thrived in school. He got a great deal of encouragement at home. He understood at an early age that his mother and I believed in striving for excellence in everything that is worthwhile. His standardized test scores were high enough that Mrs. Nichols had him skip one of the lower elementary grades. They recommended later that he skip an upper elementary grade or two, but we would not allow that, because we were concerned that he was already one and a half to two years younger than everyone else in his class. By the time he was in the fifth grade, the teachers put him to work on the high school annual staff. In everyone's estimate, Gilbert, Jr., was a bright child who could obviously benefit from the advanced college preparatory science and math courses that were available at Biloxi High School but not at Nichols.

Many times in later years people have asked me why it took so long after the *Brown* decision in 1954 for us to get into court to challenge Mississippi's segregated school system. They point out that we did not actually file suit in federal court until 1963, almost nine years after the *Brown* decision. In response, I point out that I had talked about school desegregation from the time I arrived in Biloxi in 1955, but I had no actual standing for filing suit until my own child entered school. In the spring of 1960, while Gilbert, Jr., was in the first grade, we actually petitioned the Biloxi school board for desegregation for the first time. Nothing came of this petition. After the bloody wade-in, and after the Biloxi branch came into existence, I undertook serious discussions with Medgar Evers about school desegregation. On October 11, 1960, Medgar Evers wrote to Robert Carter, the NAACP legal counsel in New York, requesting on our behalf national NAACP assistance for "a group of citizens in Biloxi, Mississippi, who would like to file suit to desegregate the schools for the second semester term, 1960–61."[2] This is likely to have been the first request for assistance in desegregating a Mississippi public school district that the national NAACP office received. The timetable which Medgar suggested for attaining our goal was reasonable, but it turned out to be unrealistic. We soon discovered that the courts would expect us to exhaust all administrative remedies within the school system before petitioning a judge for a hearing on our complaint. The Biloxi branch petitioned the Biloxi school board again in 1961, before the Ole Miss desegregation crisis and while the arch-segregationist Ross Barnett was still governor of Mississippi and still shoveling money to the State Sovereignty Commission to fight desegregation. It was the spring of 1963 before we had exhausted local school board administrative remedies without producing any results. Only then could we go to court. Even though we had the *Brown* precedent in hand, and the law was on our side, it took almost three years from the time of our first inquiry to Robert Carter for us to get into the courts. It then took nine additional months of litigation to obtain the appeals court ruling that finally opened the Biloxi schools under a freedom-of-choice desegregation plan.

Because white elected officials at the time were quick to blame "outside agitators" for any signs of local black discontent with Jim Crowism, the question often arises as to where the initiative came from for school desegregation. Was it outsiders, or was it truly local folks with gumption who started the ball rolling for school desegregation? The answer should be clear at this point. We in Biloxi initiated every phase of our struggle. We looked to the national and state NAACP organizations for advice and legal assistance, but we set our own priorities and chose our own targets and tactics. In the matter of school desegregation, I believe that our example and determination in Biloxi played a role in inspiring Medgar Evers's decision to file on behalf of his children in Jackson. The courts eventually consolidated what came to be known as the Mason case in Biloxi with the Evers case in Jackson and the case of Mrs. Winston Hudson and her sister Dovie for Dovie's daughter in Carthage, Mississippi. Thus, the plaintiffs in all three of Mississippi's first school desegregation cases gained federal court relief simultaneously in 1964.

In Biloxi, the Masons intended to file suit whether anyone else did so or not. However, as we discussed the school situation with our friends, we discovered many kindred spirits who felt as strongly as we that it was an affront to the dignity of mankind to deny a person equal protection under the law. In this case our children were being denied an equal opportunity for a full educational curriculum. The beach case had taught us about the harassments and risks that anyone challenging Jim Crow would have to be ready to face. I had that inspiring October 18, 1960, letter from Medgar Evers announcing his own desire to join a desegregation suit on behalf of his children, and telling me of the depths of his commitment to the point that he was "willing to risk even life itself."[3] School desegregation was risky business. It required a showing of faces and a signing of names to petitions. Any black person who went public as a plaintiff in a lawsuit could expect white employers to immediately label him or her a trouble-maker, and bring economic pressure to bear or do worse. Mrs. Winston Hudson told us about the harassment which she endured connected to school desegregation up in Leake County. The atmosphere in Carthage grew so threatening that she sat up all night with a shotgun literally across her lap so that others could sleep.

As we began to move toward a court confrontation over the schools in Biloxi, I contacted some of the parents of school-age children that I knew through my medical practice to determine their interest in joining a suit. Others came forward on their own when they heard that there was a move afoot to desegregate the Biloxi schools. Many families expressed an early interest in the suit, and many people showed up at our home for meetings. Everyone had to be serious about the risks involved and the punishments that could come down on us, and they had to consider the possibility of losing their jobs. When it came time to actually sign petitions, the group had narrowed down considerably. In the end, thirteen families felt able to join our school desegregation suit on behalf of their twenty-five children. All of us were insulated from the kind of economic pressure that white employers so often brought to bear on blacks who bucked the system. Beyond the Mason family, the final group included two full-time ministers, Reverend Thomas Davis and Reverend Oscar (Orange) Harris, Mrs. Johnnie Brown, a waitress whose husband owned a dry cleaning business, and another nine who were were totally beyond the reach of any local economic blackmail because they were federal employees working as instructors or blue collar laborers at Keesler Air Force Base. These were Mr. Lewis Black, Mr. Harold Boglin, Mr. Samuel Edwards, Mr. John Elzy, Mr. Rehofus Esters, Mr. Jack Martin, Mr. Clifton Nunley, Mr. Christopher Rosado, and Mr. James E. McKinly.[4] Four of the thirteen school desegregation plaintiffs, John Elzy, Sam Edwards, Harold Boglin, and Clifton Nunley, were also active members of my volunteer bodyguard group.

Over a period of many months, the parents and sometimes the children met often at my office or in our home. All of these plaintiffs held a deep loathing for segregation. They were united in their determination to secure for their children the best education possible through the Biloxi school system. These were hardworking people who had dignity. The plaintiff families shared a strong Christian faith and viewed segregation as morally wrong. In our meetings we discussed the problems that we could expect, and we developed plans for transporting the children to the desegregated school and for making sure that every child had proper school supplies and clothing. We discussed ways that we could support the children in this new and possibly intimidating educational environment. We wanted to insure their academic success, but we also wanted the children to be prepared for any taunting, exclusion from extracurricular activities, or other hostility they might encounter. We cautioned children not to respond to acts of hostility in kind, but rather to report negative incidents and names of perpetrators to their parents. Parents were in turn to report incidents to the Biloxi branch. We concluded that it would be even more important than ever for the black parents to be actively involved in PTA in the desegregated schools.

Of course, there could be no desegregation case until we established through petitioning and negotiation that the Biloxi school board would not act to bring the schools into compliance with the *Brown* decision and the Fourteenth Amendment. So, we got on the board's agenda and sat down face-to-face and eyeball-to-eyeball to try to negotiate desegregation. When we met, we simply proposed that the board come up with a good faith plan to totally dismantle all vestiges of the dual school system based on race. Superintendent Robert D. Brown was hostile to the desegregation proposal from the beginning. Superintendent Brown talked like Ross Barnett. Brown would not admit that Negroes were discriminated against and remained basically negative in his dealings with us throughout. At first, the five-person board dug in its heels, too. Dr. D. L. Hollis had a "segregation forever" outlook. The board's disposition, no doubt, reflected that of the majority of white citizens in Biloxi, who had put Laz Quave into office as mayor in 1957. There was a tendency for the board to try to avoid the real issues of federal law and the Constitution with the argument that the black folks they knew weren't interested in integration, and that our group somehow did not represent overall black feelings about the matter. Odd that they would think that a segregationist all-white board in Mississippi would be more able to read the minds of black folks and represent their true feelings better than the community's own black physician and its own black NAACP executive committee. With staggered terms, the board's makeup changed, and we dealt with several board members whose names did not appear on the list of defendants when we finally filed suit.

However, over time, we discovered some spirits of moderation among the school board members. Mrs. Dudley Andrews, for example, was friendly and had an open mind. Dr. Peter Pavlov, a white dentist who treated both black and white patients in an office with a nonsegregated waiting room, was sort of a moderate. Dr. J. A. Graves, the board's president when we filed suit, was also a moderate. Mr. C. T. Switzer, Sr., was harder to read. Perhaps he was ambitious for elective office and held his cards close to the vest. Our meetings were generally moderate to friendly in tone. I think that Biloxi officials were concerned for the tourist trade. The 1960 riot over beach desegregation had hurt business. The local powers that be wanted no more bad publicity. Officials at Keesler Air Force

Base weighed in on the side of moderation and an easing of racial tensions in the town. Especially after the 1961 election of Mayor Guice, it was evident that city leaders wanted things handled peacefully. Nonetheless, however friendly their outward deportment in our meetings, the board refused to act. The state of Mississippi, in the person of Governor Ross Barnett, made public statements prohibiting any desegregation during this time. The board's delays and failure to act meant that we actually wound up petitioning them several times. By the fall of 1962, we thought that it was evident that the board would not act on its own accord, and we were ready to file the lawsuit.

Meanwhile, in September of 1962, Governor Barnett's demagogic resistance to federal court orders mandating the admission of James Meredith to the University of Mississippi set off the shameful riots at Oxford that left two persons dead and dozens wounded. Some thirty thousand federal troops had to be deployed on the university campus to bring things under control. The NAACP financed Meredith's legal fight to desegregate the university. Because our home had by this time become a familiar stopover place for civil righters, James Meredith spent some time with us before his admission to Ole Miss. As Medgar Evers had done, James Meredith slept in my den. Meredith met with attorney Constance Baker Motley at our house.[5] It was apparent to me that James Meredith had guts. A veteran, he was very intelligent, and he had a rare sense of feeling not only for his own people but for all of the citizens of Mississippi. Meredith had a very strong ego. He knew that as the first black to attend Ole Miss he would be making history. A strong ego was probably necessary for anyone to succeed in making the kind of stand that Meredith made; unfortunately, however, a later consequence was that he became alienated from the NAACP.

The Ole Miss riot demonstrated just how explosive the school desegregation issue could become in Mississippi in 1962, if a deceitful demagogue decided to use it to build a racist following. On October 2, 1962, two days after the Ole Miss riot ended, attorney J. Francis Pohlhaus, the NAACP's Washington bureau counsel, wrote me to suggest that if we wanted to go ahead with a suit for desegregation of elementary schools in Mississippi, we "should seek the maximum Federal protection." Pohlhaus believed that the best way to ensure maximum protection would be for the federal government itself to become the moving party in the lawsuit. I was aware that the Justice Department had filed suit in Virginia seeking desegregation of schools in Prince George County, which received large sums in federal impact aid. The presence of Keesler Air Force Base and a veterans hospital in Biloxi meant that the Biloxi schools also received substantial federal impact aid. This suggested the possibility that we could get the Department of Justice to file suit in Mississippi. Pohlhaus argued that even if the Justice Department would not file suit, a case involving children of military personnel would be less likely to subject the parents and children to physical violence.

We took these suggestions to heart. The Justice Department agreed to undertake school desegregation suits in Biloxi and Gulfport on the same premise upon which they had undertaken the Virginia suit. Therefore on January 18, 1963, when the first Mississippi school desegregation suit was filed, the Justice Department filed as the plaintiff seeking to prevent both the Biloxi and Gulfport school systems from segregating any dependents of military personnel or federal employees. Judge Sidney Mize once again put up predictable barriers. In April he ordered the division of the suit, mandating separate hearings for the Gulfport and Biloxi issues. On May 16, 1963, Judge Mize dismissed the Gulfport case, holding that the federal government had "no standing as plaintiff in this court and does not have the requisite interest in the subject matter to maintain the action. . . ." The trial judge held that "only natural persons are entitled to the privileges and immunities of the Fourteenth Amendment . . . ," and that the federal government was not a person and "could not sue for the deprivation of civil rights of others." On June 18, 1963, Judge Mize dismissed the Justice Department's Biloxi school case on the same grounds.[6]

Since we had known from at least May 16 that Judge Mize would dismiss the government's case, we prepared a separate school suit with NAACP support and filed it on June 5, 1963, on behalf of the thirteen parents and twenty-five children in Biloxi. We thought that in contrast to the Justice Department, we most definitely had, in Judge Mize's words, the standing of "natural persons." We, of course, had decided to assume whatever risks might come with our action. These continued to be potentially very serious. Within the next three weeks after our school suit was filed, Medgar Evers was assassinated, and we staged the June 23, 1963, wade-in. Moreover, it had been less than a year since the rioting at Ole Miss. My hospital privileges had been threatened after the 1960 wade-in, and the officers of the local medical society had threatened to go after my medical license when I had protested my exclusion from a meeting with a gubernatorial candidate. On a personal level, I was aware that challenging Jim Crow in Mississippi could be like challenging a rattlesnake. While I was not afraid, I believed in being prepared. If the authorities went after my medical license in retaliation for my civil rights activities, I owed it to my family to be prepared to make a living elsewhere. We knew that if there was a cloud hanging over me from having a license revoked in Mississippi, it would be difficult to get a license in another state. We decided that I should take out and maintain an Ohio medical license in 1963, as a kind of insurance against the Jim Crow rattlesnake striking at our vulnerable spot. I had no intentions of leaving my home unless forced out, but with an Ohio medical license as a backup, I was now prepared to continue making a living whatever retaliations might come to us in the wake of the school suit or any other activities we might choose to undertake.

Over the months after the school desegregation suit was filed, I came to know and respect the NAACP education and legal defense attorneys who were associated with our case. Marian Wright Edelman handled matters for a time. Constance Slaughter-Harvey was active in our case, as was Constance Baker Motley, who is now a federal judge. Attorneys Jess Brown, Derrick Bell, Cassandra Flipper, Jack Young, and Carsie Hall worked with us for a time. Then there was the young black attorney Fred Banks, who also came aboard to handle part of the case. Fred Banks was a distinguished graduate of my alma mater, Lanier High School, and of Howard University School of Law. After assisting us and after laboring in the vineyards of civil rights for many years, Fred Banks went on to become a member of the Mississippi Supreme Court. I am proud to have been associated with each of these attorneys early in their careers.

Once in court, in June of 1963, we asked Judge Sidney Mize for a speedy trial on the merits of the case. We petitioned the judge to issue an injunction to permit our children to attend school on a nonracial basis beginning in September of 1963. We argued that the Biloxi school board should be required, within sixty days, to submit a plan to accomplish the complete conversion of the dual-race school system into a unitary, nonracial system over a three-year period. We held that such a plan should reassign children, teachers, administrators, and school staff on a nonracial basis, and that the plan should eliminate racial distinctions in budgets, facilities, school curricula, and extracurricular activities.[7] Notwithstanding the recent integration of Ole Miss and the nine years of case history and precedents under the *Brown* decision which insured that segregated schools would not stand, and notwithstanding the state's poverty, Mississippi's attorney general, Joe Patterson, put the world on notice that the state would fight us. On behalf of the state and the Biloxi schools, on June 10, Patterson filed a motion to dismiss the suit. The attorney general and the school board had the audacity to argue that, after almost three years of petitioning and negotiating with the board, the Negro plaintiffs had not exhausted "any of the administrative remedies available." The state also argued that the federal court had no jurisdiction in the matter, and that we as parents had no standing for undertaking a legal action on behalf of our own children.[8]

Given his previous behavior in desegregation cases, no one should have been surprised that on July 5, 1963, Judge Mize upheld the state's petition and ordered the case dismissed. This did not stop us. Ten days later, we put up a $250 cash bond and filed notice of appeal to the Fifth Circuit Court of Appeals. On July 26, the court of appeals denied our request for an immediate injunction against the Biloxi schools pending their ruling, but within seven months the appeals court announced a decision. In the interim between the time of our appeal and the time of the final ruling, two other Mississippi cases were combined with ours. The Carthage or Leake County desegregation case of Mrs. Winston Hudson and her sister Dovie on behalf of Dovie's daughter, Diane, and the Jackson case in behalf of Medgar Evers's children, Darrel, Rena, and James, had also been dismissed by federal district judges in Mississippi. Of course I retained a special affection and deep respect for Mrs. Myrlie Evers and her children. I also developed a great admiration and fondness for Mrs. Hudson, who took to calling me her wade-in doctor. With our cases combined, one unified Mississippi case was presented to the Fifth Circuit Court of Appeals.

On February 14, 1964, the Fifth Circuit Court of Appeals reversed Judge Mize's lower court ruling and ordered that the Biloxi Municipal Separate School District and others be condemned, *in solido*, to pay court costs. On March 4, the appeals court issued a preliminary injunction, subsequently made permanent, restraining and enjoining the Biloxi Municipal Separate School District from requiring segregation of the races and ordered the district to make arrangements for admission of children to its schools on a racially nondiscriminatory basis "with all deliberate speed, as required by the Supreme Court in *Brown v. Board of Education of Topeka*." The appeals court ordered the district to submit a plan by July 15, 1964, ending the dual race system in at least one grade by September 1964, along with plans to dismantle the dual system in at least one additional grade each school year thereafter. Within a few months, the courts ordered the Biloxi system to develop a plan for extending desegregation to at least three additional grades for the 1965–66 academic year, and the court later ordered that the dual school system in Biloxi be disestablished in its entirety in 1967.

Having won this initial victory in the spring of 1964, we wanted to refine our plans for supporting our children when school opened in the fall. Friends told us that the Biloxi school system had long before developed its desegregation plan. We were told that during the local petitioning process, when my son was in the second grade, school officials had called for his permanent records and transcripts as if they believed desegregation to be imminent. Natalie always believed that the board was determined to purposefully develop a plan that would leave our son's grade segregated as long as possible. That is the way it worked out. Gilbert, Jr., the lead plaintiff, wound up waiting about three years after the original court victory for the opportunity to desegregate the formerly all-white Michel Junior High School. However, in the spring and summer of 1964, we were not privy to any school board contingency plans that may have been drawn before the courts ruled. For this reason, our preparations of children and parents could not be exact until after July 15, 1964, when the board presented its plan to the judge. Only then did we know which schools and which grades would be desegregated beginning that fall. As it turned out, only the first graders were admitted to school on a nonracial basis in the fall of 1964, but second, third, and twelfth grades were opened the next year.

In our preparations for school desegregation, we coached students and parents on nonviolent responses to harassment. We did not want any incident to ignite a disturbance that might threaten the safety of the children. The newspapers quoted Biloxi school superintendent R. D. Brown as saying that "the NAACP wanted a confrontation." After years of negotiation with us, I thought that was a rather foolish statement for an educator to make. These were our children, our loved ones. We wanted no confrontation. In fact, a smooth and secure integration was in the best interests of the black community at large and might help others who wanted to choose a different school overcome their reticence and come forward to claim their right. However, we believed that segregationist die-hards in the white community might try to provoke an incident in order to discredit integration. We tried to anticipate such things and prepare ourselves to react in a nonviolent way.

As fate would have it, one week before the opening of the first desegregated school in 1964, a dreaded incident of the type for which we had tried to prepare occurred at Howard Memorial Hospital. I had been up most of the night with a laboring mother who delivered her baby just before 7:00 A.M. After the delivery, I went down to the hospital cafeteria to get a cup of coffee and a biscuit. Just as I sat down at a table, some young white punk came up behind me and poured hot scalding coffee down my neck and back. Stunned, I bolted out of that chair, and loudly demanded, "Man, was that an accident, or did you do that on purpose?" When he coolly replied, "It was no accident," I let him have it with a left-cross jab. I punched him so hard that it knocked him down and slid him across the floor like he was a mop. My watch went flying off my arm. I picked up a chair and was ready to hit him again if he tried to retaliate. The other people in the cafeteria began saying, "Don't hit him with that chair." The white guy made no move to attack me again, so I put the chair down and ran upstairs to the emergency room to get someone to look at my back and document the burns. Dr. Maurice Taquino was in the emergency room, and he quickly determined that I had first-degree burns on my back and neck. They said that my assailant had a broken nose. Someone called the police, and the white guy charged me with assault. When the policeman inquired, no one in the cafeteria at the time would own up to having seen how the incident developed. While the officer investigated, I went on back to my Division Street office and began seeing patients. A short while later, a Biloxi police officer appeared at my office to inform me that I was under arrest, scalded back and all. They took me down and booked me for fighting in a public place.

No one ever likes being arrested, but the bigger threat was that the publicity coming out of the incident would create a negative atmosphere for school desegregation, or that the medical staff at the hospital might rescind my staff privileges or press the state to revoke my medical license. Melvin Zar from the NAACP Legal Defense Fund, along with Knox Walker, handled the case for me. At the time, I believed that the hot coffee was thrown on me in a deliberate effort to provoke an incident that would discredit the impending desegregation of the schools in Biloxi. However, since serving blacks in public accommodations such as a hospital cafeteria was a very new feature of Mississippi life in the summer of 1964, the scalding coffee may have been a protest of my very presence in this formerly all-white eating place. My defense was fairly simple. I was acting in self-defense. My attacker had assaulted me with a dangerous weapon— scalding-hot coffee. We had case law to support this defense. When the medical staff called me in for a hearing on charges of fighting in a public place, one physician, now retired, rebuffed my defense, stating, "You can't say that a hot cup of coffee is a dangerous weapon." There are now some famous cases involving fast food restaurants that affirm our contention that hot coffee is dangerous, and as such it would be classified as a dangerous weapon if used in an assault of the type that was perpetrated against me. In the end, the majority of the hospital medical staff stood by me. I did not lose staff privileges, and no one attempted to go after my medical license. Likewise, the authorities later dropped the public fighting charges that had been filed against me.

On Monday, August 31, 1964, for the first time in Mississippi history, black children and white children started to school together in desegregated first-grade classrooms in Biloxi. Our own planning as well as the federal and local planning for a smooth and incident-free school opening paid off. We expected that up to twenty-three Negro children would exercise their right to enter the first grade in desegregated classrooms. White House documents show that in the days leading up to desegregation, FBI agents stayed in constant contact with the Biloxi police. The Justice Department sent twenty deputy U.S. marshals to Biloxi to augment local law enforcement and to be available to protect the children in any emergency. The deputy marshals were equipped with two-way radios and tear gas. With the Ole Miss riots just twenty-four months behind us, the U.S. marshals were prepared to delay the black children's entry into school until it was clear that the situation was completely under control. Backup federal contingency plans called for a select force of eighteen hundred Mississippi National Guardsmen to be deployed to Biloxi under presidential orders within a few hours of any significant disturbance. A similar federal security plan was developed to back up desegregation for the two to five black children expected to enter school in Carthage, Mississippi, later that week. However, as the date for the desegregation of the Biloxi schools drew near, Justice Department officials were confident that our local authorities could and would preserve law and order.[9]

On August 31, 1964, desegregated classes opened in Biloxi in an atmosphere of calm. Twenty-one black children presented themselves[10] on the first day for enrollment in four previously all-white elementary schools. U.S. marshals were stationed in strategic places around the schools, such as Mrs. Madge Curet's attic, which overlooked the playground at Gorenflo Elementary School. Biloxi police were visibly present at each of the schools. Our transportation committee drove the children right up to the school door, where a marshal met them to usher them inside. Thankfully, no hostile white crowds materialized to create a sense of tension or crisis. Our desegregation went along peacefully. In fact, even though U.S. marshals remained on the scene for nine months, there was not a single school-based incident the entire first year of desegregation. There were some fairly predictable incidents of harrassment of parents away from the school grounds. Mr. Alexander Bellamy, the treasurer of the Biloxi branch, whose first-grade daughter was in the group that broke the color line, was approached by ruffians who threw refuse and urine on him one evening outside his home. About one-third of the parents reported harrassing or threatening phone calls. Two years later, after I was appointed to the Mississippi Advisory Committee of the U.S. Civil Rights Commission, I heard of serious incidents in other places in Mississippi, such as parents losing their jobs or welfare benefits or being kicked out of rental housing because they chose desegregated schools for their children. But to my knowledge there were no reprisals of this type perpetrated upon any of the Biloxi plaintiffs.

During the second year of desegregation, when the twelfth grade desegregated, there were some minor incidents at school. Natalie heard about it most because she ran a sort of homework support group at our house several nights a week for the kids involved in desegregation. At the high school there was some name-calling. Occasionally some white kids would purposefully step on the heel of a black kid in crowded hallways. There were even episodes of white kids ganging up around a black kid in the rest room to bully or intimidate him. One high school student, John Robert Esters, who went on to become a medical doctor, was so upset by the harrassment one day that he vomited and lost a dental appliance in the toilet. Some three years after the original court order, urine and feces were thrown on Mrs. Delores Rankin outside Central Junior High as she waited for her son, Don.

On the other side though, there were examples of white children reaching out in kindness to these black students. When Gilbert, Jr., started at the formerly all-white Michel Junior High School, his name sometimes appeared in the paper as the lead plaintiff on the desegregation suit against the school board. One day some of the white kids saw his name in the paper and came up to him, wanting to know what he had done to get into trouble with the school board. It was amazing to us that he ran into a lot of young white kids who wanted to know what they could do to help him. Gilbert, Jr., was very considerate of others and always had a lot of friends, but in high school he had white friends who would offer him rides home after school. Some of these white kids spent time with him in our home and invited him to their homes. Several of those friendships have endured for decades now.

In spite of the vicissitudes of those early years, I think that we as parents concluded that desegregation was worth the sacrifices made. I know that Gilbert, Jr., for example, got access to the best science labs and the best advanced math courses available in the Biloxi schools. He excelled and went on to become a medical doctor himself. Students who wanted to learn office skills got access to training on office machines that was just not available at Nichols. The children themselves, surrounded by a sea of white faces, got the satisfaction of knowing that they were blazing a trail for others and knowing firsthand that they could compete with white students on an equal basis. They got the advantage of coming to know students and teachers of a different ethnic group, and they learned that, while racism had a mean face, not all whites shared the race hatreds that made so many white Mississippians sick. These children and their parents did a lot to move race relations forward in Mississippi. They proved that desegregation could be made to work peacefully. Our children did not have to give up their black identity to do this. Gilbert, Jr., stayed very involved with his church, the NAACP Youth Branch, and with his neighborhood Scout troop. Because our child got the best high school education available, and because he learned to cultivate friendships among every race of people, I considered school desegregation a success.

Under a legal precedent called *Singleton*, the first desegregation plans in Biloxi were so-called "freedom of choice" plans. No one was forced to do anything. In later years, as integration progressed, the Biloxi branch became very active in seeing that black teachers did not lose their jobs as a result of declining enrollments in black schools. We insisted that teachers be transferred with the students. In 1970, when massive integration and the total dismantling of all vestiges of the dual school system was decreed, these guarantees to black teachers became a part of the court orders governing the process, along with the requirement that no school in the system have a black enrollment that exceeded 40 percent of the student body.

Busy as we were locally with planning for school desegregation, the summer of 1964 saw some signal gains for the larger civil rights movement in Mississippi and in the nation. Under the umbrella of the Council of Federated Organizations, of which Aaron Henry was president, the Freedom Summer voter registration projects got under way across the state, culminating in the formation of the Mississippi Freedom Democratic Party. The Freedom Democrats, led by Aaron Henry and Fannie Lou Hamer, launched an unsuccessful nationally televised challenge to the all-white, hand-picked regular Mississippi delegation at the 1964 Democratic National Convention in Atlantic City. The Freedom Democrat challenge failed to dislodge the regulars, but did effect a change in party rules which made possible a successful Freedom Democrat, or "Loyalist," challenge to the regulars in Chicago four years later. The summer also saw the passage of the sweeping Civil Rights Act of 1964, which utterly destroyed the legal foundations of state laws dictating segregated public accommodations.

With intensive preparation for school desegregation under way in Biloxi, with voter registration drives going, and with the task before us of organizing the Biloxi branch to systematically test restaurants, hotels, and theaters for compliance with the new civil rights law, I was too busy to make it to Atlantic City with the Freedom Democrats. From Biloxi we elected Reverend A. A. Dickey.

Just as soon as President Johnson signed the Civil Rights Act of 1964 into law, the Biloxi branch formed a Food and Restaurant Commitee, an Entertainment Commitee, and a Public Accommodations Committee to test local compliance with the new federal requirement that businesses end segregation in public accommodations and open to all citizens without regard to race. The Biloxi branch's Food and Restaurant Committee developed a plan called Operation Food. We listed the restaurants and hotels on the coast and systematically sent people to ask for service and report the result. Most of these tests went along without incident, because white businessmen were ready to comply. One of the first establishments we tested was the Longfellow House restaurant in Pascagoula. Someone had led us to suspect that this elite restaurant might not open its services to us. James Crawford, who later got a medical degree, and his wife, June, now a psychologist, reported that when they arrived at the Longfellow House, to their surprise, the waiters and maitre d' were standing at the door with their arms open, welcoming them and saying that the management wanted the NAACP to know that black diners were welcome. Natalie and I drove over to the Longfellow House without reservations a few days later and found Charles and Myrtle Davis already there. We were all served courteously.

Other establishments at first resisted or showed signs of tension. The Crawfords reported that while they were being served at the Howard Johnson restaurant on the beach, sheriff's cars kept coming by to check, almost as if there were a fire. When Mrs. Burnell Burney Fletcher, Mr. Joe Edmonds, and Mr. A. E. Mitchell were sent for a second test at Howard Johnson, the tension produced a little humor. When the waitress came to take their order, Mrs. Fletcher decided to have whatever Mr. Edmonds was having. However, when she looked across the table, she saw that a nervous Joe Edmonds was holding the menu upside down and had not made a choice. They've gotten many a good laugh out of recalling that episode over the years.

I became the troubleshooter for any establishment that resisted desegregation, or if we could not get anyone to go to a particular place, it fell my lot to go there and see that we got served. At first the Sun 'n' Sand in

Biloxi refused to serve blacks. I had just gotten a brand-new, canary-yel-low, 1964 1/2 Mustang prototype, one of the first off the assembly line. James Crawford and Clemon Jimerson, one of our NAACP Youth Branch officers, along with Charles Davis and Lee Oscar Johnson, piled into that brand-new Mustang with me and headed for the Sun 'n' Sand. We went in, sat down, and got ready to order. The waitress, as if getting the lay of the land, said, "You're that doctor from Biloxi, aren't you?" I replied, "Yes, I am a doctor from Biloxi." We got served a wonderful meal, but when we returned to the Sun 'n' Sand parking lot, we found that someone had taken a knife and scraped a line in the paint all the way around that brand-new Mustang. Like the Sun 'n' Sand, the Buena Vista gave some folks trouble the first time it was tested. Then Sam Edwards and I showed up. Sure enough, the Buena Vista staff resisted, but we insisted. We got served at the Buena Vista. Mr. Gus Stevens, a man whom I later got to know as a friend, ran a first-class nightclub on the beach in Biloxi. Gus Stevens brought some big-name acts and nationally known entertainers to his Biloxi club on a regular basis in the 1960s. When Mr. and Mrs. Crawford showed up to test Gus Stevens's compliance, Gus refused them service. We reported it to the Justice Department, and Gus Stevens was indicted for violating the Civil Rights Act. Subsequently, Gus Stevens began serving on a nonracial basis in compliance with the law.

Sometimes we got served but found our stay uncomfortable. I remember the first time that we tested desegregation of the Saenger Theater. There were a couple of ramshackle black theaters in town, and no black had ever been into the Saenger before 1964. Mrs. Marie Anderson, Mr. Lonnie Ducksworth, and teenage twin boys accompanied our group to see *Robin and the Seven Hoods.* The tension was so great outside the box office that one of the teenagers suffered a grand mal seizure. The rest of the group went on into the theater. Inside we had the unique experience of trying to watch a motion picture in a dark theater with folks in the back throwing ice at us and rolling cans under our feet. However, this type of harrassment soon faded away, and later groups attending the Saenger reported no problems. We tested everything that summer from ritzy res-taurants to the bus station. Clem Jimerson and some of the other mem-bers of the Biloxi NAACP Youth Branch got served in the bus station uneventfully, and then bought tickets on a bus to New Orleans to verify the end of the back-of-the-bus rule. I followed the bus to New Orleans and brought the group home after an uneventful ride. Very quietly, a meaningful local revolution in adult race relations got under way in the summer of 1964, as a direct result of the Biloxi branch's systematic demanding of full compliance with the new federal civil rights laws.

During that same summer, I met Roy Wilkins personally and had the honor of introducing him at a meeting at the New Bethel Baptist Church; he was touring the South as part of the COFO Freedom Summer voter registration emphasis. The year before, Dr. Felix Dunn and I both had attended the 1963 meeting at the Dooky Chase Restaurant in New Orleans where COFO was born. It had become apparent in 1963 that the major civil rights organizations in the country—the NAACP, the Southern Christian Leadership Conference (SCLC), the Congress of Racial Equality (CORE), and the Student Nonviolent Coordinating Committee (SNCC)—needed some mechanism by which to coordinate their efforts. The famous March on Washington in support of President Kennedy's civil rights bill was being planned. All of these different groups were appealing to people for personal or financial support for their pet projects. The NAACP was the big dog, and when the other groups got into financial difficulties there was a tendency for them to appeal to the NAACP to bail them out. In June of 1963, Roy Wilkins had publicly expressed his frustration at an NAACP convention, charging that other groups "furnish the noise," while the NAACP "pays the bills." Wilkins was frustrated enough with the lack of coordination to advocate that NAACP members refrain from giving money to the other groups.[11] Through the creation of an intergroup council, COFO attempted to bring some strategic coordination to the movement. Aaron Henry, the president of the Mississippi Conference of the NAACP, was elected president of COFO. All of the organizational members of COFO found that they could agree on the need for black political empowerment through voter registration in the South as a top priority.

COFO's 1963 and 1964 voter registration efforts brought the appearances not only of Roy Wilkins but also of James Farmer from CORE, Bob Moses from SNCC, and Lawrence Guyot, a Pass Christian native, also with SNCC. As in other places in Mississippi, freedom schools were organized in Biloxi and Gulfport and at the Methodist Gulfside Assembly at Waveland near Bay St. Louis. In Biloxi the United Benevolence Association Hall was made available for a freedom school under the coordination of SNCC. COFO brought hundreds of white students from the North to work on voter registration projects in the South that summer. Many of them worked in Gulfport and Biloxi. Some stayed in the home of Reverend A. A. Dickey in Biloxi. The freedom schools taught people how to register and vote, and they taught basic literacy skills as well. These activities brought Michael Schwerner, Andrew Goodman, and James Chaney to Mississippi, where they wound up giving their lives for freedom. We were all shocked and saddened at their murder up in Neshoba County that summer.

As part of their voter education program, COFO and SNCC decided to hold mock county and state conventions to teach new voters how the national party convention delegate selection process was supposed to work. In Mississippi at the time, there was no presidential primary, so in the Mississippi Democratic Party, the delegate selection process began at precinct caucuses where delegates to county conventions were elected. County conventions then elected delegates to congressional district conventions and to the state convention, where delegates to the national convention were elected. This outcome was undemocratic on two counts. The delegates were for the most part handpicked by local power brokers, and literacy tests and other discriminatory devices systematically excluded blacks from the voter rolls and thus from participation in the delegate selection process. The teaching process that SNCC created paralleled the process in the state Democratic Party. It was widely known that the delegates picked in the regular party process that year would be bound by the unit rule to act as little more than pawns for Mississippi's segregationist establishment politicians who meant to oppose civil rights planks in the proposed platform of the national Democratic Party.

The kind of political awareness that had developed among black citizens of the Mississippi Gulf Coast in 1960 and 1961 came to the rest of the state in 1964. The frustrating unfairness of the delegate selection process that would mean that no Mississippi convention vote would be cast for a strong civil rights plank in the Democratic platform led COFO leaders to organize the Freedom Democratic Party to challenge the credentials of the all-white regular Mississippi delegation at the Democratic convention in Atlantic City. From Biloxi, Reverend A. A. Dickey was elected a Freedom Democrat delegate.

In Atlantic City, Mrs. Fannie Lou Hamer and Ms. June Johnson took the national spotlight and told of the beatings and threats they and others had received while trying to register to vote in the Mississippi Delta. The national television networks carried parts of Mrs. Hamer's testimony live. President Johnson was reported to have been very disturbed by the Freedom Democrat challenge, because he feared losing the formerly solid Democratic South to the Republicans. Johnson's operatives were said to have offered the Freedom Democrats the compromise of two seats in the state's regular delegation. I understand that NAACP officials and COFO officials like Aaron Henry favored accepting the president's compromise. SNCC leaders and Mrs. Hamer, whose pure charisma had given her great sway with the group, determined to reject the compromise. Having worked so hard to get to Atlantic City, the Freedom Democrat delegates and their supporters were disappointed, and many were deeply disillusioned with this outcome. From their perspective the evils of Mississippi voter registration had been laid out before the nation, and there should be no compromise with that evil. The Mississippi Freedom Democrat delegation accepted Mrs. Hamer's view and walked out rather than compromise.

Lyndon Johnson went on to win a landslide victory over Republican Barry Goldwater in the fall of 1964, but the president won without the backing of five traditionally Democratic southern states. Among southern whites, the 1964 Civil Rights Act produced a backlash against the national Democratic Party and President Johnson. In Mississippi, President Johnson carried only 20 percent of the vote. The voting rights issue gained new life during the next few months. The Selma-to-Montgomery march in 1965 further dramatized the serious difficulties which blacks encountered in voter registration in the South. The cumulative effect of Mrs. Hamer's 1964 testimony together with events at Selma led to the passage of the Voting Rights Act of 1965, which sent federal registrars south and put an end to literacy tests and other machinations devised to deny blacks the vote.

In hindsight, we can now see that the Civil Rights Act of 1964 and the Voting Rights Act of 1965 set in motion a real civil rights revolution. When we saw the crumbling of so many long-standing racial barriers in education, public accommodations, and voting rights, for many veteran civil rights activists it was if the walls of Jericho were tumbling down. Many of us experienced the mid-to-late 1960s as years of important breakthroughs for desegregation, black opportunity, and black political empowerment. In Biloxi, while we endured the legal maneuverings over the beach, we achieved notable successes in voter registration and peaceful school desegregation. We also tested fully the guarantees of free access to public accommodations set forth in the Civil Rights Act of 1964. These were difficult but meaningful achievements. The price that we paid for these gains reinforced my respect for every human being who sacrifices to expand the realm of human freedom and dignity.

However, where we saw important breakthroughs, others saw these years as filled with frustration and disillusionment, ending with the assassination of Dr. King in 1968. For the disillusioned among us, the slow but steady gains won in the courts, in the Congress, and through vigorous local activism in a thousand cities and towns paled beside the yet unsatisfied three-hundred-year hunger for black opportunity. Reflecting this mood in Canton, Mississippi, in 1966, Stokely Carmichael raised the cry of "black power." Other voices of black separatism arose out of frustration, extolling us to turn inward and reject the dream of one America. In the late 1960s, much to the distress of Mrs. Fannie Lou Hamer, whose Christian conviction made her hate racism of any kind, SNCC voted to expel its white members. CORE renounced integration as a goal, and the Black Panther Party announced an antiwhite program. These developments gave black separatist connotations to the term "black power" in the late 1960s.[12]

On a personal level, my faith never waivered that the judicial and legislative destruction of Jim Crow, the desegregation of the public schools, the opening of public accommodations, and the attainment of free access to the ballot across the South would set in motion profound, permanent, and positive changes in the quality of life for black Americans and for all Americans. I never lost faith in the goals and philosophy of the NAACP. I believed then and believe now that every honorable means must be used to combat all of the forms of discrimination that scar, deform, and distort American life. However, as technology shrank the world in the space age and the information age, I could see no realistic place for economic, political, or even social separatism.

Some in the movement lost patience with long court contests. No one had experienced any more fully than we in Biloxi the depths of frustration involved in litigation strategies to advance the cause. However, I believed then and I believe now that you must be prepared to speak a language that your adversary will understand. Your adversary may not understand a street demonstration or a long negotiation, but in America your adversary will always understand a court order. In the end, no advance is secure in America unless it is enforceable in court. Therefore, though I grew impatient, I never lost faith in the ultimate wisdom of court strategies to advance the cause of human rights.

Similarly, no one had learned the difficulties and limitations of political coalition building any better than we did in Biloxi. The 1964 Democratic convention's rejection of the Freedom Democrats was very difficult for some of us to understand. Whereas by the late 1960s, some had grown totally disillusioned with the movement's alliance with white liberals and were questioning the so-called "integrationist" goals of the traditional civil rights organizations, I believed that I saw the fruits of our hard work and perseverence in a righteous cause being slowly realized. We, too, were disappointed when white moderates could not or would not steer a steady course toward justice and fairness with the speed and exactitude we wanted. However, if we were disappointed with the pace of progress, we were encouraged by the general direction of the changes which we were able to effect in both the temper and substance of local politics. In Biloxi we employed every tool known to the civil rights movement. We put on the whole armor of God, from public demonstrations and civil disobedience to court battles, economic boycotts, and political empowerment. By the late 1960s, each of these tools had borne at least some fruit at some time in Biloxi. None of these tools was taken up without suffering or sacrifice on someone's part. Yet the Biloxi branch of the NAACP persevered, and, in staying its course, it grew in power and influence in both the black community and the white community.

Black separatism has never had any real appeal to me. In the late 1960s, a Black Muslim separatist group led by Imari Obadalli made a down payment on some property out from Bolton, Mississippi, that had once belonged to my great-great-grandfather, Harrison Mason. Obadalli proposed to set up the Republic of New Africa there. This experiment never had any broad appeal in Mississippi. In trying to shed some light on why separatism has had so little following among blacks in general or Mississippi blacks in particular, I can only speak for myself. No one loves the distinctive cultural life of African Americans more than I. No one takes greater pride in the outstanding achievements and contributions of black artists, craftsmen, educators, scientists, and statesmen than I, and no one is more determined to see those contributions duly recognized than I am. Yet, I abhore racism of any kind, black or white. I am proud to be a black man and an African American man, but, with W. E. B. Du Bois, I aspire to a pride of self that is "so deep as to scorn injustice to other selves. . . ." With Du Bois, I also want to hold to a "pride of lineage so great as to despise no man's father. . . ."

As a purely practical matter, I also believe that any group that closes itself to the larger world and fails to develop the skills to interact with others will inevitably cripple itself and restrict its own opportunities for creativity and growth. I have always supported, honored, admired, and encouraged black entrepreneurship. I have worked to destroy artificial constraints on equal economic opportunity. However, economic interdependence is a fact of American life and a fact of global life. Our task is to make sure that black Americans are equipped to compete on an equal footing with all others so that our genius and hard work are rewarded with a fair share of the national economic pie that we have helped to create.

In summary, the village I have always wanted for myself and my family is the village called America. The village of which I want to be a part is a village of many faces and many races. It is a village where people of widely varied backgrounds work together and associate freely and without fear. It is a village where difference can be celebrated and understood as contributing to the creativity of the group. It is a village where we know enough about each other to respect and learn from each other. In the village of my dream, no person is second class. It is a village where every generation of its different and complementary peoples dedicates itself to the hard work of combating fear, prejudice, and misunderstanding in order to make the collaboration productive and meaningful. That is the only dream that I was willing to work for and die for in the early 1960s.

NINE

Community Action and Hurricane Camille

*Then shall the King say unto them on his right hand, Come, ye
blessed of my Father, inherit the kingdom prepared for you from the
foundation of the world: For I was an hungred, and ye gave me
meat: I was thirsty, and ye gave me drink: I was a stranger, and ye
took me in: Naked and ye clothed me: I was sick, and ye visited me:
I was in prison, and ye came unto me. Then shall the righteous
answer him, saying, Lord when saw we thee an hungred, and fed
thee? or thirsty and gave thee drink? When saw we thee a stranger,
and took thee in? or naked, and clothed thee? Or when saw we thee
sick, or in prison, and came unto thee? And the King shall answer
and say unto them, Verily I say unto you, Inasmuch as ye have done
it unto one of the least of these my brethren, ye have done it unto
me.*

—Matthew 25:34–40.

ON THE NATIONAL LEVEL, THE DISILLUSIONMENT OF THE
left wing of the civil rights movement after 1965 was balanced by a tendency of some moderates and conservatives to conclude that the passage
of the Civil Rights Act of 1964, the Voting Rights Act of 1965, and the Open
Housing Act of 1968 meant that the movement was finished. Comfortable
conservative voices argued that there was now no more need for a civil
rights agenda. To those on the left who argued that the alliance with white
liberalism was useless and that traditional organizations such as the
NAACP were ineffective and out of touch with the grassroots, I said, "Let
them come to Biloxi." Let them see how an activist local branch re-

sponded and continues to respond to every need of the community it serves. To those on the right who argued that there was no further need for a civil rights movement, I also said, "Let them come to Biloxi," and see a local branch busy with the larger world of human rights which extended beyond the destruction of legal Jim Crow to encompass equal employment opportunity, decent housing, and early childhood health and education.

The great and menacing bastions of Jim Crowism, poll taxes and literacy tests, along with their attendant indignities and disenfranchisements, had presented obvious and easily identifiable targets for destruction in the late fifties and early sixties. The new frontier of civil rights presented more abstract and diffuse targets, but targets that were no less insidious. A malnourished child whose mental capacity is unnaturally and irreversibly constricted by the ravages of hunger has suffered a civil rights deprivation every bit as serious any imposed by segregation. Teenagers or adults who find their employment opportunities limited by prejudice, lack of training, or lack of information about training opportunities have suffered a loss in their quality of life and in their right to liberty and the pursuit of happiness. The child who starts school unprepared to learn and who falls behind and ends up a dropout has suffered an unnatural and unfair deprivation that should compel our attention with the same strength as any back-of-the-bus rule that ever humiliated a person of color. The new frontier of civil rights which emerged in the mid-to-late 1960s presented issues and concerns of a more abstract nature which required new and different types of effort undertaken and sustained over long periods of time. Affirming the basic humanity of all persons required and still requires attention to a broad array of issues—social and economic as well as legal and political. For me, the transition was natural. Our idealism never ceased to include political rights and the possibility of litigation, but it was not limited to the arena of courts or electoral activity alone. After all, when I had returned to Mississippi in 1955, I had set three goals for my medical practice: healthy babies, healthy mothers, and decent housing for mothers and children. The agenda of the Biloxi branch expanded to touch each of these areas.

My first glimpse of the potentialities for a new direction for local activism came in a November 1964 White House conference which I, as a vice president of the Mississippi Conference of the NAACP and president of the Biloxi branch, attended along with Aaron Henry, Charles Evers, Felix Dunn, and a number of other community leaders from across the South. In 1964, under President Johnson's leadership, Congress had passed the Economic Opportunities Act, which created the Office of Economic Opportunity. Many of the antipoverty programs which OEO envisioned, under the leadership of Sargent Shriver, were designed to use local initiative in the guise of community-based groups to set local antipoverty agendas and strategies. One of the key OEO initiatives was the Head Start program, which was set up to lift economically disadvantaged preschool children into health and educational readiness. The White House conference was designed to acquaint the participants with the possibilities of the Head Start program and stimulate grant applications.

I cannot say for sure exactly why I was chosen to attend the White House meeting. The Biloxi schools had begun desegregation that fall, and my reputation as an activist was by now well established in NAACP circles in Mississippi and the South. In any case, I was ready for what I heard in Washington. I discovered that Sam Yette, a former classmate of mine at Tennessee State, was working as an assistant to Sargent Shriver. I got the presentation that the other conferees received, but Sam Yette made sure that additional firsthand information got to me. The group stayed overnight in Washington and had a chance to discuss the merits of the proposal over dinner. The next day, at the conclusion of the conference, we all met with President Johnson on the South Lawn of the White House to hear personally of the president's commitment to Head Start.

However, even as we Mississippians began forming a new vision of a local antipoverty agenda, we were also doing some high-level politicking for a federal appeals court appointment for Biloxi attorney Howard McDonnell. As a state senator, Howard McDonnell had distinguished himself by introducing legislation outlawing use of the Black Annie, or bullwhip, at the State Penitentiary at Parchman. McDonnell had proven himself to be a man of character, moderation, and fairness during the many crises in Biloxi in the early 1960s. We hoped to inspire President Johnson to appoint McDonnell to a vacancy on the Fifth Circuit Court of Appeals. As I moved through the receiving line to shake President Johnson's hand, I mentioned my hope that he would give serious consideration to Howard McDonnell. The president, however, had made up his mind and did not mince his words. "It's going to be J. P. Coleman," Johnson said. Coleman had been the governor of Mississippi when the Sovereignty Commission was created and when the first Biloxi wade-in took place in 1959. Rather than follow extremist segregationists like Ross Barnett into the desert of unpledged electors or Goldwaterism, Coleman had remained loyal to the national Democratic ticket in 1960 and 1964. Still, I was not enthusiastic about this prospective appointment. Little could I have suspected that it would be J. P. Coleman who, as a federal appeals judge four years later, would write the opinion which declared the Harrison County beaches public and opened them to all citizens without consideration of race.

Of course, Head Start was the main concern at our meeting with President Johnson. Upon my return to Biloxi, I met with several persons in the black community, including Mr. John Pettus, Mr. Robert Fortner, Mrs. P. I. Green (a local kindergarten teacher), and the trustees at First Missionary Baptist Church of Biloxi. We met at Nichols High School and decided to send forward a Head Start application in the name of First Missionary Baptist Church for a program to serve seventy-five children. This was the first Head Start grant proposal forwarded from the coast. The Back Bay Mission and the Biloxi Municipal Public School System also soon made application. The Biloxi school system's application was funded at a very high level. The school system was able to get its program implemented in the summer of 1965, making it the first operational Head Start program on the Mississippi Gulf Coast. Elsewhere in our county, the Child Development Group of Mississippi, operating out of Jackson, organized some Head Start centers in Gulfport working through Mr. Robert Hoskins. Over in Pass Christian, the parochial school under the direction of Father Philip McCloone received a Head Start grant. The Systematic Training and Rehabilitation Act (STAR) was another part of the OEO community-based program package; we got it going at the old Our Mother of Sorrows school, which had just closed, on Division Street. The STAR program was focused on reaching out-of-school adults with GED and other adult education and literacy courses. My wife, Natalie, wound up as a social worker for the STAR program, and Mrs. Rosa Martin was the program writer. It is my understanding that, because of the vigor of various groups in putting forward proposals, Mississippi was funded for more Head Start slots than any other southern state. There were five different Head Start grant projects operating in Harrison County plus the STAR program.

By November of 1966, many of us on the coast who were involved in these initiatives saw a great disadvantage in several groups writing local grant programs that were, in effect, in competition with each other. The more we talked, the more logical it seemed that we would form an umbrella organization to go after a larger piece of the pie in order to serve more children. In fact, the initial federal legislation authorizing these programs envisioned local community action agencies to harness and coordinate neighborhood-based activity. The Harrison County Board of Supervisors attempted to create a community action agency topdown—that is, as a semiofficial arm of county government—with state representative Jim Simpson as its chairman pro tempore and Dr. J. O. Tate, Dr. Milas

Love, and others as board members. This county-backed agency went no-where. Energy, initiative, and commitment to the new OEO programs were coming from grassroots people across the county and not from the politicians. As community activists saw the need for coordination, we turned to Thomas Rafferty, director of the STAR program. One of the duties outlined in Rafferty's job description was to act as a community organizer. Therefore, with Rafferty's help, we sent out notices for a meeting to be held at the Harrison County courthouse in Gulfport. Beginning with this November 1966 meeting, we completely transformed the community action agency. We rewrote its constitution and bylaws to create genuine grassroots representation through a region-wide forty-five-person board. NAACP members were at the forefront of this reorganization; thus they obtained a guaranteed NAACP slot on the new board. Every effort was made to create equitable representation for each of the municipalities and areas to be served. Moreover, all of the existing grantees in the county were guaranteed representation on the new board. As president of the Biloxi branch, I was elected to the guaranteed NAACP slot on the board. As the reconstituted board for the new Harrison County Community Action Agency took shape, I was elected its chairman, and Father Philip McCloone from Pass Christian was elected vice chair; among the new board members were Mayor Francis Hursey of Pass Christian, funeral director Lang from Gulfport, and Reverend Kaufman and Reverend Regier from the Mennonite mission in Gulfport. The Harrison County Community Action Agency was later renamed the Gulf Coast Community Action Agency.

I am very proud of the accomplishments of the Harrison County Community Action Agency in its early years. We had an enthusiastic and hard-working board. Some of our meetings would convene at 7:00 P.M. and not wind up until 2:00 A.M. For the most part they were good, productive meetings. Our first director was Mr. Ray Fernandez. We quickly applied for a state charter of incorporation. Our largest program continued to be Head Start. One of the ways the Harrison County Community Action Agency fought poverty was to provide solid employment to adults caught up in poverty. We absorbed the employees of the preexisting Head Start programs and retained neighborhood-based oversight boards for each Head Start center. The neighborhood boards were answerable to the over-all community action agency board.

The poverty-stricken children we served got stimulation and training which their parents could not otherwise afford or provide. In addition to taking field trips, the kids learned the alphabet, numbers, colors, shapes, and directions—all essential to their later success in school. Beyond the classroom, we provided nutritious meals and free medical treatment to the children. At first, only Dr. Felix Dunn and I would treat Head Start children, and only Dr. J. O. Tate and Dr. George Powers would attend to their dental needs. I helped Dr. Dunn with physicals for the initial class of children, but stepped aside from any direct personal involvement in the medical program for about two years in order to avoid any semblance of conflict of interest with my role as chairman of the board. However, the workload, especially the required paperwork, became too great for Dr. Dunn, so after a couple of years I applied for and received a waiver that allowed me to resume assisting him with giving the Head Start children their physicals. One of my most poignant memories of this time is of a little black child who came in with his mother for his pre-Head Start physical. The little fellow looked at me and then turned to his mom and asked, "Mama, Mama, is he a doctor?" "Yes," the mother replied, "he's the one that brought you and your brothers and sisters into this world." Without skipping a beat the little boy said, "Well, he ain't white." Sadly, in less than four years of life this black child had concluded that you had to be white to be a doctor. I immediately saw the need these children had for positive black role models to help expand their vision of possibilities for themselves.

The agency branched out in several new directions. We administered a program called Operation Bootstrap to assist teenagers and young adults in finding employment or appropriate job-related training. We also launched ourselves into a project to develop low-income housing units. In the housing arena, the Community Action Agency acted as a broker, negotiating with OEO and the U.S. Department of Housing and Urban Development to bring their resources to the table with the Council of Negro Women and local contractor Frank Collins. The result was the TurnKey housing project in North Gulfport. With advice from Mrs. Unita Blackwell, the mayor of Mayersville, along with Dr. Dorothy Height and Mrs. Dorothy Duke, we were able to get seventy-seven new TurnKey homes constructed with sweat-equity from the new homeowners as part of the package.

Of course, as with any new institution, we had our moments of administrative difficulties as an inexperienced board trying to find its way. Our first executive director resigned in a controversy over making major supply purchases without consulting the board or gaining its consent. A gentleman named Kochek then served briefly as our director. When Mr.

Kochek left, Reverend John Aregood of the Back Bay Mission shared executive duties with Father Philip McCloone for a time. Before I stepped down from the Harrison County Community Action Agency board in 1969, we employed Mr. Doyle Moffett as agency director. The agency was stable and in good hands. It found effective ways to supply the needs of "the least of these." I took great pride in the fact that the Biloxi branch of the NAACP was the prime mover in bringing the Harrison County Community Action Agency into being.

The year I left the Harrison County Community Action Agency Board, 1969, was the year that Mother Nature sent an unparalleled calamity to Mississippi Gulf Coast residents, regardless of their race, creed, or color. On the night of August 17, 1969, Hurricane Camille struck the coast with 230-mile-per-hour winds which drove the waters of the Mississippi Sound across low-lying zones in a 30-foot storm surge. The worst-hit area was to our east in Pass Christian, but there was plenty of wind and water damage to go around. Practically the entire black community back-of-town in Biloxi was inundated with four to six feet of floodwater from the storm surge. Some 6,000 homes were destroyed along the Mississippi Gulf Coast, where 132 people were killed before the storm went inland and wreaked havoc with flooding as far away as Virginia, where an additional 200 persons lost their lives. Chaos and crisis stalked our lives for months after the storm, as all kinds of people, white and black, rich and poor, who had lost everything struggled to put their lives back together again.

The Masons at 873 Fayard Street in Biloxi struggled with all the rest. Before the storm, in good Boy Scout fashion, we had prepared a family plan to ascend to our partially floored attic in case rising waters entered the house. Gilbert, Jr., had the job of making sure the Coleman lantern was in working order and that it got to the attic. Natalie was in charge of our battery-powered radio. We watched storm news on the local television station until our electrical power went out as lines snapped in the storm's fury. As we sat in the darkness with the wind howling outside, we heard the sound of water lapping at our kitchen door. When we went to the back to check it out, we found that two inches of murky saltwater had already seeped through the door to cover the kitchen floor. We decided it was time to go to the attic, but access was through a ladder and crawl space on the back porch. When we opened the door to go out onto the porch, water poured into the house at a rapid pace. I sent Natalie and Gilbert, Jr., on up the ladder and turned back into the house to try to save a few things by lifting them off the floor. I went to the bedroom to try to save Natalie's clothes, but water was already in the chest of drawers, dresser, and closet. I could do little good. Ironically, in a surge of energy, I did manage to lift a heavy console-type television off the floor and onto a couch. By this time the carpeting was floating up, and I had to literally fight my way through the living room, back to the kitchen and on out to the porch to climb to safety in the attic with my family. Our house was eleven feet above sea level. When daylight came, the extent of our personal disaster became apparent. Our home had been invaded by four and a half feet of sea water. As the water receded, it left a briny mud coating on floors and walls and all that it had touched. Everything we owned was destroyed. Our two automobiles had been completely submerged in water and ruined. My office was ruined and all of my medical equipment was destroyed by four and a half feet of water. I was unable to see patients at the office for two weeks. We had money in the bank, but no change of clothes, no food, no water, no electric power, and no transportation to take us to where these items could be obtained. However, we were not alone. Thousands of people, white and black, rich and poor, were in the same predicament. Common loss evoked a spirit of camaraderie that mitigated some of the suffering of those awful days immediately following the storm.

Once the enormity of the devastation had sunk in, I called an immediate meeting of the executive committee of the Biloxi branch of the NAACP. We had a dynamic branch executive committee, including Mrs. Natalie Mason (a trained social worker), Mr. Robert Fortner (a civil servant), Mrs. Myrtle Davis, Mrs. Marjorie Reese, Mr. Jack Martin, Mr. E. E. Jackson, Mr. Charles Davis, and Mr. W. O. Hill. We quickly identified food, drinkable water, and housing as the most urgent needs of the community, and we began actively seeking and disseminating information on when and where these necessities might be available. Natalie and Mrs. Elzy began organizing the social service by surveying the community for its most urgent needs. In these days of disaster, the Biloxi branch reached out to the needy not only in the black community but in the low-income white neighborhood on "the Point" to the east of us on the Biloxi peninsula. During the first couple of days, the disaster looked like it had drawn everybody together, black and white, to create a true spirit of community. Matt Lyons, director of the Biloxi Housing Authority, called a meeting, which I attended. We respected each other, but we had often been adversaries on issues related to the desegregation and proper upkeep of public housing units in Biloxi. The spirit of that meeting following the hurricane was so good that I complimented Matt Lyons on the direction in which he appeared to be going. The personnel of Keesler Air Force Base were gallant in distributing water. They had water flown in, delivered it to the hospital, and made it available to the general public in large cans that looked like gasoline cans. Although they could not go onto private property, heavy equipment operators from the Naval Construction Battalion Base in Gulfport began clearing the worst of the storm debris that blocked the streets. All of this made me hopeful. The Red Cross opened up for emergency food and clothing distribution at the Howard Avenue Community Center. The mood was so positive to start with that I even telegrammed Roy Wilkins at the national NAACP offices to say that it looked as if everybody was working together.

However, once the most pressing survival needs of the community were addressed, that initial surge of almost euphoric emergency cooperation receded, and a bureaucratic nightmare ensued. The federal Office of Emergency Preparedness set up an office in Biloxi but staffed it with people who proved to be totally unprepared for a disaster of the magnitude of Camille, and who did not know what to do for folks looking for money or materials to begin making home repairs. There was virtually no provision for emergency food stamps or medical services for the displaced. Had not the weather been unusually dry in the days after the storm, our water-related losses would have been much greater. Some private relief groups such as the Salvation Army performed beautifully. Others like the Red Cross brought in staffers with dehumanizing, denigrating attitudes toward those in need. No doubt the primitive state of governmental disaster relief programs placed too much responsibility on private charities and over-burdened their staffs. However, Red Cross workers in Biloxi developed a reputation for needlessly humiliating those seeking relief, especially black folks, whom they often seemed to make beg, cajole, or grovel for assistance. In the bureaucratic maze, victims of the disaster were treated not as people with feelings and a deep need to preserve their dignity but as if they were almost invisible. Over time, an emerging pattern of ill treatment of blacks and poor white people at the hands of the Red Cross required the Biloxi branch to become a virtual mediator and advocate in seeing that individual needs were fairly met. We became again the community advocates for the powerless, the voiceless, the poor, the unemployed, and the dispossessed who were in every sense "the least of these."

Insensitive Red Cross staffers administered a system of vouchers which were apparently intended to make relief available on the basis of need, but there appeared to be no rhyme or reason behind their decisions to grant clothing or goods vouchers to one family but not to another similarly situated or worse off. I had lost my automobiles and all of my clothing except two jumpsuits. My home and office were badly damaged. I had a pair of flip-flops but no shoes. There were no stores open in our area, and no transportation was available to take us elsewhere. In this situation, I attempted to get a pair of shoes from the Red Cross. Red Cross relief workers denied me any shoes, because, as the Red Cross worker put it, "Well, you're a doctor and you don't need help." I said, "Yeah, but Camille did not know that when she took everything I own." Family members eventually sent us some shoes and clothing. However, others were denied who had no family resources to fall back upon. Families in need of relief found themselves bounced from the Red Cross to the Small Business Administration and back to the Red Cross for recovery loans and grants for housing repairs or to replace clothes, furniture, and household items. If a family qualified for an SBA recovery loan, the Red Cross was no longer involved. Only after the SBA found a family ineligible would the Red Cross step in with long-term assistance. My nurse, Mrs. Melvina Davis Smith, received emergency food aid from the Red Cross right after the hurricane, as did thousands of others like her. She, like other victims, was then sent to the SBA to determine her loan eligibility. The SBA denied her husband and her a loan because she was considered too old; at fifty-two, she could not be relied upon to pay back a ten-thousand-dollar loan before retirement or death overtook her. Denied at the SBA, she and many others were thrown back on the Red Cross for long-term help.

The local Red Cross chapter, like most Mississippi institutions, had a recent history of discrimination. Only in 1969 was the first black person, Dr. John Kelly, named to the local Red Cross board. Now, as events unfolded after Camille, old attitudes and habits reappeared. Black folks appeared to be the last to be waited on and the last to receive Red Cross services. Clothing and food came to us last. Many people, worn down by the red tape, intricate bureaucratic processes, and sense of humiliation, just gave up, saying, "I don't want to be made to feel like I am begging." By September 9, 1969, so few black folks had been served, and of these so many complained of bad treatment at Red Cross hands, that the NAACP branch conducted a survey of 143 families to determine their needs and the responsiveness of the Red Cross in meeting those needs in the three weeks after the storm hit. We discovered that almost all of the 143 families surveyed were dissatisfied. We found that twenty families had received emergency aid from the Red Cross immediately after the storm, but had not been told that they would have to register again for long-term recovery assistance. Twenty-five other families had been given forms to fill out for long-term assistance but had not returned the forms because the need to return them had not been emphasized. The Red Cross made it a prerequisite that individuals apply to the Small Business Administration for loans before completing their Red Cross applications for long-term aid. The Red Cross had not called any public meetings to explain these procedures to residents in the storm impact area. Sixty families had returned forms requesting long-term assistance, but no Red Cross caseworkers had called upon them by September 19. Another thirty-two families had their cases closed, and most were not satisfied with their disposition and wanted the cases reopened.

With these facts in hand, the executive committee of the Biloxi branch met with the director of Red Cross operations on September 19, 1969, to present our findings and try to effect changes in the Red Cross approach to our community. We demanded that Red Cross personnel stop denigrating black folks seeking help. We demanded that more local blacks be hired to work with Red Cross relief services as a means of helping the agency present a fair and friendly face to those in need. We asked that either the Biloxi branch of the NAACP be permitted to bring handicapped, elderly, and disabled persons to Red Cross headquarters for immediate service, or that the Red Cross allow NAACP volunteers to take necessary forms, information, and services to these victims. Finally, we asked that the Red Cross files be opened to the branch so as to cross-index Red Cross information with our survey information. We made it known that we would be prepared to stage street demonstrations if the problems were not resolved. As a consequence of this confrontation, which was coupled with follow-up letter writing and branch meetings, business really picked up at the Red Cross. Three local blacks were hired. The Biloxi branch was permitted to aid the elderly, handicapped, and disabled, and the Red Cross files were opened for our research and inspection.

However, the grudging demeanor and denigrating attitudes of Red Cross service workers did not go away. Many poor persons, white and black, made four, five, six, or more visits to the Red Cross. Each time they were made to wait in line for a considerable time and then turned away and told to return another day. After repeated appointments many found themselves denied aid, or they were given such small amounts of assistance as to make the time invested in waiting appear to be a wasted effort. Our Biloxi NAACP began investigating cases closed unsatisfactorily as they were brought to our attention. When we thought there were good grounds for reopening a case, we wrote letters asking the Red Cross to reconsider its decision. These efforts usually produced positive results. However, because local NAACP intervention was vital to so many people, there were days when my office looked more like a social welfare agency than a medical practice. We were certainly willing to take on these chores as part of our broadened human rights commitment, and we undertook interventions on behalf of white as well as black citizens. However, we felt that a more rational, professional, systematic, fair, and courteous Red Cross effort would have made it unnecessary for us to expend so much energy and time in this way.

These problems were compounded by the fact that large numbers of people in the black community were left unemployed because of damage to local businesses, and state government failed to make information available on how to file for unemployment compensation in such an emergency situation. Further, few citizens on the Biloxi peninsula and fewer black citizens had flood insurance on their dwellings and household furnishings. Those of us who did have insurance were caught in a bind between urgent needs to make repairs and the machinations of adjustors and insurance companies who often offered immediate checks for those willing to take low-estimate settlements. Those who could afford to hold out longer often found that their insurance benefits somehow magically increased, but not usually to the full value of items lost or needing repair. We therefore had an immediate need for legal services. There was a legal aid office operating on a federal legal services grant in the Biloxi court-house. We were concerned that the fact that there were no black attorneys on staff tended to make needy black persons reticent about seeking help there. We were able to get several black attorneys from the Lawyers' Committee for Civil Rights Under Law to come down from Jackson to offer assistance, but the district attorney declined their offers to assist the county's own legal aid attorneys. In fairness, I must say that there were no reports of discrimination on the part of local legal aid attorneys in handling these many insurance claims. Our concern was that the lack of black faces might discourage people from seeking the legal aid they needed in dealing with insurance companies.

Emergency housing was another pressing need. The U.S. Department of Housing and Urban Development responded by sending hundreds of mobile home units to the affected area. However, when the trailer units first arrived, there was little information about the conditions on which this form of long-term housing assistance would be made available. The result was far fewer black applicants than would have been expected given the serious damage to dwellings in the black neighborhoods. Mr. Matt Lyons of the Biloxi Housing Authority consulted the Biloxi branch's executive committee. We were quick to identify a serious lack of communications and the existence of inaccurate rumors that kept black folks from applying for these units, which were set up on existing housing authority sites. The specter of long-term unemployment in the wake of the storm damage made many families fearful of taking on additional rent or house payments, which were rumored to range as high as sixty-five to eighty-five dollars per month. The Biloxi branch took responsibility for distributing accurate information about the more generous terms available based on need. The response from HUD was sufficient to insure that, within a few weeks, no one was without adequate shelter for the winter. We did raise complaints about continuing patterns of segregation in public housing. Three of Biloxi's four existing public housing developments were desegregated, but one site remained virtually all white despite our constant protests.

On another front, black community leaders across the coast held out hope that clean-up and reconstruction efforts in the wake of the storm would be a stimulus to black entrepreneurship. With plenty of work to go around we hoped that small contractors and black contractors would get a fair share. However, for a small operator to be successful in a clean-up or reconstruction bid, a substantial up-front capital outlay was often necessary in order to purchase additional tractors, trucks, or other equipment and tools. The SBA seemed just the agency to provide loans for such capital outlays, and with lots of work guaranteed it looked like minority operators might now easily qualify for equipment loans. Dr. Felix Dunn, the president of the Gulfport branch of the NAACP, became the point man for gathering and distributing SBA information to minority contractors. Unfortunately the great hope felt at early SBA staff meetings with minority contractors in Gulfport and Biloxi went largely unfulfilled. Red tape at the SBA was as bad or worse than Red Cross red tape. The SBA proved to be difficult in its insistence on collateral to back loans to expand minority operations. Even where sufficient collateral existed, there were long delays between application submissions and loan approvals. Dr. Dunn's personal SBA application for loans to repair his home and office entailed at least a five-month waiting period for approval. As a result there were far fewer minority SBA loans than our assumptions of fairness had led us to expect.

Local NAACP leaders brought these problems to the attention of local authorities where appropriate, but we also laid our observations boldly before the U.S. Senate Special Subcommittee on Disaster Relief, which held hearings in Biloxi in January of 1970. The subcommittee was chaired by Senator Edmund Muskie and included Senator Bob Dole, Senator

Birch Bayh, and Senator William Spong. From three days of hearings in Biloxi and additional hearings in Virginia, this subcommittee proposed legislation which totally reformed federal emergency responses and led to the creation of the modern Federal Emergency Management Agency. I gave lengthy testimony, as did Mrs. Marjorie Reese of our branch, Dr. Felix Dunn of the Gulfport branch, and Dr. J. O. Tate of Pass Christian. Our local NAACP leadership candidly and publicly brought each of our concerns to the senators. We gave voice to the dispossessed. We felt that we were heard. We had the satisfaction of seeing federal legislation enacted to meet many of our concerns. The responses of FEMA and the Red Cross to recent storms have shown a vast improvement in speed, fairness, and sensitivity. We think that the candor and assertiveness of a dedicated group of local civil rights activists in Mississippi in the late 1960s and early 1970s contributed substantially to that improvement.

In addition to dealing with deficiencies in private and federal disaster relief, the Biloxi branch became concerned with the state of Mississippi's own tardy recovery response. In the fall of 1969, Governor John Bell Williams appointed a special Governor's Emergency Council to help plan for and coordinate the Mississippi Gulf Coast's long-range reconstruction. As first announced, the Governor's Emergency Council was all white and all male. Having endured the storm of the century, which ignored no person based on race or gender, the Biloxi branch was determined that the state's recovery planning should not ignore any significant segment of the community. Our local black political power had been growing with increasing voter registration throughout the 1960s. On the coast, because of a sufficient black turnout in the Regular Democratic Party caucuses leading up to the 1968 Democratic National Convention, I was elected a national convention delegate in the Regular (rather than the alternative Freedom Democrat) delegate selection process. The Biloxi branch flexed that political muscle by lodging a vigorous protest when Governor Williams announced the appointment of his all-white, all-male emergency council. We enlisted the assistance of state representative Robert Clark, the first black elected to the Mississippi legislature since the end of Reconstruction. We complained both to the governor and to the Senate Committee on Public Works as it was making plans for the Gulf Coast hearings of the Special Subcommittee on Disaster Relief. Others joined us in objecting to the lack of representation of the total population on this potentially vital recovery board.

Just days before the U.S. Senate Special Subcommittee on Disaster Relief opened its hearings in Biloxi, Governor John Bell Williams decided to expand his emergency council by adding three black men and a white woman to its composition. I was appointed to the expanded Governor's Emergency Council, along with Dr. Douglas Conner of Starkville and Mr. Travillion, a black funeral director from Pascagoula. We joined prominent bankers and businessmen to help shape the coast's future. I had just stepped down as chairman of the board of the Harrison County Community Action Agency, and I felt that I was able to bring to the table significant insights about the community that would be unavailable to other members of the council. I hoped that my own familiarity with individuals in high and low places would serve as a leveling influence as we reviewed reconstruction proposals, grant applications, and loan requests.

As a member of the Governor's Emergency Council, I came to know and respect several other members whose attitudes transcended the state's image of recalcitrant resistance to change. I was particularly impressed with Meridian businessman Gil Carmichael, who was one of the founders of the modern Mississippi Republican Party. It is sad that many right-wing elements in that party today reject Carmichael's moderation. Over the past twenty years, the Republican Party in Mississippi has become a comfortable home for many former Democrats who are conservative and segregationist. I never for a moment saw a hint of any racial bias in Gil Carmichael. Gil Carmichael combined a businessman's acumen and a scholar's habit of careful thought with a genuine love for humanity. He was in many respects a visionary who held out the hand of friendship to all. I had no doubt that Gil Carmichael shared my view that positive race relationships and a climate affirming human dignity would be keys to Mississippi's future progress and success in economic development. I was proud that Mississippi could produce such a fine human being. I also learned from attorney Edward Brunini's astute appraisals of the potential opportunities before us. I valued my acquaintance with Mr. Leo Seal, an important coast banker. I believe that my time on the Governor's Emergency Council was well spent. No council or committee accomplishes all that is hoped for at its inception. This group did exercise a positive influence in shaping reconstruction policy and priorities, and it was able to provide additional insight and feedback to the federal government that was used in the legislative reshaping of federal emergency responses.

I had made quite a personal journey during the decade of the 1960s. From appearing before a municipal judge and being convicted as a repeat offender for venturing onto a segregated beach, I had moved to the rarified air of the Governor's Emergency Council. My commitment to civil rights and to local activism remained unchanged. If anything, these broadening experiences made me even more cognizant of the importance of the struggle for human dignity and opportunity to the overall well-being of Mississippi and America. While the nature of the civil rights agenda had changed, the importance of carrying on the struggle had not. The destiny of the nation is, after all, tied inextricably to the fate of "the least of these."

TEN

Inclusion, Influence, and Public Responsibilities

If you can trust yourself when all men doubt you,
But make allowance for their doubting too;
If you can wait and not be tired by waiting,
Or, being lied about don't deal in lies,
Or, being hated, don't give way to hating,
And yet don't look too good, nor talk too wise: . . .

If you can talk with crowds and keep your virtue,
Or walk with kings—nor lose the common touch; . . .
If you can fill the unforgiving minute
With sixty seconds' worth of distance run—
Yours is the Earth and everything that's in it. . . .
—Rudyard Kipling, from "If"

WHEN GEORGE WASHINGTON'S RAGTAG ARMY TOOK THE surrender of the British troops at Yorktown during the American Revolution, a British army band played a tune called "The World Turned Upside Down." As a part of the second American Revolution, the civil rights revolution of the 1960s, I never heard that tune played, but I certainly understood its meaning. The world of Mississippi politics literally turned upside down in the late 1960s. A poor black boy delivered by a midwife on Riggins Alley in Jackson, Mississippi, had made his way from sitting in the back of the bus to receiving a presidential invitation to the White

House, and, with some insistence, to obtaining a state governor's appointment to his emergency council. This did not happen in a vacuum. It happened because freedom-loving Mississippians in Biloxi and elsewhere filled every "unforgiving minute / With sixty seconds' worth of distance run. . . ." By the time of Hurricane Camille, political inclusion was before us. Our influence was rising, and with that influence came responsibility. Beyond the Governor's Emergency Council, there were other federal, state, and local appointments on the horizon as we moved slowly and sometimes haltingly from systematic exclusion to systematic inclusion. There were new lessons to be learned that could only be learned in taking up a share of the responsibility in decision making for the community at large. From the outside we had learned to diagnose the ills of official policy. Now, we had to make the leap from diagnosis to treatment. African American southerners had to undertake the hard work of helping to build and revitalize their cities, their states, and their nation from inside the political and governmental arena.

To me, the most powerful symbol of a world turning upside down was the appearance of several of President Richard Nixon's closest advisors visiting in my home in back-of-town Biloxi, Mississippi, to discuss an appointment to serve on the president's Mississippi Advisory Committee to the Cabinet Committee on Education. In 1970, the Justice Department called a halt to any further delays in school desegregation in the South. Seven southern states with five hundred public school districts faced a crisis of their own making. In Biloxi, we had successfully desegregated the schools beginning in 1964. However, there were plenty of predictions of doom across the South. Some thought that the Citizens' Councils would create massive white resistance or violence. Others speculated that there would be a nearly total white abandonment of the public schools across the Deep South. In places where there had been little effort toward school desegregation, emotions were running high. To his credit, President Nixon decided to create a special Cabinet Committee on Education, headed by Robert Mardian, to recruit local leaders in the affected states to advise and assist federal and local school officials in making safe and peaceful transitions from segregated to unitary school systems.

The president sent several of his closest assistants to Mississippi to interview me and other potential committee members. I, Gilbert R. Mason, Sr., great-grandson of a slave, welcomed into my den at my home at 873 Fayard Street, back-of-town in Biloxi, Mississippi, presidential assistant Robert Mardian, Postmaster General Red Blount from Alabama, Nixon advisor Fred Larue from the Mississippi Gulf Coast, and Attorney General

John Mitchell. There in my home we talked about school desegregation and the background to our local school desegregation suit.

The next thing I knew, in June of 1970, I received an invitation to come to the White House to meet with President Nixon. The president had invited sixteen Mississippians to serve on this, the first of the state advisory committees. In the East Wing of the White House, six black Mississippians and ten white Mississippians sat down with federal officials to discuss school desegregation.[1] I sat at the table with Mr. Warren Hood, a Mississippi furniture manufacturer with fourteen factories who also sat on the Mississippi Oil and Gas Board and on the boards of the Masonite Corporation, Deposit Guaranty National Bank, and Standard Life Insurance of Jackson. Mr. Hood had a reputation as a moderate in Mississippi politics. In the middle of lunch, he leaned over to me and said, "We want you to be chairman of the Mississippi Advisory Committee." I was flattered, but I declined his suggestion. I told Mr. Hood that we, meaning black leaders in Mississippi, respected him for his civic activities and his reputation for fairness. "We want you to be our chairman," I said. Mr. Hood agreed to accept the chairmanship of the committee, if I would accept the vice chairmanship. On that basis we went forward with the work. We hired Dr. Kirby Walker, retired superintendent of the Jackson public schools, as our executive director. Dr. Walker had been Jackson's school superintendent when I finished at Lanier. He had signed my diploma. Now, I was vice chair of a committee that hired him.

This was an interesting committee. Its makeup pointed to the possibilities for cooperation across racial lines that might build a new day in Mississippi. On the president's Mississippi Advisory Committee, I and other NAACP activists like Jack Young and Doug Conner sat with white moderates like Warren Hood, Gil Carmichael, and Owen Cooper. There were rumors that one of our other white members held less moderate views. I never knew if that was true or not. However, at our press conference in Washington, a reporter asked President Nixon, "How could you get an active member of the white Citizens' Council to join a committee with the president of the Biloxi branch of the NAACP and the president of the Jackson branch of the NAACP?" President Nixon answered, "Because all of them are good men."

Over the next several months, a part of the work of the committee involved receiving input and advice on controversial matters such as school busing. Sometimes we heard from ordinary citizens, parents, and school officials. We met again with President Nixon and Attorney General John Mitchell and representatives from the other state advisory committees in New Orleans in August of 1970. Our wives were invited to join us there and meet Mrs. Nixon. There was a big regional meeting in Atlanta where Elliot Richardson and George Schultz led us in a discussion of busing. I wrote a paper on busing in which I concluded that the good to be gained from desegregation and the opportunities for children to interact with persons of all races fully justified using this and every available tool. I found the opportunities to exchange ideas and experiences with members of other state advisory committees to be a valuable part of this committee's work.

Closer to home, from 1970 to 1973 the Mississippi Advisory Committee worked to make Mississippi school districts and citizens' groups aware of the emergency assistance funds which the federal government made available for distressed school districts to aid them in making successful desegregation transitions. Our role was to act as a liaison between the president's cabinet and local schools, PTA groups, and others interested in strengthening public education in Mississippi. We surveyed school superintendents to gain insight into their opinions and recommendations. We listened and sent advice back to the cabinet and to the Department of Health, Education, and Welfare. In turn, we passed on to local school districts the information and insights that we had gleaned. We conducted the initial review of grant applications from local school districts under the federal Emergency School Assistance Program of 1970 and made recommendations as to which proposals merited funding. The first such grant application was approved in July of 1970, and, by the end of the year, 95 of Mississippi's 150 school districts had received aid under the Emergency School Assistance Program. We met frequently with representatives of the Mississippi School Boards Association and made grants to strengthen the work of PTA groups throughout the state.

The result of these efforts between 1970 and 1973 was a transition to desegregated schools that was smoother and much more peaceful than most people had anticipated. Most important, the level of tax support for the public schools remained constant. I believe that our influence was positive in every way. I regret only the resegregation that has occurred in Jackson and the Delta region of the state as whites have continued to show a decided tendency to flee from black-majority public schools and school districts in favor of private academies. Still, close to 90 percent of Mississippi schoolchildren attend the public schools of Mississippi in 1999, some twenty-nine years after the final desegregation decree came down.

In the late 1970s, as we put the Mississippi Democratic Party back together, on three occasions President Carter invited me and other state party leaders from across the South to the White House. In August of 1977, President Carter invited me to be a member of a group to receive a special White House briefing on the Panama Canal treaties, then under review, which were due to expire in 1999. President Carter invited me to another White House meeting on October 25, 1978. This meeting was focused more on the status of the Democratic Party and the need to reinvigorate the party and defeat a perceived growing trend toward voter apathy. My third White House meeting with President Carter focused almost entirely on the president's 1980 reelection bid. Senator Edward Kennedy had entered the early primaries, and the president was concerned with marshalling his own forces against Kennedy and uniting the party against the Republicans in November. Each of my trips to the White House has been something of a spiritual journey, and they were probably much more useful to me as an American than to the presidents who called me to their briefings. On any visit to the White House you tend to reflect on the history of the country and the great decisions made in those rooms. You tend to think of the personal history that has brought you there. For me the political world was turning upside down. We as a people were moving from exclusion at the lowest levels to inclusion at the pinnacle of American life. All of us in Mississippi had come a long way in the ten short years between the time of my arrest for trying to desegregate a beach in Biloxi and the moment when I received that first presidential invitation to the White House to discuss and help plan for desegregation across the entire South. Being that God has put me in the company of presidents and governors and cabinet officers, I have prayed that I would never lose sight of a suffering and striving humanity to whose health and healing I dedicated myself long ago.

My visits to the Carter White House had additional symbolic meaning for me. President Carter, more than any other president before Bill Clinton, represented the promise and the potential for progress wrapped up in the black alliance with southern white moderates and liberals in state Democratic Party organizations in the South. For years, I had worked to build such a coalition in Mississippi. From 1964 to 1975 I served on the Mississippi Advisory Committee to the U.S. Civil Rights Commission. I suppose that my experiences in Biloxi, including our evolving experience with school desegregation, brought me the appointment to this body. In that capacity I saw the ills of Mississippi writ large. I heard reports of continuing intimidation and reprisals against those seeking to desegregate schools and public accommodations in other areas of the state. I had certainly seen enough myself to know that racist segregation would die a hard death in Mississippi. But sometimes in these monthly meetings of the Mississippi Advisory Committee to the U.S. Civil Rights Commission, I also saw hope for the future. I saw hope in the federal mandate that there be a single high standard of civil rights enforcement throughout the nation. I saw hope in the people of Mississippi, black and white, who were willing to show their faces and serve publicly on such a body. I especially valued my advisory committee association with fellow Alpha Phi Alpha and Lanier High and Howard University medical school alumnus Dr. Albert Britton of Jackson. I came to know and respect Dr. Powers, a white dentist from Long Beach, Dr. A. D. Beittel, president of Tougaloo College, and the courageous Mrs. Hazel Brannon Smith.

Mrs. Smith's strength and commitment amazed and inspired me. A white female newspaper owner from the small town of Lexington, in Holmes County, Mississippi, Mrs. Smith endured years of economic reprisals because she consistently advocated moderation and campaigned against fear and intimidation. The Citizens' Council and the Sovereignty Commission had tried to break her, but they failed. Like the storm-tossed flower of Robert Frost's poem, she "knelt and lay lodge but was not dead." Hazel Brannon Smith may have knelt in prayer, but racists never brought her to her knees broken. In public she stated that she "would not take crap off anyone," and I believed her. I got to know her well and thought the world of her. I knew that Mississippi was redeemable, so long as salt-of-the-earth people like Hazel Brannon Smith were willing to struggle for its soul. She gave me hope for the future of progressive biracial politics in Mississippi.

Beyond being concerned with basic political rights and rights to public accommodations, the Mississippi Advisory Committee heard many complaints about access to government services such as health and welfare. We found that the state welfare agency denied citizens access to its policy manual. There was a widespread practice of keeping welfare clients or potential clients ignorant of the relief programs for which they might qualify. I was surprised to find that poor whites, especially, were systematically kept in the dark about welfare programs in some areas of the state. Many local welfare officials in Mississippi turned needy whites away, telling them that such programs were only for blacks. When we investigated, even our civil rights advisory committee had difficulty in getting the state welfare agency to supply us with their handbook. The powers that be in Jackson acted as if we were after some closely guarded national security secret. In the end, it was a volunteer, a Dr. Retta from Maryland, who supplied us with a copy of the Mississippi handbook on welfare. We in turn copied this material and distributed it so that our citizens might know their rights to assistance under these programs.

Some of our work on the civil rights advisory committee brought us into contact with employers. The two largest employers in south Mississippi were Ingalls Shipbuilding in Pascagoula and Keesler Air Force Base in Biloxi. When the committee received complaints about discrimination in these places, I took them home to the Biloxi and Moss Point branches of the NAACP for action. We on the coast were able to resolve these complaints locally. General Bryan Shotts, the commander at Keesler Air Force Base, proved to be a man of goodwill in working with us to resolve complaints about discrimination in hiring and promotion and in the treatment of servicemen of different races. General Shotts's moderating influence regarding equity and justice, both on and off base in Biloxi, was much appreciated. In the midst of grave challenges that came before us, my occasional encounters with responsive and sensitive employers gave me glimmers of hope for my Mississippi and glimmers of hope for biracial coalition politics.

Political empowerment and court action emerged as the most solid foundations for my hope. It was plain that white moderates or liberals by themselves could not guarantee a sane future for the state, for they were in a minority within their own dominant ethnic group. Moreover, black Mississippians alone, even if fully empowered, would constitute only a 37 or 38 percent block of votes statewide. Blacks could not control statewide offices on their own. However, it was equally plain to me that a coalition of perhaps one-third of the state's white voters, the moderates, in combination with a truly empowered black voting block could combine to create a biracial progressive coalition that could control state politics. For coalitions to work, all partners must reap benefits from the partnership. In coalition politics was the hope for reconstruction and political renewal in Mississippi. In south Mississippi from 1964 to 1968, we worked hard to build the black voter base for such a coalition. We registered new voters with impunity. We worked to turn out the vote for every election from dogcatcher to coroner. When the 1968 presidential campaign rolled around, we were ready for those precinct and county caucuses in the Fifth Congressional District where the selection process for Democratic National Convention delegates was to begin. As I later told the Democratic National Convention's Credentials Committee in Chicago, some came walking, some came running to those precinct caucuses. In Harrison County, we had one of the heaviest precinct caucus turnouts of any presidential convention year in history. The strength of the black precinct turnout gave us black strength in the county convention and strength in the congressional district convention where the first batch of national convention delegates were to be elected. From the Fifth Congressional District in 1968, I was elected a delegate to the Democratic National Convention, along with District Attorney Boyce Holleman. All this took place in what became known as the "Regular" party process. In the Fourth Congressional District, the "Regular" party process elected Charles Evers a delegate. Up in the Delta, Dr. Matthew Page was elected. These outcomes guaranteed that, for the first time in history, there would be blacks in the Mississippi delegation at the Democratic National Convention.

In 1968, black voters made up something approaching 20 percent of the electorate in Harrison County and the Fifth Congressional District in southeast Missisippi. My election from the Fifth Congressional District made for a reasonably fair and equitable representation of black voters in the convention delegation from our particular region. However, elsewhere in the state, black representation was not at all reflective of black voting strength. In the first, second, third, and fourth congressional districts, blacks were in some cases excluded from the precinct caucuses or systematically underrepresented in the county convention processes. This exclusion rekindled the "Freedom Democrat" movement, which took to calling itself "Loyalist" as opposed to the so-called "Regulars" who would control the state convention, in which the remaining convention delegates were to be selected. The Loyalists conducted a separate caucusing process across the state and produced a competing delegation that sought to replace the so-called Regular delegation at the Chicago convention. The Loyalist decision to pull out of the Regular delegate selection process was not communicated to us in the south end of the state. However, by the time we assembled for the state Democratic convention in Jackson, it was apparent that there would be a challenge to the state's Regular delegation, unless action were taken to remedy the inequities that had surfaced in the early part of the delegate selection process.

I hoped that the state party convention could be brought to draw the Loyalists into a coalition by electing the remaining delegates in such a way as to guarantee the Loyalists half of Mississippi's national convention delegation. At the 1968 state convention, I became the author of a motion to suspend the rules and elect a slate of delegates that would include Matt Page, Aaron Henry, Charles Young, R. L. T. Smith, Sam Bailey, Andrew and Oscar Carr (two white businessmen who were in sympathy with the Freedom Democrats), myself, and enough others to give blacks and Loyalists half of the twenty-two-member delegation. I thought it was a sensible compromise that would save the state the embarrassment of having its delegation challenged and unseated in Chicago. Columnist Robert Novak was sitting next to me when I made the motion. He asked me if I thought this motion had a chance of passing. I said, "I hope so."

Senator Burgin from Columbus, who presided over the state convention, was presumed to be doing the bidding of Governor John Bell Williams. Williams, a former congressman, had come home to run for governor in 1967, after the Congressional Democratic Caucus stripped him of his seniority and committee chairmanships for publicly supporting Barry Goldwater for president in 1964. I think my motion to include the Loyalists in the delegation would have passed if it had been put to a vote. There had been a lot of preconvention talk about such a compromise in the south end of the state, and there had been talk along these lines at the convention itself. The Williams forces, however, were in no mood for compromise. Even though there appeared to be some considerable convention sentiment in favor of my motion, Senator Burgin would not allow it to come to a vote on the floor. After hearing my motion, Senator Burgin responded, "I am going to rule that motion out of order." This ruling was met with a chorus of cries of "Why? Why? Why? Why?" I went forward to question the ruling, but to no avail. A slate of delegates acceptable to the governor was quickly put before the convention and elected to the slots that remained to be filled. Near the front of the auditorium, I met columnist Bill Minor, who said in his always frank and candid way, "Doctor, did you really think that they were going to seat any of the Loyalists or Freedom Democrats?" I said, "I had hoped so." He retorted, "You're really naive." Of course, the test of whether or not I was naive would have been a state convention debate and floor vote on my motion. The powers that be were not willing to risk it. My hope was that the majority of the state convention delegates would be sensible. Senator Burgin and the governor merely proved that they were not ready for compromise, nor were they ready to risk entrusting the matter to a vote of the convention. In 1968, the day of genuine biracial coalition politics had not yet arrived for us in the Mississippi Democratic Party.

Understandably, the Loyalists, led by Aaron Henry, proceeded to challenge the credentials of the Regular delegation. Aaron sent me word that if I wished to have a Loyalist spot reserved for myself, I would be elected a Loyalist delegate. Even though I knew that the Regular delegation, of which I was a duly elected member, would in all likelihood not be seated, I decided that I could not accept the Loyalists' offer. I told Aaron that the Loyalists certainly would go to Chicago with my full sympathy, but, having worked within the rules and gotten elected in south Mississippi, I did not want to appear to be running with the foxes and hunting with the hounds.

I believed that the Regular delegate selection process had worked fairly in Harrison County. I agreed to testify to my own personal and local experience before the Credentials Committee in Chicago in advance of the national convention. My dad's old example of criticizing those things and persons that needed improvement and complimenting those who had done a good job came to my mind. I did not believe that my county deserved to be tarred with the same brush as the rest of Mississippi. I had not gone soft in any way. We had made some notable strides in Harrison County, and my sense of honor bound me to point that out. Charles Evers and Dr. Matt Page, who had been elected in the regular process in other areas of the state, declined the invitation to testify. I do not judge them in any way. They saw what they saw in their areas, and I saw what I saw on the coast. We each had a truth to uphold.

I made a special trip to Chicago for the Credentials Committee hearing along with Mayor Bobby Galloway of Lumberton, a small town in the Fifth Congressional District located about fifty miles north of the Mississippi Gulf Coast. A young white man from rural Mississippi, Bobby Galloway had never spent much time with a black man. In Chicago Bobby and I were roommates for one night. We talked into the wee hours. I took him to school in black history—every facet of it, social, political, and economic. We became genuine friends. The next day, we both gave testimony about the substantial extent of black participation in the delegate selection process in the Fifth Congressional District in southeast Mississippi. We made no apologies for the rest of the state. Still, I will always remember Congresswoman Barbara Jordan's vigorous cross-examination. I love Barbara Jordan, but she gave me a tough time. As a point in fact, I had previously advocated for absolute fairness in the entire delegate selection process. I was merely there attesting to its fairness in my own neighborhood. Of course, Barbara Jordan had no personal knowledge of me, the Biloxi struggle, or the details of the civil rights movement in Mississippi, nor did she know about the delegation compromise motion that I had attempted to broker at the state convention in Jackson. I took my lumps and admired her style.

Given what I understood to be the national party's commitment to create a level playing field in delegate selection, I was certain that the regular delegation would not be seated. As I had expected, the Credentials Committee ruled that, statewide, the Regulars had failed to carry out in good faith the national party's delegate selection mandate. Therefore, the Loyalists succeeded in unseating the Regulars when the delegates went into session a few days later. Within just three years of the passage of the Voting Rights Act of 1965, the world of national Democratic Party politics turned upside down.

I certainly understood and accepted Aaron Henry's statement that "none of us is free until all of us are free." Before leaving for Chicago, Aaron and the Loyalists again offered me a spot in their delegation, but, having testified for the Regulars, I felt that I should decline this honor. However, I did accept with enthusiasm the Loyalists' invitation to come to Chicago as their guest to stay in the Midland Hotel with the delegation. Natalie and I decided to take Gilbert, Jr., and make the trip on the train with the Loyalist delegates. In Chicago, the delegation presented us with guest passes that allowed us to observe all sessions of the convention. Gilbert, Jr., was a sophomore at Biloxi High School, so this was a great learning experience for him. Outgoing as he is, he got himself acquainted with some members of the national press and landed a job pulling television cable around the floor for CBS News. For Democrats, this turned out to be a terribly divisive convention. Antiwar demonstrations outside the convention hall erupted into violence. Mayor Daley's insensitive comments and the rough tactics of the Chicago police made a bad situation much worse. The convention nominated Vice President Hubert Humphrey for president, but went on to suffer a humiliating defeat in the fall at the hands of Richard Nixon and the Republicans. The independent candidacy of George Wallace in 1968 fractured the solid South and guaranteed the delivery of the White House to the Republicans.

The aim of a political party is, above all else, to win elections. At home in Mississippi we faced the task of trying to build or rebuild the Mississippi Democratic Party into a true biracial progressive coalition. Just as an all-white faction could not succeed within the national Democratic Party, an all-black state party would have no hope of winning statewide office or exercising any real influence with statewide elected officials. The task of salvaging a biracial party coalition was not easy. A lawsuit was filed contesting which faction, Loyalist or Regular, had the legal right to use the party name. This produced the specter of a trial in Biloxi featuring the ACLU defending the president of the state NAACP, who also happened to be chairman of the Loyalist Democrats. The courts refused to deal with the case, leaving it to the state's Democrats to grope their way toward some type of resolution on their own.

The election of Bill Waller as governor in the fall of 1971 was helpful.

Waller, a former district attorney from Hinds County, had earned broad respect for carrying forward two unsuccessful prosecutions of Klansman Byron De La Beckwith for the murder of Medgar Evers. As governor, Bill Waller broke new ground in appointing a significant number of blacks to state boards and commissions. He appointed my wife, Natalie, with her master's degree in social work, to the board of the Youth Department, which oversees youth correctional facilities and other programs for troubled children. Under Governor Waller's moderate leadership, we began slowly and haltingly to put things together.

The state party conformed to the national party's mandates in the delegate selection process in 1972, and at the state convention meeting in Jackson, we debated things out. I was once again elected a state and national convention delegate from south Mississippi. I, along with Boyce Holleman (our Gulf Coast district attorney), state senator Stone Barefield from Hattiesburg, and Ben Stone, the Fifth Congressional District's Democratic candidate for Congress, participated in the attempt to hammer out a solution that would let the state party go forward united in 1972. I was elected parliamentarian of the state Democratic Executive Committee in 1972 and was reelected to that position in every election cycle for the next twenty years. We went to the Miami national convention in 1972 in a Mississippi delegation that included a number of Loyalists such as Mrs. Fannie Lou Hamer, Mr. Charles Young, Mrs. Winston Hudson, Ms. Pat Derian, newspaperman Hodding Carter III, and a number of Regulars from both 1964 and 1968. Many of the white Regulars supported the failed presidential primary bid of George Wallace, who was wounded in an assassination attempt in the Democratic primaries of 1972. I, of course, was a McGovern man. At Miami, George McGovern was nominated for president, and the national party went down in a humiliating presidential defeat for a second consecutive time.

Following the 1972 national presidential defeat, Aaron Henry continued as the Loyalist chairman. The Regulars continued with a slate of party officers of their own, and the two factions continued with their tiffs at the interim convention at Kansas City in 1974. As titular head of the Regulars, Governor Waller showed a grace and courtesy which eased tensions at critical moments in Kansas City. The candidacy of Jimmy Carter for president in 1976 occasioned a final healing of the Loyalist versus Regular split. With much friendly advice from the national party, Loyalists and Regulars agreed to create two state party cochairpersons, one black and one white. This decision turned out to be the key compromise that brought the Regulars and Loyalists into the same fold. I was elected a national convention delegate for Jimmy Carter in 1976 and again in 1980, and I was elected an alternate for Jesse Jackson in 1988.

The Mississippi Democratic Party has had to really struggle to build and keep its biracial coalition together since 1976. In 1980, under the guidance of Governor William Winter, we abandoned the black and white cochair arrangement in favor of a single state party chairperson, Danny Cupit. It was a very difficult decision, and I am not sure that we have yet sorted through all of its distressing side effects. In 1988, after a painful intraparty struggle, a black and white majority coalition on the one-hundred-person Mississippi Democratic Executive Committee overrode Governor Ray Mabus's handpicked choice for party chairperson and elected Ed Cole, an aide to Senator Stennis, as the nation's first black state party chairperson.

Despite some very difficult times, the Mississippi Democratic Party managed to hold most of Mississippi's statewide elective offices through the era of Reagan-Bush realignments in southern congressional politics. Every succeeding Democratic governor since Bill Waller has appointed substantial and increasing numbers of blacks to state boards and commissions. Since 1968, four different Democratic governors have honored me with appointment or reappointment to state board service. When the state legislature created an agency called the Division of Comprehensive Health, a forerunner to the Medicaid Commission, Governor John Bell Williams appointed me as one of the two physicians to sit on its governing board. I remember wondering when the appointment to the Division of Comprehensive Health came down if the governor was trying to assuage himself or to appease me for the debacle his forces had created in turning down my delegation compromise motion at the 1968 state Democratic convention. I like to think that the governor knew he was getting a good man for a medical board. I accepted the appointment and became one of the first black appointees to any state board or commission since Reconstruction.

When Governor Cliff Finch took office in 1976, he nominated me along with three white physicians to fill vacancies on the Mississippi State Board of Health and Medical Licensure, which regulated the state's health department and licensed and disciplined physicians. The story that then unfolded revealed to me a side of Cliff Finch that few people knew about. The man had a heart of gold. He was like a mockingbird. He did no harm to anyone, but he was determined to see that justice was done. The state constitution requires that all gubernatorial appointees be confirmed by the Mississippi Senate. The black Mississippi Medical and Surgical Association, of which I was an officer (I served two terms as president, 1977 and

1978), endorsed my candidacy. The senate, however, balked and refused to confirm any of Governor Finch's state health board appointments. The senate reasoned that the state constitution required that nominees to the state board of health must be approved by *the* medical association. Well, I was approved by *the* Mississippi Medical and Surgical Association founded in 1900, but I was not the choice of the predominantly white Mississippi State Medical Association founded in 1840. So, the senate refused to confirm me or any of the governor's four other appointees.

Unfortunately, the nine-member Mississippi State Board of Health and Medical Licensure could not conduct its business without the proposed new members. Governor Finch, a white Democrat, stuck with me, his black nominee. The governor refused to submit new nominees to the senate. Instead he issued temporary commissions appointing us to serve on an interim basis until such time as the senate acted to confirm his nominees. For almost four years, I served on the state board of health on this basis. Governor Cliff Finch even joined Dr. Al Britton and me in a lawsuit, arguing that it was wrong for one medical society to have the exclusive right to endorse state health appointments. Seeing it as a constitutional issue, the governor did not believe that his hands should be tied in making appointments because of politics in rival professional associations. The case wound its way from circuit court all the way to the Mississippi Supreme Court.

However, before the supreme court ruled, the legislature had brought Mississippi into conformity with the practices of other states by dividing the Mississippi State Board of Health and Medical Licensure into two separate boards. One board was created to handle medical licensure and the policing of the medical profession, and the other was given the task of overseeing the work of the state department of public health. In 1980, Governor William Winter appointed me, along with Dr. Matt Page, a black physician from Greenville, to the new nine-member Mississippi State Board of Medical Licensure. This time the senate confirmed the nomination. This black doctor from Biloxi, who in 1955 was given only "courtesy" staff privileges without voting rights at the Biloxi Hospital, was now helping determine who was to be admitted and expelled from medical practice in the state.

The increasingly favorable minority appointment record of statewide officeholders bears witness to growing black political strength in an evolving biracial coalition. Black political strength and the emergence of healthy white-black progressive coalitions is also increasingly visible on the local level. I have seen the hard labor of the civil rights generation bearing its political fruit in all corners of the state. In the River Region, the Delta, and Jackson, where blacks are in the majority, the number of black officeholders rapidly expanded in the seventies, eighties, and nineties. Charles Evers, whom I was proud to recommend to the national NAACP board to walk in his brother's steps as our state NAACP field secretary, was elected mayor of Fayette, Mississippi. Robert Walker, a former employee of the African Bureau of the U.S. State Department who became the first black faculty member at the University of Mississippi and served later as an outstanding state NAACP field secretary, was elected mayor of his hometown of Vicksburg. Another former NAACP field secretary, Cleve McDowell, the first black to attend the Ole Miss law school, was elected mayor of Drew, Mississippi.

Even more impressively, exclusion has given way to inclusion in Harrison County on the Mississippi Gulf Coast, where black voters make up barely 20 percent of the electorate. Here, where I still practice medicine, in 1998, black-white coalition politics delivered county-wide election victories to county judge Robin Alfred Midcalf and circuit judge John Whitfield, both of whom happened to be black. This Gulf Coast, where the civil rights movement had its bloody beginnings in Mississippi in 1959 and 1960, became, in the 1990s, the first place to demonstrate that black candidates can win elections in an overwhelmingly white majority district in Mississippi. The world of Mississippi politics, especially Mississippi Gulf Coast politics, has indeed turned upside down in the past thirty years.

Although I stepped down from state party office in 1992, I still believe in the absolute necessity of biracial coalition politics for Mississippi's overall future health, wealth, and well- being. Democratic coalition politics produced Governor William Winter's landmark Education Reform Act of 1982. In the 1990s, while Mississippi elected its first Republican governor since Reconstruction, Democratic coalition politics continued to dominate the state legislature, which enacted, over the Republican governor's veto, the Mississippi Adequate Education Program to equalize funding between rich and poor school districts. Neither white moderates nor black activists could have passed this monumental legislation by themselves. Together, they have been able to begin the difficult process of building the state anew.

Biloxi municipal politics has also undergone gradual but revolutionary change. In city government, if Mayor Guice's election in 1961 represented a kind of 1960s budding of a new southern politics of respect for minorities, Mayor Jerry O'Keefe and Mayor Gerald Blessey in the 1970s and 1980s brought that trend to a full flowering in Biloxi. O'Keefe, a World War II ace pilot, and Blessey, a highly decorated Vietnam-era infantry officer, brought real vision and a true and deep personal commitment to the highest ideals of inclusion to the mayor's office. The introduction of the mayor-council form of government to replace the at-large mayor-commissioner system in 1981 gave an additional positive boost to the evolving political climate of the city. In this transition, the Biloxi branch of the NAACP helped draw the boundaries for the new city council wards. In 1981, the new black-majority ward in back-of-town elected Michael Esters the first black city councilman in Biloxi's history. Shortly thereafter, under Mayor Blessey, Biloxi employed its first black police chief, Tommy Moffett. The appointment of black citizens to municipal committees and boards is now commonplace and rarely controversial. We've come a very long way in Biloxi from the old days of Laz Quave.

Significant and meaningful municipal appointments have come to me and others as this new Biloxi evolves toward racial inclusion. In 1968 Mayor Guice appointed me to the Biloxi Planning Commission, and I was reappointed by Mayor O'Keefe in the 1970s. In this capacity, inclusion brought real responsibility. All of us together on the planning commission learned that our best intentions and our most creative efforts could not bring back the business health of the old downtown area of Biloxi when the Edgewater Mall opened on the west end of town. As businesses within walking distance of the old black and poor white neighborhoods folded up or went to the mall, black people and poor people were placed at a great disadvantage. Moreover, when stores closed in the old part of town, service workers, custodians, and stock helpers lost their jobs. Our concerns with these negative side effects of the loss of downtown business led us into an urban renewal effort that in the end only exacerbated the problem. We determined to make an effort to bring back the old market area along Howard Avenue, the so-called Vieux Marche, by creating an outdoor pedestrian mall and closing two blocks of this storefront business district to automobiles. I had seen a beautiful pedestrian mall in Boston that appeared to be reviving an old part of that city. Architects and planners from Tennessee convinced us all that just such a revival might be possible for Biloxi.

Closing Howard Avenue to automobiles turned out to be a great mistake. Businesses that were barely hanging on in this location now lost almost all of their customer base. Stores closed right and left, and old downtown virtually died as a shopping district. Shopping options for the poor people, white and black, in east Biloxi were greatly diminished. Many elderly people or those on the bottom rung could not afford cars. To get the best choices in food or dry goods on the west side of town, they now had to either pay for bus transportation or take pain and walk (TP and W, as black folks say). The mistake was a hard one for all of us. We had to face the limits that the laws of economics imposed on the best intentions and best judgements and best efforts of planners. Through the many meetings of the planning commission and the Citizens Participation Organization, I learned much about building codes and the ways in which neighborhoods function, or why they fail to function and fall into decay. We made our share of mistakes, but we learned from them, or at least we learned that when one approach did not work, we should admit it, pick ourselves up, and try another.

Still, inclusion has not always been automatic. Sometimes we still have to speak emphatically to assure that minority concerns will be heard. However, a little story of a late 1970s struggle for black inclusion on the Mississippi Coast Coliseum Commission illustrates an interesting change in the tone of coast politics. The first coliseum board, appointed to build this facility after Hurricane Camille, was all white. In 1976, NAACP chapters across the coast took it upon themselves to remedy this oversight. I well remember meeting with Les Newcomb, the director of the South Mississippi Regional Planning Commission and one of the mayors, in the new Hilton Hotel in Biloxi at two in the morning to make them aware that we intended to do our best to see that a black was appointed to this board. I did not expect to be chosen myself, but I was soon surprised with a mayoral appointment to the Mississippi Coast Coliseum Commission.

A short time later, Governor Cliff Finch appointed a local white businessman, Mr. Lawson Gallotte, to the coliseum commission also. On the occasion of our first commission meeting with Mr. Gallotte in attendance, Gallotte made a pointed public statement that I, who had long served on the Biloxi Planning Commission and the Governor's Emergency Council, was there only because I was black. In Mr. Lawson Gallotte's view, Dr. Gilbert R. Mason was a token who was otherwise unqualified to sit on the commission. Well, that public statement provoked an immediate verbal challenge from me. Furthermore, the publication of Mr. Gallotte's remarks in the newspaper created a furor for several weeks. The more the man said in public the more the public turned its wrath upon him. The press quoted Mr. Gallotte as saying that he was a very "liberal" man, because he owned a business in "jigtown" in Gulfport. Soon the *Daily Herald* and a host of both black *and* white civic groups were calling for Gallotte's resignation and urging Governor Finch to replace him. After several weeks of controversy, Mr. Gallotte resigned. The most influential members of the white community, the folks who in 1959 would not let me swim on the public beaches, were now, eighteen years later in 1977, embarrassed, up in arms, and rising to my defense over a foolish public racial insult delivered to me by an insensitive white businessman. The winds of change were indeed remaking the political atmosphere of the Mississippi Gulf Coast.

As Natalie would say, it's been quite a life. Because the sweat of the committed and the blood of the martyrs has turned this world upside down, a poor boy born on Riggins Alley in Jackson, Mississippi, has seen boardrooms and cabinet rooms, the Governor's Mansion and the White House. However, the most meaningful service has been that to which I felt called as a boy. It has come where I have been able to ease the births of babies, help heal the sick, and give comfort to the dying now for forty-five years. In this, my cherished practice of medicine, I have seen dramatic changes, too—changes that fulfill the hope of America in ways that I could only dream of in 1955 when I opened for service. The hospital staff, a sizeable minority of whom seemed ready to withdraw my staff privileges twice in the 1960s because of my civil rights activities, in the 1980s elected me its staff president and chose me to rewrite its staff bylaws and constitution.

Institutions do change, and so do individuals. Beginning in 1970 or 1971, I started seeing large numbers of white patients in my practice. This revolutionary change took place when I won the bid to provide U.S. Public Health Service medical benefits to seamen, fishermen, and other offshore workers. The government had long provided medical coverage to seamen and fishermen, because their vessels and services were subject to conscription in time of war. The previous physician who held this contract in Biloxi continued to run a segregated practice with separate waiting rooms for his black patients and white patients. The U.S. Public Health Service preferred my bid. So it was that until the early 1980s, when the Reagan administration ended this program, about one-third of my practice was made up of a combination of white seamen and fishermen and white Medicaid patients. It was said that some of these white patients or their families had been involved in the rioting over desegregation of the beach in 1960. However, as I got to know them individually, and as they got to know me, we developed mutual respect. I found that many of these hardworking men and their families had their good qualities. After the U.S. Public Health Service dropped the seamen's program, a number of these white patients from the poor neighborhoods of east Biloxi continued to use me as their family physician.

In my medical practice, and in my experiences of public service, I have seen that individual relationships built one-on-one are capable of helping many of us bypass or rise above the tendency to view others exclusively through a racial filtering lens. Reaching for each other as individuals, we can often connect with that common humanity that lives just beneath the surface.

Worlds can turn upside down.

Epilogue

Last year, in preparation for the tricentennial of the founding of the first French settlement on the Gulf Coast, the Mississippi Department of Archives and History opened an exhibit in the Old Capitol Museum celebrating the three cultures which came together with the colonial settlement of Mississippi and Louisiana—Native American, European, and African. As a member of the board of the department of archives and history, I attended the opening ceremony. The Old Capitol is a building whose bricks were laid by slave hands. It is the building where the secession vote was taken at the beginning of the Civil War and where John R. Lynch presided as the first black speaker of the house. The Old Capitol is the place where the infamous 1890 Mississippi State Constitution was written, disenfranchising blacks.

There in that packed rotunda, a remarkable public tribute unfolded as representative citizens of Mississippi's various present-day ethnic groups—black, white, and red—enacted a ceremonial smoking of the calumet. Former governor William Winter represented the English, Edmond Boudreaux of Biloxi stood in for the French, Choctaw and Chickasaw chiefs smoked the peace pipe for their people, and my friends C. C. Bryant and Barbara Middleton represented African American Mississippians. Here was C. C. Bryant, a long-time NAACP state and local officer whose house had been bombed during the civil rights movement, smoking in peace for all of us, along with William Winter, Native American chiefs, and all the others. The scars of the past being what they are, there was a spiritual beauty in this moment that moved me to tears. It represented an affirmation of respect for the character and value and contributions of all of our peoples in making us who we are as Mississippians and Americans. I think I have seen hope for healing in such affirmations—public and historic affirmations of human dignity and worth that could not have happened in Mississippi forty years ago.

I have seen the power of affirmations of worth and respect accorded persons both in private lives and in public places. In 1986, when I began serving on the board of the Mississippi Department of Archives and History, I took my place as a great-grandson of a slave sitting at the table of history alongside the great-grandsons and great-granddaughters of slave owners. I have always loved history. During my days in medical school in Washington, D.C., I found great personal inspiration in the monuments and museums celebrating our national heritage. I have been witness to a time of momentous change. The opportunity to promote the collection of archival resources for a broad-based and inclusive history based on facts appealed to me. Too many people have been ignored in our historical writings, and too much has been written from a narrow perspective or selected to perpetuate some myth of a superior race. I believe that broadening the types of archival materials available to scholars will make possible histories which extol the common humanity of us all. As a member of the board of the Mississippi Department of Archives and History, I tried to serve this ideal.

In this role, I saw the power of affirmation at work when that Mississippi board, made up of eight whites and one black, voted unanimously to induct outstanding black citizens into the Mississippi Hall of Fame. A portrait of J. R. Lynch, Mississippi's black Reconstruction-era speaker of the state house of representatives and U.S. Congressman, now hangs, forever enshrined, where future generations can see the worth accorded to the life of a brilliant, self-taught ex-slave who reached the heights of Mississippi and national politics a century ago. Later, the same Mississippi board unanimously inducted my friend and inspiration, Medgar W. Evers, into the Mississippi Hall of Fame, announcing to the world the accolades appropriately bestowed on a black martyr to the cause of human rights and the highest ideals of freedom. Actions like these have potentially powerful symbolic and healing significance.

Recently at a meeting of the Mississippi Medical and Surgical Association, Dr. Robert "Bob" Smith and I were noticing how much healthier looking the children and teenagers are today than when we first began our medical practice in Mississippi. We attributed those improvements to the health care and treatment afforded through Head Start and various women's and infants' nutrition and health programs and to the efforts of the dedicated professionals who work with them. However, we observed that somehow we had not obtained optimum psychological health and wellbeing for many of the children and young adults we see. Herein lies the challenge of the present and the future. Psychological well-being requires a fertile environment filled with appropriate affirmations of worth and respect for persons and their known or unknown potentialities.

While the hard lesson of history is that we cannot underestimate the potential viciousness and destructiveness of racism, neither should we forget the potential redeemability of our adversaries. There is hope for the future in individuals, in political coalitions, and in the courts of these United States. The road we have trod in Biloxi and in Mississippi has proven this hope. However, we have not yet reached the promised land. The nasty head of racism lurks near. There is work yet to be done. But I believe that there are brighter days ahead and that the struggles and progress of the recent past have enabled members of a new generation to make their way to the starting gates, and some are away and running.

To the new generation taking the first steps up the ladder of work and study toward the fulfillment of dreams, I would say, in the words of Langston Hughes in "Mother to Son," that "life for me ain't been no crystal stair," but I'm "still climbin'." Now, you keep climbing, too. There remain steps to take, challenges to meet, and races to be won, but we've come a long way. For the generations yet to come I pray for health and healing. Seeing how much we have progressed in one lifetime, I see a world coming where great promise exists. I believe that America is moving toward a truer reflection of the beauty of its ideals.

Looking over the horizon just a short distance ahead, I see possibilities for our children and grandchildren beyond what our fathers could have hoped for. I feel comfortable about foreseeing Dr. Gilbert R. Mason, Jr., founding and heading some great medical foundation of the future, or imagining Angela Rose Juzang as a future Constance Baker Motley, or Yolanda Marie Juzang Craft owning her own art gallery and studio, or David and Adam Owen producing epic films equivalent to *The Ten Commandments* through their own movie production company. I feel good about a future in which Gilda Yvette Sizor can head her own diversified enterprises, and Omar Mason, a recent graduate of Loyola Law School, can be elected to the Louisiana state legislature, and Aria Monette Mason can become a thespian or terpsichorean worthy of her proven abilities. For Carolyn Mason Stamps, Shonda Alean, Gia, Ranjie, Helema, Shyare, and Little Willie, I want and can see a world where they will be able to excel at business entrepreneurship and investment. I see a world coming where Reginald can make his way as a large electrical contractor, and where Arthur will receive respect for the value of the work of his hands. For Willie Arthur Mason and Hiram, his brother, I want a world where they can aspire to own a shipping line, and I foresee a world where Little

Hiram can become director of the FBI. For our nurses Yvonne and Yvette, I foresee a world where they can own their own home health services or become nursing directors at a large hospital. The world I see is a world where Diane Marcelin can develop her math skills sufficiently to explain some unknown equation or theory and be acclaimed for it, and where Vanessa can win international acclaim as a photographer and Surayel can give flute concerts at Carnegie Hall. The thought of a world where Paul Atwood can rise to great heights in landscape and design and where Philip can become a fire chief in a large city thrills me. A world where each and all of the children—Amber Layne, Tai, Jaylan, English, Sedrick, Little Philip, Numia, Darian, Ranjie and Sheru—can realize their fullest potential is just ahead. That is the future for which I have struggled.

The future that I have worked for is one in which attorney Curtis Hays can become a Mississippi appellate court judge, Judge Robin Alfred Midcalf and Judge John Whitfield can become Mississippi Supreme Court justices, and state supreme court justice Fred Banks can become a judge of the U.S. Supreme Court. I see a time when a man of God like the Reverend James Black may freely expand the boundaries of his ministry. It is a future in which an aspiring black political leader like Eric Dickey can become a mayor, or Bill Stallworth can become secretary of state, or Boyd James III can become a state representative, or state representative Frances Fredericks can become a U.S. congresswoman.

May we pray and work and live and dream in the faith that these possibilities are real. And may we affirm the children, and so give them unconquerable spirits and the faith and determination to keep on climbing.

INVICTUS

Out of the night that covers me,
Black as the Pit from pole to pole,
I thank whatever gods may be
For my unconquerable soul.

In the fell clutch of circumstance
I have not winced nor cried aloud.
Under the bludgeonings of chance
My head is bloody, but unbowed.

Beyond this place of wrath and tears
Looms but the Horror of the shade,
And yet the menace of the years
Finds, and shall find, me unafraid.

It matters not how strait the gate,
How charged with punishments the scroll,
I am the master of my fate;
I am the captain of my soul.

—William Ernest Henley

Notes

Chapter 4

1. The Biloxi police reported this first wade-in to an agent of the Mississippi State Sovereignty Commission on May 27, 1959. However, the Biloxi Police Department had first reported to the Sovereignty Commission that I, along with Wilmer B. McDaniel, a funeral director, was a member of the NAACP in response to an agent's inquiry on February 16, 1959. See Van Landingham to Director, State Sovereignty Commission, 16 February 1959, State Sovereignty Commission Files (SSC Files), Victim Classification, ID: 2-56-1-6-1-1-1, Mississippi Department of Archives and History, Jackson, Mississippi; and Van Landingham to Director, State Sovereignty Commission, 27 May 1959, SSC Files, Victim, ID: 2-56-1-11-1-1-1.

2. *Daily Herald* (Biloxi), 5 October 1959, pp.1–2.

3. Van Landingham to Director, State Sovereignty Commission, 14 October 1959, SSC Files, Victim, ID: 2-56-1-16-2-1-1.

4. Van Landingham to Director, State Sovereignty Commission, 4 November 1959, SSC Files, Victim, ID: 2-56-1-19-2-1-1.

5. Van Landingham, Memo to File 5-4, 4 May 1960, SSC Files, Victim, ID: 2-56-1-33-5-1-1, p. 6.

6. *Daily Herald* (Biloxi), 11 January 1965, p. 2.

Chapter 5

1. Bob Thomas, Investigative Report, "Beach Disturbances, Biloxi, Harrison Co., Mississippi," 22 April 1960 to 2 May 1960, SSC Files, Victim ID: 5-4-0-50-11-1-1, pp. 2–3.

2. "Police Accused of Aiding Mob," *Commercial Appeal* (Memphis), 10 August 1960, p. 28.

3. Bob Thomas, Investigative Report, "Beach Disturbances, Biloxi, Harrison Co., Mississippi," 22 April 1960 to 2 May 1960, SSC Files, Victim, ID: 5-4-0-50-11-1-1, p. 5.

4. *Clarion-Ledger* (Jackson), 26 April 1960, p. 1.; *Jackson Daily News*, 26 April 1960, pp. 1–2.

5. *Daily Herald* (Biloxi), 26 April 1960, p.1.

6. Van Landingham to Director, State Sovereignty Commission, 20 October 1959, SSC Files, Victim, ID: 5-4-0-10-7-1-1, p. 6.

7. Bob Thomas, Investigative Report, "Beach Disturbances, Biloxi, Harrison Co., Mississippi," 22 April 1960 to 2 May 1960, SSC Files, Victim, ID: 5-4-0-50-11-1-1, p. 3.

8. Ibid., p. 4.

9. *Clarion-Ledger* (Jackson), 26 April 1960, pp. 1–2.

10. *Daily Herald* (Biloxi), 25 April 1960, pp. 1–2; *Amsterdam News* (New York), 30 April 1960, pp.1, 10–11, and 34–35.

11. *Daily Herald* (Biloxi), 25 April 1960, p. 2.

12. Ibid., p.1.

13. *Commercial Appeal* (Memphis), 26 April 1960.

14. *Jackson Advocate*, 30 April 1960.

15. *Clarion-Ledger* (Jackson), 26 April 1960.

16. Ibid.

17. *Commercial Appeal* (Memphis), 26 April 1960.

18. *Jackson Daily News*, 26 April 1960, p. 2.

19. *Daily Herald* (Biloxi), 27 April 1960, p.1, and 30 April 1960, p.1; *Jackson Daily News*, 29 April 1960, p.1.

20. *Daily Herald* (Biloxi), 27 April 1960, pp.1–2.

21. Van Landingham, Memo to File 5-4, "Beach Integration, Harrison County, Mississippi," 4 May 1960, SSC Files, Victim, ID: 2-56-1-33-6-1-1, p. 5.

22. *Daily Herald* (Biloxi), 10 May 1960, pp. 1–2.

23. Van Landingham, Memo to File 5-4, "Beach Integration, Harrison County, Mississippi," 5 May 1960, SSC Files, Victim, ID: 9-22-0-9-2-1-1, p.1.

24. Thomas to Governor Barnett, "Beach Disturbances," 2 May 1960, SSC Files, Victim, ID: 5-4-0-51-4-1-1, p.4; *Clarion-Ledger* (Jackson), 2 May 1960; *Jackson Advocate*, 7 May 1960.

25. Van Landingham, Memo to File 5-4, "Beach Integration, Harrison County, Mississippi," 5 May 1960, SSC Files, Victim, ID: 2-56-1-34-1-1-1.

26. *Daily Herald* (Biloxi), 9 May 1960, p.1.

27. *Jackson Advocate*, 21 May 1960.

Chapter 6

1. Thomas to Director, State Sovereignty Commission, 27 June 1960, SSC Files, Victim, ID: 2-56-1-41-1-1-1, p. 2.

2. Thomas to Director, State Sovereignty Commission with enclosure, 27 June 1960, SSC Files, Victim, ID: 2-57-0-24-3-1-1 and ID: 2-56-1-36-1-1-1.

3. James W. Silver, *Mississippi: The Closed Society*, new enlarged edition (New York: Harcourt, Brace & World, 1966), p. 271.

4. Ibid.

5. Van Landingham to Director, State Sovereignty Commission, "NAACP, Gulfport, Mississippi," 16 February 1959, SSC Files, Victim, ID: 2-56-1-6-2-1-1.

6. Undated four-page handwritten list, SSC Files, Victim, ID: 99-93-0-77-4-1-1; undated two-page typed list titled "Negro Drug Stores in Mississippi," SSC Files, Victim, ID: 99-202-0-10-2-1-1; Thomas to Barnett, attachment to memorandum "Beach Disturbances," SSC Files, Victim, ID: 5-4-0-51-5-1-1; and Robert C. Thomas, report dated 7 July 1960, "Investigation of Disturbances at DeSoto National Forest Park," SSC Files, Victim, ID: 2-56-1-51-4-1-1.

7. Van Landingham to Director, State Sovereignty Commission, 14 October 1959, SSC Files, Victim, ID: 5-4-0-1-3-1-1.

8. Ibid.

9. Van Landingham to Director, State Sovereignty Commission, 20 October 1959, SSC Files, Victim, ID: 5-4-0-10-1-1-1

10. *Daily Herald* (Biloxi), 19 April 1960, p. 2.

11. Van Landingham, Memo to File 5-4, "Beach Integration, Harrison County, Mississippi," 4 May 1960, SSC Files, Victim, ID: 5-4-0-54-6-1-1; and audiotapes of April 28, 1960, meeting of Felix Dunn, Knox Walker, and Nap Cassibry with Sovereignty agents Bob Thomas and Zack Van Landingham, SSC Files, uncataloged tapes 1–8.

12. Ibid.

13. Ibid.

14. Van Landingham, Memo to File 5-4, "Beach Integration, Harrison County, Mississippi," 5 May 1960, SSC Files, Victim, ID: 5-4-0-55-1-1-1.

15. *Jackson Daily News*, 19 May 1960.

16. Van Landingham, Memo to File 5-4, "Beach Integration, Harrison County, Mississippi," 5 May 1960.

17. Editorial, *Jackson Advocate*, 30 April 1960.

18. Editorial, *Jackson Daily News*, 3 May 1960.

19. Van Landingham, Memo to File 5-4, "Beach Integration, Harrison County, Mississippi," 5 May 1960, SSC Files, Victim, ID: 5-4-0-55-1-1-1.

20. Van Landingham to Director, State Sovereignty Commission, 16 February 1959, SSC Files, Victim, ID: 2-56-1-6-1-1.

Chapter 7

1. Thomas A. Bailey and David M. Kennedy, *The American Pageant: A History of the Republic*, 7th ed. (Lexington, MA: D. C. Heath and Company, 1983), p. 868.

2. Van Landingham to Director, State Sovereignty Commission, 16 February 1959, SSC Files, Victim, ID: 2-56-1-6-2-1-1; and report by Tom Scarbrough, "Harrison County," 16 January 1961, SSC Files, Victim, ID: 2-56-1-77-3-1-1.

3. Silver, *Mississippi: The Closed Society*, p. 250.

4. *Daily Herald* (Biloxi), 11 April 1961.

5. Ibid., 10 May 1961.
6. Ibid., 15 May 1961.
7. Ibid., 10 May 1961 and 15 May 1961.
8. Ibid., 17 May 1961.
9. Ibid., 18 May 1960.
10. Ibid., 21 May 1960.
11. Ibid., 20 May 1960.
12. Ibid., 19 May 1960.
13. Ibid., 25 May 1960.
14. Ibid., 9 June 1960.
15. Ibid., 23 June 1960.
16. Ibid., 9 August 1960.
17. Ibid., 19 August 1960.
18. Ibid., 8 August 1960 and 9 August 1960.
19. *Commercial Appeal* (Memphis), 10 August 1960.
20. *Daily Herald* (Biloxi), 7 September 1960.
21. Ibid., 8 September 1960, 14 September 1960, and 1 November 1960.
22. Ibid., 21 September 1960, 23 September 1960, and 28 September 1960.
23. Ibid., 1 November 1960.
24. Ibid., 19 December 1960 and 23 May 1961.
25. Carter to Mason, 20 February 1961, Mason Papers, privately held by author.
26. *Daily Herald* (Biloxi), 23 May 1961.
27. Ibid., 7 May 1962 and 27 July 1962.
28. Ibid., 11 September 1962, 27 December 1962, and 1 March 1963.
29. Ibid., 28 June 1963.
30. Ibid., 20 November 1963 and 21 November 1963.
31. Ibid., 21 November 1963.
32. Ibid., 22 February 1965.
33. Ibid., 9 March 1967.
34. Ibid., 16 August 1968.

Chapter 8

1. Dr. Gilbert R. Mason, Millsaps College Oral History Memoir, recorded 10 August 1965, p. 9.
2. Evers to Carter, 11 October 1960, Mason Papers, School Desegregation Documents, privately held by author.
3. Evers to Mason, 18 October 1960, Mason Papers, School Desegregation Documents, privately held by author.
4. The twenty-five child plaintiffs included Gilbert R. Mason, Jr., Gary Black, Jerry Black, Diane Black, Daryl Boglin, Linda Gail Davis, Jessica Denise Davis, Henry Lee Davis, Glorhea Diane Edwards, Janice Elzy, John Elzy, Reho-

fus Esters, Jr., John Robert Esters, Michael Esters, LaValeria Esters, Barbara Jean Harris, James McKinly, Jr., Sylvia Yvonne McKinly, Adrienne Martin, Patsy R. Mumford and Rosa M. Mumford (daughters of Mrs. Johnnie Brown), Clifton Nunley, Jr., Gretchen Nunley, Bernardo Rosado, and Ernest Rosado.

The first black children to enter school on a nonsegregated basis in 1964 were first graders. The first-grade group included only the very youngest of the group above, plus some children not listed as plaintiffs in the original suit, including Cynthia Fletcher, Frederick Gibbs, Brenda Payne, Evangeline Bellamy, Brenda Tennort, and others.

5. Many other noted attorneys of the civil rights era spent time in our home, including Marian Wright Edelman, William Kunstler, Jean Fairfax, Derrick Bell, Constance Slaughter-Harvey, and Cassandra Flipper.

6. *Daily Herald,* 18 June 1963.

7. Ibid., 5 June 1963.

8. Ibid., 10 June 1963.

9. Deputy Attorney General Katzenbach to President Johnson, 28 August 1964, Johnson Presidential Papers, WH40445, Lyndon B. Johnson Presidential Library, Austin, Texas.

10. Newspaper accounts mistakenly state that sixteen black children started to previously all-white schools in Biloxi in 1964. Actually sixteen children known to the local NAACP started that fall, but five other children whose parents were stationed at Keesler Air Force Base joined the original sixteen. Thus, a total of twenty-one black children desegregated the Biloxi schools that fall.

11. *Daily Herald* (Biloxi), 23 June 1963.

12. Thomas R. West and James W. Mooney, eds., *To Redeem a Nation: A History and Anthology of the Civil Rights Movement* (St. James, NY: Brandywine Press, 1993), pp. xxiv–vi; and Steven Thernstrom and Abigail Thernstrom, *America in Black and White: One Nation Indivisible* (New York: Simon and Schuster, 1997), pp. 166–71.

Chapter 10

1. The Mississippi Advisory Committee to the Cabinet Committee on Education included the chairman, Warren Hood, the vice chairman, Dr. Gilbert R. Mason, R. R. Lampton of First National Bank in Jackson, Dr. T. B. Brown of Jackson (a minister), businessman Gil Carmichael of Meridian, Dr. Douglas Conner of Starkville, Owen Cooper of Mississippi Chemical Corporation, pharmacist Alvin Fielder, Jr., of Meridian, businessman Leslie Lampton of Jackson, Paul W. McMullan of First Mississippi Bank in Hattiesburg, Dr. Sylvester Moorhead of the School of Education at the University of Mississippi,

plantation owner and city councilman Henry Self of Marks, Rowan Taylor of Mississippi Valley Title Insurance Company in Jackson, businessman Walter Williams (a past president of the Jackson Urban League), attorney Jack Young (president of the Jackson branch of the NAACP), and James Hines, president of Deposit Guaranty National Bank in Jackson.

Index

Index 219

Esters, Dr. John Robert, 158
Esters, Councilman Michael, 199
Esters, Rehofus, 86, 149
Evans, Mary Williams Jackson, 11
Evers, Charles, 109, 141, 191, 193, 198
Evers, Darrel, 154
Evers, James, 154
Evers, Medgar W., 1, 7, 49, 59, 71, 85–86, 92, 102, 107, 114, 115, 130, 132–35; school deseg-regation, willingness to risk life for, 147–48, 152, 154; induction into Mississippi Hall of Fame, 204
Evers, Mrs. Myrlie, 154
Evers, Rena, 154

Fallo, Dominic, 121
Farish Street District (Jackson, Miss.), 2, 9
Farmer, James, x, 162
FBI, 68, 135
federal registrars (voting rights), 164
FEMA (Federal Emergency Management Agency), 181
Ferdinand, Reverend John, 74, 85, 172
Fielder, Gilmore, 68, 71, 76
Fifth Amendment, 126
Fifth Circuit Court of Appeals (U.S.), 130, 139, 154, 170
Finch, Governor Cliff, 196–97, 200
first aid, 7
First Amendment, 58
First Missionary Baptist Church (Biloxi, Miss.), 46, 53, 62, 77, 107, 171
First Missionary Baptist Church (Handsboro, Miss.), 111
Fisk University, 25
Fitzgerald, Ella, 23
Five Points area (Jackson, Miss.), 6
Fletcher, Ms. Burnell Burney, 69, 160
Flipper, Ms. Cassandra, 153
Flood of 1927, Mississippi, 8, 12
Flowers plantation, 142
Floyd, Dr. Charles, 40
Floyd, Otha Lee, 52
Ford, Emma Lou, 38
Fortner, Robert, 171, 175
Fourteenth Amendment, 49, 126, 146, 150, 152
Fourth St. Drug Store (Clarksdale, Miss.), 99

Fox, Reverend, 111
Franklin, John Hope, 33
Frazier, E. Franklin, 33
Fredericks, State Representative Frances, 206
Freedmen's Hospital (Washington, D.C.), 31
Freedom Democratic Party, Mississippi, 159–60, 163–65, 191
freedom of choice (desegregation), 148, 159
freedom riders, 7, 130
freedom summer (1964), 120, 159, 162–64
French colonial settlement, in Mississippi, 203
Frost, Robert, 189
"Full Gospel" Baptist Churches, 12, 20

Gallagher, Reverend Roger, 111, 135, 138
Gallinger Hospital (D.C. General), 31
Gallote, Lawson, 200–01
Galloway, Mayor Bobby, 193
Galloway, Mr. Dorothy, 69
Garvey, Marcus, 27, 44; Garveyism, 81
Gettysburg Address, Lincoln's, 13, 146
Gill Avenue, Biloxi 1963 wade-in site, 135
Gillam, James, 61
Gilmore, Mrs. (LPN), 36
Goldwater, Barry, 164, 170, 192
Goodman, Andrew, 163
Gorenflo Elementary (Biloxi, Miss.), 157
Goudy community (Jackson, Miss.), 12
Governor's Emergency Council (Hurricane Camille), 181–82, 185, 200
Governor's mansion, 201
Grant, General Ulysses S., 12
Graves, Dr. J. A., 150
Great Migration (African American), 9
Green, Mrs. P. I., 171
Green, P. I., 46, 56
Green, R. H., "Colored Annex" Baptist Hospital, 4
Greene, Percy, 98, 99, 106–07
Greensboro, N.C. (1959 sit-ins), ix
Grimes, S. E., 42–43
Gruich, Dr. Charles, xvii
Gruich, Dr. Frank, xvii, 39, 40, 82
Gudan, Uz, 3
Guice, Mayor Daniel, 121–25, 131–32, 135–37, 151, 198–99
Guice, Mrs. Lee Dicks, 125, 128–29